Who Speaks for
America's Children?

Edited by Carol J. De Vita
and Rachel Mosher-Williams

# Who Speaks for America's Children?

## The Role of Child Advocates in Public Policy

THE URBAN INSTITUTE PRESS
Washington, D.C.

**THE URBAN INSTITUTE PRESS**
2100 M Street, N.W.
Washington, DC 20037

Library of Congress Cataloging in Publication Data
    Who speaks for America's children? : the role of child advocates in public policy / edited by Carol J. De Vita and Rachel Mosher-Williams.
        p. cm.
    Includes bibliographical references and index.
    ISBN 0-87766-704-7 (pbk. : alk. paper)
    1. Child welfare—United States. 2. Children—Government policy—United States. 3. Social advocacy—United States. I. De Vita, Carol J. II. Mosher-Williams, Rachel.
HV741.W6725 2001
362.7'0973—dc21

                                                                2001003807

Printed in the United States of America

**THE URBAN INSTITUTE** is a nonprofit policy research and educational organization established in Washington, D.C., in 1968. Its staff investigates the social, economic, and governance problems confronting the nation and evaluates the public and private means to alleviate them. The Institute disseminates its research findings through publications, its Web site, the media, seminars, and forums.

Through work that ranges from broad conceptual studies to administrative and technical assistance, Institute researchers contribute to the stock of knowledge available to guide decisionmaking in the public interest.

Conclusions or opinions expressed in Institute publications are those of the authors and do not necessarily reflect the views of officers or trustees of the Institute, advisory groups, or any organizations that provide financial support to the Institute.

# Contents

## Figures

## Tables

## Appendixes

# Acknowledgments

A book of this breadth reflects the work of many people. The suggestion to study the topic of nonprofit advocacy, and child advocacy in particular, came from Elizabeth T. Boris, director of the Center on Nonprofits and Philanthropy (CNP) at the Urban Institute and Ruby Takanishi, president of the Foundation for Child Development (FCD). Their interests in exploring the mechanisms for citizen participation in the political process and improving the lives of children found common ground and synergy. Their ideas and critical input throughout the project were invaluable.

We would also like to thank the authors who contributed to the volume. They worked with us in a variety of ways—sharing early drafts of their papers at an authors' conference, presenting formal papers at the Urban Institute's December 1999 conference "The Roles of Child Advocacy Organizations in Addressing Policy Issues," and revising their papers. Their patience throughout the process was greatly appreciated.

Other individuals who contributed to this work include our national advisory committee, which helped us narrow an extensive list of important topics related to child advocacy to a manageable few, and the discussants and participants at the conference, who gave us valuable feedback and recommended further issues to consider. Pho Palmer of CNP provided administrative support for the conference. Finally, we are grateful for the financial support provided by FCD that enabled us to undertake this important study.

Carol J. De Vita
Rachel Mosher-Williams

# Introduction

## How Are the Children?

*Emmett D. Carson*

M embers of the Masai tribe in Africa always greet each other in the same way. They ask, "How are the children?" The customary response is, "The children are well."

With this tradition, the members of the tribe have achieved the two most important goals of every child advocacy organization. First, the tradition ensures that every member of the community continually asks about each child's well-being as if that child were his or her own. Second, the reply—"the children are well"—reinforces the community's goal of protecting and nurturing its children.

Unfortunately, most child advocacy organizations in the United States have yet to mobilize the necessary level of public interest to make the welfare of children an overriding concern in every citizen's life. Especially disturbing is how much work remains to be done before we can say that all of our children, regardless of race or household income, are well. Despite the unprecedented economic prosperity of recent years, here are some sobering statistics to consider:

- 17 percent of all children in 1999 (12.1 million children) lived in households where family income was below the federal poverty level ($17,200 or less for a family of two adults and two children) (U.S. Bureau of the Census 2000b).

- 14 percent of all children in 1999 (10.0 million children) did not have health insurance (U.S. Bureau of the Census 2000a).
- 37 percent of fourth graders scored below basic reading levels in 2000 (National Center for Education Statistics 2001).
- One in six boys had been sexually abused before the age of 16, according to a review of studies in 1996 (Hopper 2001).
- Approximately 1 million children were victims of substantiated or indicated child abuse and neglect in 1995 (U.S. Department of Health and Human Services 1997).

This volume examines the history and experiences of child advocacy organizations in safeguarding and improving the welfare of children. Its objective is to explore how child advocacy organizations can more effectively raise the public's awareness of children's issues and advance public policy at the federal, state, and local levels.

The volume is divided into two sections. The first section examines the current infrastructure for child advocacy organizations, including the scale and scope of child advocacy organizations, the extent to which these organizations can rely on financial support from foundations, and the role of these organizations in the democratic decision-making process. The second section looks at how child advocacy organizations have historically worked at creating and maintaining constituencies and at the prospects for creating a self-sustaining, constituent-based child advocacy movement in the future. Before discussing each section in more detail, it is useful to briefly examine how child advocacy organizations have shaped the public's evolving perspective of the government's role in protecting children.

## Historical Background

The prevailing view of what best serves the interests of our children has evolved along with society. As popular views changed, so did the policy agenda of child advocacy organizations.[1] Concerns about protecting poor children can be traced to colonial times and the English Poor Law of 1601. At that time, most people believed that misbehaving children needed to be removed from the negative influence of their parents. Accordingly, troubled children were placed in institutions or indentured to other families and forced to work. Many children were sent to almshouses, which emerged in the 1800s to assist the poor and where many died or were subjected to significant abuse. Child advocacy organizations raised public concern over these abuses and helped prompt several states to enact laws providing public financing for the care and support of children. By the late 1800s, owing to the advocacy of anticruelty societies, many states had also enacted laws outlawing abuse of children. Before such laws existed, there were more legal safeguards for animals than for children.

By the early 1900s, more than 300 anticruelty societies had emerged. These groups worked from the belief that, in most cases, children should not be permanently removed from their parents, but that the overall family unit should be strengthened to enable the parents to properly care for their children. Such assistance was seen as especially important for widows raising small children (but not yet for divorced or unwed mothers). These views contributed, in part, to the Social Security Act of 1935, which contained provisions for aid to widowed women with children and funding for state programs to develop protective services for children (U.S. Congress 1998).[2] Other laws have followed, including Head Start (1964), the Child Abuse Prevention and Treatment Act (1974), Title XX of the Social Security Act (1975), the Social Services Block Grant (1975), the Indian Child Welfare Act (1978), the Adoption Assistance and Child Welfare Act (1980), the Family Preservation and Support Initiative (1993), and the Adoption and Safe Families Act (1997).

Child advocacy organizations can take considerable credit for both the passage of these laws and the positive impact each has had on improving children's lives. As discussed in the sections that follow, future successes will depend largely on strengthening the infrastructure for child advocacy, developing and sustaining a constituency for child advocacy groups, and understanding the implications of various legislative strategies to further advance the welfare of children.

## The Infrastructure for Child Advocacy

It is not easy to identify the universe of child advocacy organizations or to determine what kinds of advocacy methods are the most effective for advancing children's issues. Advocacy encompasses a variety of activities, including lobbying in support of specific legislative action, public policy research and its dissemination to influence public opinion and policymakers, advertising campaigns to educate the public, and efforts to mobilize citizens to vote for specific candidates or otherwise participate in the political process. Each of these methods has been used in the past to help improve children's quality of life. The chapters that make up this first section examine the breadth and scope of child advocacy organizations, the extent to which they receive financial support from foundations, and how they contribute to the political process and civil society.

In "Nonprofit Organizations Engaged in Child Advocacy," Carol J. De Vita, Rachel Mosher-Williams, and Nicholas A. J. Stengel identify the organizations that are speaking out for children's rights today. They use a statistical database constructed from several sources to describe the broad scope and activities of nonprofit organizations engaged in child advocacy. Although the authors are careful to note methodological limitations, they estimate that "one nonprofit service provider and child advocacy organization exists for every 1,300 children in the United States." These nonprofit groups cover an array of services, including education, human services, recreation, youth development, health, and the arts. This statistic is likely to heighten existing concerns about the effectiveness and duplication of effort by so many organizations and the difficulty of marshalling their collective strengths to advance a child policy agenda.

Sally Covington, in her chapter "In the Midst of Plenty: Foundation Funding of Child Advocacy Organizations in the 1990s," contends that the type of financial support received by organizations might weaken child advocacy outcomes. Through a review of existing data and a collection of supplemental information, she finds that foundation support for advocacy work is limited. Follow-up interviews with selected child care advocates suggest that foundations' focus on single issues, their reluctance to fund community organizing for constituency-building activities, and an emphasis on grants for specific projects rather than for general operating support have contributed to the frailness of the children's movement.

Limitations in funding often lead child advocacy organizations to focus their advocacy efforts on one level of government (federal, state, or local municipalities). Although many large child advocacy groups advance policies that ultimately lead to national legislation, some observers assert that because of the recent devolution of social programs, meaningful action on children's issues will occur at the state and local levels. Regrettably, few national organizations have the state-level infrastructure to advocate for children in all 50 states simultaneously or to coordinate the activities of potential coalition partners. While influencing change from the state and local levels appears daunting, child advocates have had significant success in securing protections for children this way. In many instances, local successes have provided the measurable results that led to the passage of similar laws at the national level.

Sara Rosenbaum and Colleen A. Sonosky provide a compelling case study of the State Children's Health Insurance Program (SCHIP), in "Medicaid Reforms and SCHIP: Health Care Coverage and the Changing Policy Environment." The authors describe how two groups of child advocates found themselves holding very different views about the values and long-term impact of SCHIP, which gave states a non-Medicaid option to provide insurance to poor children. The chapter also highlights the issues inherent in devolving greater responsibility to the states for creation and management of programs under broad federal guidelines. Child advocates will likely find themselves increasingly divided on future issues of federal versus state program management when the long-term outcomes for children are unclear.

The broader role of child advocacy organizations within the democratic decisionmaking process is explored in Elizabeth Reid's chapter, "Building a Policy Voice for Children through the Nonprofit Sector." The chapter explores advocacy's multiple facets and discusses how these ideas have been implemented by national and local child advocacy organizations. Reid suggests that child advocacy organizations should consider pursuing more active involvement in the electoral process, including full participation in the campaign and agenda-setting process. She also believes that child advocacy organizations should better use parents' and children's input to influence the decisions of elected officials.

## Creating and Sustaining a Movement for Child Advocacy

One major challenge to child advocacy groups has been the breadth of issues they cover and the limited interaction between advocacy organizations that work on different issue areas. This has been a major barrier to developing and sustaining a unified focus on children's issues. As child advocacy has evolved to consider children's well-being within the context of the family structure, an increasing number of organizations have become involved in issues that touch children's lives. Education, health care, child protection services, and housing, for example, have each spawned advocacy groups that focus on particular issues and, at times, voice concerns or promote policies aimed specifically at children. While the variety of institutions may help ensure that children's interests are considered, such a broad mix of organizations pursuing different strategies makes it more difficult to develop and sustain a cohesive children's movement.

The history of child advocacy organizations is the subject of Theda Skocpol and Jillian Dickert's "Speaking for Families and Children in a Changing America." Skocpol and Dickert trace the evolution of the child advocacy movement from its early reliance on volunteers to the development of organizations that use full-time professional staff to implement programs and strategies. The authors provide case studies on the formation and development of top-down national organizations, such as the Parent-Teacher Association and the Children's Defense Fund, as well as bottom-up organizations, such as the Texas Industrial Areas Foundation. Skocpol and Dickert suggest that both types of organizations face tremendous challenges in moving a child advocacy agenda forward because of cultural, demographic, and political factors.

Barbara Beatty's "The Politics of Preschool Advocacy: Lessons from Three Pioneering Organizations" describes how early advocates rose to such challenges. Drawing on advocates' successful efforts to universalize kindergarten programs, she derives several lessons that will be useful to today's child advocates. She compares the philosophical perspectives of the National Federation of Day Nurseries, the National Kindergarten Association, and the National Association for Nursery Education, and finds that the success of the kindergarten movement was the result of focusing on a single issue, creating an inclusive coalition across different income groups, and connecting the provision of early childhood care to the resolution of other public concerns, such as securing support for women in the labor force and eliminating the stigma of out-of-home care. Beatty provides several examples of local actions that were initially supported by local government and private financing alone but that ultimately won enough political support to secure public tax dollars.

All of these chapters bring us to a larger question: What combination of social, political, and economic factors is needed to foster the development of a new social movement for children? Doug Imig looks for an answer in "Mobilizing Parents and Communities for Children." Imig is perplexed as to why the relatively high poverty rate of children has not resulted in the development of a parent-led mass movement for children. He reasons that three developments have hampered the emergence of a children's movement. First, the growing distance between urban centers and outer suburbs has prevented parents from organizing around common concerns for the welfare of their children. Second, child advocacy organizations have not developed the necessary national and state infrastructure that could help parents identify common issues affecting their children. Third, advocacy organizations' prior legislative successes may have had the unintended consequence of eroding the very passion and energy volunteers need to sustain momentum for new advocacy efforts.

## Concluding Observations

In many ways, the conclusions in these chapters reflect several larger issues confronting child advocates: There is no consensus on the central issues facing children. There is little agreement on the long-term value of community organizing or on the most successful strategies that child advocacy organizations should consider. There is also no agreement about whether child advocacy organizations should focus their efforts at the national, state, or local level, or about the implications of pursuing one or more of these approaches. Each chapter suggests that significant changes in how organizations conduct their work will have to occur before children will get the effective advocacy that they deserve.

These statements are not intended to diminish the enormous dedication or past successes of existing organizations. Rather, they suggest that the most significant challenge to keeping children's issues on the public and legislative agendas is managing the conflicting interests and strategies of the large number of child advocacy organizations. Indeed, groups whose primary motivation is looking out for children's interests may need to consider whether the existence of fewer child advocacy organizations could lead to better coordination, more effective advocacy, and increased, stable funding.

Without question, America's poorest children remain in desperate need of an effective voice to speak on their behalf. Child advocacy organizations need to undertake the difficult process of identifying the two or three critical issues that they believe will most improve the lives of children, given the current political and economic climate. The identification of a few strategic issues might help to pierce the media noise related to other issues that compete for the public's attention. As the chapters in this volume document, child advocacy organizations have already made several successful efforts to collaborate and share information. But until we can reply that all of the children are well, no one should be content with maintaining the status quo.

## NOTES

1.  See Schene (1998) for a discussion of the changing role of child advocacy groups.
2.  These laws are documented in U.S. Congress (1998) on pp. 109, 772, 723, 723, 814, 734, 781, 738, respectively.

## REFERENCES

Hopper, Jim. 2001. "Prevalence of the Sexual Abuse of Boys." At *Child Abuse: Statistics, Research, and Resources.* Http://www.jimhopper.com/abstats. Boston University School of Medicine and The Trauma Center at HRI Hospital, Brookline, Massachusetts.

National Center for Education Statistics. 2001.*The Nation's Report Card: Fourth-Grade Reading Highlights.* Http://www.nces.ed.gov/nationsreportcard/reading/results.

Schene, Patricia A. 1998. "Past, Present, and Future Roles of Child Protective Services." *The Future of Children: Protecting Children from Abuse and Neglect* 8 (1): 23–38.

U.S. Bureau of the Census. 2000a. *Health Insurance Coverage, Consumer Income: 1999,* P60-211. Washington, D.C.: Government Printing Office.

———. 2000b. *Poverty in the United States: 1999,* P60-210. Washington, D.C.: Government Printing Office.

U.S. Congress. 1998. House Committee on Ways and Means. *Green Book.* Washington, D.C.: Government Printing Office.

U.S. Department of Health and Human Services. 1997. *Child Maltreatment 1995: Reports from the States to the National Child Abuse and Neglect Data System.* Washington, D.C.: Government Printing Office.

# SECTION ONE:
## Assessing the Environment for Child Advocacy

# 1

# Nonprofit Organizations Engaged in Child Advocacy

*Carol J. De Vita*
*Rachel Mosher-Williams*
*Nicholas A. J. Stengel*

The past decade has yielded mixed results for America's children. Some are doing quite well; others are struggling to overcome barriers and challenges that impede their efforts to compete in tomorrow's world. Their story is complex, filled with good- and bad-news scenarios. Recent statistics illustrate the uneven progress of America's children:

- Both the number and rate of infant deaths declined during the 1990s. But infant mortality rates for African Americans remained twice as high as those of white Americans (U.S. Center for Disease Control and Prevention 2000, table 31).
- The percentage of low-birth-weight babies increased from 7.0 percent in 1990 to 7.6 percent in 1999, suggesting that a greater share of children face the risk of slower development and even death (U.S. Centers for Disease Control and Prevention 2001, table 44).
- High school dropout rates hovered around 13 to 14 percent throughout much of the 1990s, with Hispanic youths almost three times more likely than white youths to drop out (U.S. Bureau of the Census 2000, table 290).
- The child poverty rate was trending downward as the decade closed, but despite this hopeful sign, one in six children (12.1 million) lived in poverty (U.S. Bureau of the Census 2001, table 3).

3

These statistics raise several troubling questions: Who is speaking for America's children? What do we know about the organizations that work on behalf of children? Will some of America's children flourish as others are left behind?

While the indicators of child well-being show that progress has been mixed, the policy-making environment has undergone a transformation. "Devolution," the policy buzzword of the 1990s, has shifted responsibility for social legislation from the federal government to state and local governments. This trend has fundamentally altered the advocacy and policy-making process. Because the locus of activity has changed, policies and outcomes for children are likely to vary across different states and localities. Devolution has increased the need to analyze the number and characteristics of child advocacy organizations and to assess how well these organizations are positioned to speak out on behalf of children.

Nonprofit organizations have always played an integral role in advancing child and family well-being. Not only do they provide essential social services, they also are key players in the advocacy process. Nonprofits generally provide a venue for citizen participation and give voice to concerns about issues that affect the lives of children and families. Although much research has been devoted to the substantive aspects of children's issues—such as poverty, child care, abuse and neglect, and education—few studies have focused directly on the advocacy efforts of nonprofit organizations.

The lack of attention to organizations that promote children's well-being partly reflects a lack of data. Very little information is available on the number, types, geographic distribution, or financial resources of nonprofit groups that direct their attention to children and child advocacy issues. Using data from the Urban Institute's National Center for Charitable Statistics, this chapter profiles the characteristics of nonprofit organizations that advocate on behalf of children. It provides a rough measure of the capacity of these organizations and identifies information gaps that limit our understanding of who is speaking for our children. The chapter also profiles two leading child advocacy organizations—the Children's Defense Fund and the National Association of Child Advocates—to illustrate the historical and socioeconomic factors that affect the development of child advocacy organizations.

## Defining Advocacy

The term "advocacy" is often considered synonymous with "lobbying," but such a narrow definition captures only one function in a much broader set of advocacy activities. Bruce Hopkins (1992) defines advocacy as "active espousal of a position, a point of view, or a course of action" (32). Lobbying, in contrast, means directly addressing legislators to influence their votes on particular issues.

Nonprofit advocacy can encompass a broad spectrum of activities, including public education, provision of opportunities for civic participation, lobbying, and direct promotion of electoral candidates. Within this spectrum, many nonprofit organizations provide a venue for "voices for dissent; . . . [they] encourage government and nongovernmental structures to respond to the needs of the poor, people of color, women, and others who face significant odds in their pursuit of a quality life" (Harmon 1996). The nonprofit sector allows many voices to be heard, even those with unpopular viewpoints.

During the 1990s, some politically conservative members of Congress raised questions about the amount and type of advocacy that nonprofit organizations can legally undertake. Although these questions alarmed many members of the nonprofit community, attempts to define and regulate nonprofit advocacy have occurred throughout most of the last century. Understanding the political and regulatory context of nonprofit advocacy provides important insights into the difficulties of measuring and assessing the advocacy activities of nonprofit organizations.

## Legislative and Regulatory Markers

Two important pieces of federal legislation and regulatory code shape the way nonprofit organizations engage in advocacy: (1) Section 501(c) of the Internal Revenue Code provides the framework for defining nonprofit, charitable organizations; (2) 501(h) status, created as a result of the Tax Reform Act of 1976 and subsequent Internal Revenue Service (IRS) regulations, defines the scope and limits of political advocacy by nonprofit organizations. In addition, proposed legislation by Representative Ernest Istook (R-OK) and others during the 1990s reflects concerns about the role and practice of nonprofit advocacy in the policy arena. These legislative and regulatory markers demonstrate the difficulties of defining advocacy. Indeed, attempts to clarify the term have met with limited success, and sometimes outright resistance, from the nonprofit sector.

### Distinguishing Types of 501(c) Organizations

Federal oversight of nonprofit organizations occurs primarily through the federal tax system. The defining feature of the nonprofit sector is its tax-exempt status. This feature also shapes the way advocacy is perceived by the public and conducted by nonprofits.

The first federal law regarding tax-exempt status was passed in 1894. However, not until the Revenue Act of 1913, adopted after ratification of the 16th Amendment to the U.S. Constitution, did tax-exempt status become fully established. The Revenue Act exempted private nonprofit organizations from paying federal income tax. It also made individuals contributing to tax-exempt religious, educational, and charitable groups eligible for a tax deduction on their federal income taxes.

The Revenue Act led to the creation of Section 501(c) of the Internal Revenue Code, which defines different types of nonprofit entities and provides guidelines for each group. Nonprofit categories initially encompassed groups with a charitable, religious, or educational purpose, but the growth and complexity of the nonprofit sector has expanded these designations over time (Bremner 1988); for example, groups that monitor environmental issues or oppose cruelty to animals have been added to the list of activities classified as charitable or educational. Some types of organizations, such as labor unions, credit unions, and farmers' cooperatives, have received distinct 501(c) designations. Currently, 25 different categories exist under the 501(c) designation of the U.S. Tax Code.

Only 501(c)(3) organizations—that is, groups that serve a broad public purpose—can receive contributions that are tax deductible to the donor. Because 501(c)(3) status indicates that the organization serves a broad public purpose, this group's advocacy activities periodically receive public scrutiny.

## Tax Reform Act of 1976 and the 501(h) Election

The Cold War and the civil rights movement created considerable ferment in American life during the 1950s and 1960s. The perceived threat of communism from abroad and calls for greater social, political, and economic equality at home created a politically charged atmosphere. During this upheaval, many Americans, particularly conservatives, viewed the activities of nonprofit organizations and philanthropic foundations as fostering and underwriting a liberal political agenda.

By the early 1970s, the activities of tax-exempt groups had come under great scrutiny. Some individuals sought to rein in the nonprofit sector's perceived influence; others attempted to develop ways to create private initiatives to address public needs. To shed light on nonprofit activities, foundations and other representatives of the philanthropic sector assembled the Commission on Private Philanthropy and Public Needs (also known as the Filer Commission) to study the dimensions and contributions of the nonprofit sector. This multidisciplinary commission produced a comprehensive study on the importance of the nonprofit sector as an employer; a provider of essential health, education, cultural, and social services; and a voice in political life. The commission's report also discussed the regulatory and tax issues that affected the nonprofit sector's well-being (Hall 1987).

As it prepared legislation to revamp the nation's tax laws, the 94th Congress gave the Filer Commission's findings and recommendations serious consideration. The Tax Reform Act of 1976 (PL 94-455) provided a new framework for defining the proper scope and limits of political advocacy by the nonprofit sector. For the first time, Congress defined the term "influencing legislation" as attempts to affect the opinions of the general public through grassroots lobbying and to influence the outcome of a specific piece of legislation by lobbying Congress directly. The act also called for financial limits on nonprofit organizations' political activity. A sliding scale was created to limit lobbying expenditures to a certain proportion of an organization's total annual expenditures (U.S. Congress 1976).

Perhaps most important, the Tax Reform Act clearly *excluded* specific activities from the definition of lobbying—namely, the publication of nonpartisan studies, the provision of technical assistance, most communication with an organization's members and administrative officials, and "self-defense" lobbying. Nonprofit organizations were pleased with the final outcome of the legislation because it defined and limited government's ability to oversee and regulate advocacy activities. In addition, the act allowed 501(c)(3) groups to spend a fairly generous percentage of their time and money on lobbying (Stengel 1997).

Following passage of the Tax Reform Act of 1976, the Internal Revenue Service was charged with crafting regulations to implement the law. Working out the details of implementation proved harder than passing the act. Nearly 14 years elapsed before final rules and regulations were in place. Much of the delay was caused by nonprofit groups' fear that limits would be placed on their participation in the policy-making process.

One of the primary outcomes of this regulatory struggle was the creation of section 501(h), which contains language that allows charities either to remain under the old "substantial part" test (a vague and un-defined measure of what constitutes lobbying activity) or to elect to come under the new sliding-scale expenditures test. The IRS did not begin to clarify the rules governing this election or the forms of communication counted as direct or grassroots lobbying until 1987. The final rules appeared in 1990.

By filing a simple one-page form with the IRS, 501(c)(3) organizations can have their lobbying expenditures judged against the section 501(h) rules, which provide an easy-to-compute progressive scale for allowable expenditures toward direct and grassroots lobbying. Groups that take the election, known as 501(h) electors, need to report only dollars spent on these two forms of advocacy. Nonelectors are subject to an ambiguous test that does not define which legislation-related activities constitute lobbying and how much lobbying is permitted.[1] Table 1.1 compares the guidelines for 501(h) electors and nonelectors within the 501(c)(3) designation.

## The "Istook Amendments"

After the 1976 Tax Reform Act was passed, Congress showed relatively little interest in overseeing the nonprofit sector until the mid-1990s. Since then, several conservative legislators have introduced bills to restrict the political activities of nonprofit organizations.

During the 104th Congress, for example, Representatives Ernest Istook (R-OK), David McIntosh (R-IN), and Robert Erlich (R-MD) attempted to enact legislation that would limit or prevent lobbying among organizations that accept government grants, arguing that federal grantees engaging in advocacy were using taxpayer subsidies to promote special interests. Viewed by many liberals as an effort to defund the left, the unprecedented bill would also have restricted the amount of *privately* raised funds a federal grantee could use to advocate and lobby. Under this stipulation, a grantee spending more than a specified threshold would be barred from receiving federal grants. Similar restrictions would not apply, however, to federal contracts, loans, or tax subsidies. Thus, the bill targeted nonprofit organizations because they are more likely than for-profit businesses to receive federal grants (OMB Watch 1999).

Representatives Istook, McIntosh, and Erlich first attempted to attach their amendment to the fiscal year 1996 appropriations bill for the Departments of Labor, Health and Human Services, and Educa-

Table 1.1  *IRS Regulations for (h) Electors and Groups Using the Substantial Part Test*

| Regulation | (h) Electors | Substantial Part Test |
|---|---|---|
| Definition of lobbying | Direct lobbying generally encompasses lobbying members or staff of a legislative body; grassroots lobbying refers to efforts that urge the public to lobby. | No specific definition of lobbying; definition is at the discretion of the IRS reviewer. |
| Spending limits on lobbying | Sliding scale: 20 percent of first $500,000 in annual expenditures, 15 percent of next $500,000 of expenditures, and so on, up to $1 million. Cap of $250,000 for grassroots lobbying and $1 million for all lobbying. | No specific definition of what constitutes substantial lobbying. IRS reserves the right to measure some absolute level of lobbying activity— by dollars, time, public prominence, success, or importance to the nonprofit. |
| Reporting requirements | Report lobbying expenditures on annual IRS Form 990. | Report lobbying expenditures on annual IRS Form 990 and include a detailed narrative description of the activities. |
| Penalties for violation | 25 percent of the amount of the excess spending. | Any lobbying deemed more than insubstantial can lead to loss of tax exemption. |

*Source:* The Urban Institute, compiled from IRS Tax Code.

tion, but the amendment was stripped from the Senate version of the bill. A revised version of the Istook amendment offered in the House-Senate conference for the Treasury-Postal Appropriation became one of the nongermane riders that led to the government shutdown during the winter of 1995.

Representatives Istook and McIntosh have since tried to attach this provocative language to five more pieces of legislation. Their most recent attempt took place during the 1999 campaign finance reform debate. Efforts to pass the amendment have been unsuccessful largely because of the strong lobbying efforts mounted by national coalitions of charitable organizations such as INDEPENDENT SECTOR and Let America Speak.

Attempts to restrict the advocacy efforts of nonprofit organizations have alarmed and galvanized the nonprofit community. Many groups have spoken out against such restrictions; others are confused about which activities they can legally pursue in the policy-making arena. Not surprisingly, given the intensity of the debate, some nonprofit organizations limit or downplay their role as advocates to avoid controversy or potentially punitive actions. The politically charged atmosphere makes it all the more difficult to scientifically measure organizations' efforts to speak out on behalf of children.

## Definitions and Data

We targeted two types of nonprofit groups for study.[2] The first type was 501(c)(3) organizations, or charitable and religious nonprofits. These organizations are the main providers of services and programs for children and families. The second group was 501(c)(4) organizations, or nonprofit social welfare groups. These organizations specifically include advocacy nonprofits.

### Identifying Advocacy Groups

Although both types of organizations are tax-exempt, the regulations governing advocacy for 501(c)(3) and 501(c)(4) organizations are very different. All (c)(3) organizations are regarded as charitable, so donor contributions are tax deductible. The IRS, however, limits the types and levels of legislative lobbying activity of (c)(3) organizations. Both direct lobbying and grassroots lobbying expenses must be reported to the IRS. By contrast, (c)(4) organizations cannot receive tax-deductible contributions, and the IRS does not restrict their lobbying activities or related spending levels. As a result, these organizations are not subject to IRS reporting requirements. Neither (c)(3) nor (c)(4) organizations are required to report expenditures on public education activities.

Because the U.S. regulatory code monitors advocacy in different ways, it is impossible to capture the broad range of nonprofit activities that contribute to the policy-making process. For the purposes of this study, the definition of advocacy is limited to legislative lobbying activity. Therefore, any 501(c)(3) organization that reports non-zero expenditures for direct lobbying or grassroots initiatives to the IRS is defined as an advocacy organization. All 501(c)(4) organizations are counted as advocacy groups.

## Constructing the Database

The starting point for the study is the database of IRS Forms 990 housed at the National Center for Charitable Statistics (NCCS) at the Urban Institute.[3] Form 990, filed annually by 501(c)(3) organizations, provides data on the group's direct lobbying and grassroots mobilization efforts as well as other administrative and financial information.

To account for differences in reporting requirements among nonprofits and data processing procedures, we used slightly different methodologies to identify (c)(3) and (c)(4) organizations. Information about the 501(c)(3) organizations was obtained from the NCCS Core data files. Organizations in these files have been classified according to the National Taxonomy of Exempt Entities-Core Codes (NTEE-CC), which indicate the organization's primary service activity.[4] The 501(c)(4) organizations were identified using the IRS Return Transaction File; although based on Form 990, this file has fewer data fields and does not include NTEE-CC codes.

The next step was to identify nonprofit groups that specifically focused on children and youth. We used three filters to identify 501(c)(3) organizations that worked in this specific area. First, using the NTEE codes, we included organizations that provided child-focused services, such as child care, delinquency prevention programs, scouting programs (e.g., the Boy Scouts of America and Girl Scouts of America), and children and youth services. Groups with NTEE codes that were inappropriate or tangential to children's issues, such as Alzheimer's disease research and insurance providers, were rejected. In some cases, NTEE groupings contained child-focused organizations under a more general code. For example, children's hospitals are grouped under the code for other specialty hospitals rather than under a specific NTEE code. Because this group contained possible candidates for study, we examined the records individually to determine whether any of the organizations belonged in the study. A complete list of NTEE codes used as screening devices appears in the appendix.

The second filter was created using the IRS Activity Codes.[5] When applying to the IRS for (c)(3) status, organizations are asked to select up to 3 codes that best describe their activities from a list of more than 300.

Groups indicating an activity that was broadly related to children and youth issues were included in the study.

To create the third filter, we conducted a key-word computer search of organization names. Nonprofits with names that contained words such as adolescent, child, and youth were flagged for examination.

In total, the data filters identified more than 105,000 (c)(3) organizations focusing, or potentially focusing, on children. This total represented approximately half of all organizations in the NCCS Core 1998 file ($n = 218,649$). Using information from IRS Form 990, Web site searches, and other available resources, we checked each organization to verify whether it focused on children or children's issues. This screening process reduced the final count of child-focused 501(c)(3) organizations to 45,354 nonprofits.

We used two filters to identify 501(c)(4) organizations that belonged in the study. First, because 501(c)(4) organizations have not been assigned NTEE codes, we screened them according to IRS Activity Codes and a keyword search. A close review of the 42,017 organizations identified in this initial search showed 9,290 (c)(4) nonprofits in child advocacy. Nearly half (48 percent) of these groups were organizations such as the Kiwanis, Rotary, and Optimist Clubs. Although these organizations are not commonly considered advocacy groups, they are broadly concerned with community and social welfare and hold the (c)(4) status.

## Findings

As policy moves from the federal government to state and local governments, the locus of advocacy activity is dispersed to organizations throughout the country. Assessing how well advocates for children can respond to this change is difficult because of the limited information available on advocacy activities. Identifying the number, geographic locations, and types of nonprofit organizations focused on children is an important step in measuring the nation's capacity for establishing a strong voice for children in every state and municipality. Direct indicators, such as the number of child-focused nonprofits that take the 501(h) election or report lobbying expenditures to the IRS, also shed light on the capacity of the advocacy infrastructure that can be marshaled to speak on behalf of children.

## Number and Location

More than 45,000 nonprofit organizations that focus on children and children's issues are distributed throughout the United States (see table 1.2). The vast majority of these groups provide services rather than engage in advocacy. As table 1.2 shows, there are almost five times more nonprofit groups providing children's services (501[c][3] organizations) than child advocacy (501[c][4] groups), or roughly 45,400 versus 9,300 organizations. Although many service providers also promote children's interests—through public education campaigns, for example—advocacy is not their primary focus.

The reasons why most nonprofit groups seek 501(c)(3) ("service provider") rather than 501(c)(4) ("advocacy") status are not well documented. A particular organization's mission and scope of work may be factors; legal and regulatory criteria may also be at issue. However, public perceptions of advocacy may also steer groups away from 501(c)(4) status. In recent years, the term advocacy has acquired negative connotations. Groups may prefer classification as charitable, which indicates that they are working in the broad public interest, rather than risk being viewed by the public as a special interest seeking narrowly defined gains.

Regionally, the 501(c)(3) and (c)(4) groups are fairly evenly distributed around the country. The South has the greatest *number* of both (c)(3) and (c)(4) child-focused nonprofits in the country, while the Northeast has the fewest. This finding is not particularly remarkable, given that the South has the most states and the largest population, while the Northeast has the fewest states and the smallest population.

Table 1.2  *Distribution of Child-Focused Nonprofit Organizations and Children, by Region, 1997*

| Region | 501(c)(3) Groups | | 501(c)(4) Groups | | Children | |
|---|---|---|---|---|---|---|
| | Number | Percent | Number | Percent | Number | Percent |
| United States | 45,354 | 100 | 9,290 | 100 | 69,528,000 | 100 |
| Northeast | 9,921 | 22 | 1,746 | 19 | 12,626,000 | 18 |
| Midwest | 10,324 | 23 | 2,417 | 26 | 16,241,000 | 23 |
| South | 13,309 | 29 | 2,812 | 30 | 24,320,000 | 35 |
| West | 11,800 | 26 | 2,315 | 25 | 16,344,000 | 24 |

Source: The Urban Institute, NCCS 1998 Core Files.
Note: Numbers and percentages may not sum to totals because of rounding.

The distribution of child-focused nonprofits is surprising, however, when the distribution of children in the population is taken into account. The South, for example, is home to 35 percent of the nation's children, but it accounts for 30 percent of the child-focused nonprofit groups. In contrast, the Northeast offers a multitude of services even though its child population is relatively small. Just 18 percent of American children live in the Northeast, but 22 percent of all children's services organizations are located there (see table 1.3 for the state-by-state distribution).

On average, one nonprofit service provider and child advocacy organization exists for every 1,300 children in the United States. The provider-to-child ratio ranges from a high of approximately one organization per 1,100 children in the Northeast, to a low of one nonprofit for every 1,500 children in the South. The ratios for the Midwest and West fall close to the national average.

In the current political environment, which emphasizes regional diversity and local solutions, these ratios help identify areas where regional or local infrastructures for serving the interests of children need to be developed or enhanced. On a per capita basis, the infrastructure for promoting the well-being of children in the South is relatively weak; in the Northeast, it is somewhat stronger. Although the ratio of organizations to children does not indicate effectiveness, it is a good starting point for assessing an area's potential capacity for getting children's issues on the public agenda and developing capacity-building strategies. In a region with relatively few nonprofit groups, for example, the task of speaking out for children can be a huge undertaking. Such a locale may need to expand the number of nonprofits that make children's issues their primary concern in order to share the responsibility among a larger network. A region with more nonprofit groups might strengthen its capacity by facilitating closer cooperation among existing organizations. Knowing the number and location of child-focused nonprofits can help state and local governments, grantmakers, and advocates formulate a responsive strategy for building capacity.

## Types of Organizations

Describing the activities of the 501(c)(3) nonprofits is relatively straightforward because these groups are classified by NTEE codes. Perhaps not surprisingly, the bulk of children's services are focused on education (see figure 1.1): 40 percent of all child-focused 501(c)(3) organizations

(*text continues on page 17*)

Table 1.3  *Distribution of Child-Focused Nonprofit Organizations and Children, by Region and State, 1997*

| Location | Services (501[c][3]) Number | Percent | Advocacy (501[c][4]) Number | Percent | Children Under Age 18 Number | Percent |
|---|---|---|---|---|---|---|
| **United States** | 45,354 | 100.0 | 9,290 | 100.0 | 69,528 | 100.0 |
| **Northeast** | 9,921 | 21.9 | 1,746 | 18.8 | 12,626 | 18.2 |
| **New England** | 3,430 | 7.6 | 538 | 5.8 | 3,215 | 4.6 |
| Connecticut | 835 | 1.8 | 164 | 1.8 | 792 | 1.1 |
| Maine | 266 | 0.6 | 66 | 0.7 | 297 | 0.4 |
| Massachusetts | 1,574 | 3.5 | 180 | 1.9 | 1,451 | 2.1 |
| New Hampshire | 349 | 0.8 | 67 | 0.7 | 296 | 0.4 |
| Rhode Island | 199 | 0.4 | 27 | 0.3 | 233 | 0.3 |
| Vermont | 207 | 0.5 | 34 | 0.4 | 146 | 0.2 |
| **Middle Atlantic** | 6,491 | 14.3 | 1,208 | 13.0 | 9,411 | 13.5 |
| New Jersey | 1,451 | 3.2 | 224 | 2.4 | 1,987 | 2.9 |
| New York | 3,039 | 6.7 | 362 | 3.9 | 4,560 | 6.6 |
| Pennsylvania | 2,001 | 4.4 | 622 | 6.7 | 2,864 | 4.1 |
| **Midwest** | 10,324 | 22.6 | 2,417 | 26.0 | 16,241 | 23.4 |
| **East North Central** | 6,961 | 15.2 | 1,596 | 17.2 | 11,362 | 16.3 |
| Illinois | 1,866 | 4.1 | 353 | 3.8 | 3,175 | 4.6 |
| Indiana | 1,059 | 2.3 | 261 | 2.8 | 1,497 | 2.2 |
| Michigan | 1,242 | 2.7 | 391 | 4.2 | 2,505 | 3.6 |
| Ohio | 1,782 | 3.9 | 354 | 3.8 | 2,839 | 4.1 |
| Wisconsin | 1,012 | 2.2 | 237 | 2.6 | 1,346 | 1.9 |
| **West North Central** | 3,363 | 7.4 | 821 | 8.8 | 4,879 | 7.0 |
| Iowa | 524 | 1.2 | 159 | 1.7 | 726 | 1.0 |
| Kansas | 459 | 1.0 | 98 | 1.1 | 688 | 1.0 |
| Minnesota | 926 | 2.0 | 231 | 2.5 | 1,251 | 1.8 |
| Missouri | 836 | 1.8 | 189 | 2.0 | 1,407 | 2.0 |
| Nebraska | 317 | 0.7 | 65 | 0.7 | 444 | 0.6 |
| North Dakota | 123 | 0.3 | 40 | 0.4 | 166 | 0.2 |
| South Dakota | 178 | 0.4 | 39 | 0.4 | 197 | 0.3 |
| **South** | 13,309 | 29.4 | 2,812 | 30.3 | 24,320 | 35.0 |
| **South Atlantic** | 7,361 | 16.3 | 1,573 | 17.0 | 11,899 | 17.1 |
| Delaware | 178 | 0.4 | 26 | 0.3 | 177 | 0.3 |
| District of Columbia | 302 | 0.7 | 37 | 0.4 | 107 | 0.2 |
| Florida | 1,809 | 4.0 | 437 | 4.7 | 3,471 | 5.0 |
| Georgia | 989 | 2.2 | 207 | 2.2 | 1,988 | 2.9 |

*(Continued)*

Table 1.3  *Distribution of Child-Focused Nonprofit Organizations and Children, by Region and State, 1997 (Continued)*

| Location | Services (501[c][3]) Number | Percent | Advocacy (501[c][4]) Number | Percent | Children Under Age 18 Number | Percent |
|---|---|---|---|---|---|---|
| Maryland | 991 | 2.2 | 152 | 1.6 | 1,269 | 1.8 |
| North Carolina | 1,249 | 2.8 | 266 | 2.9 | 1,874 | 2.7 |
| South Carolina | 468 | 1.0 | 127 | 1.4 | 956 | 1.4 |
| Virginia | 1,153 | 2.5 | 268 | 2.9 | 1,645 | 2.4 |
| West Virginia | 222 | 0.5 | 53 | 0.6 | 412 | 0.6 |
| **East South Central** | 2,077 | 4.6 | 423 | 4.5 | 4,111 | 5.9 |
| Alabama | 496 | 1.1 | 119 | 1.3 | 1,072 | 1.5 |
| Kentucky | 529 | 1.2 | 102 | 1.1 | 961 | 1.4 |
| Mississippi | 289 | 0.6 | 60 | 0.6 | 753 | 1.1 |
| Tennessee | 763 | 1.7 | 142 | 1.5 | 1,325 | 1.9 |
| **West South Central** | 3,871 | 8.5 | 816 | 8.8 | 8,310 | 12.0 |
| Arkansas | 371 | 0.8 | 79 | 0.9 | 663 | 1.0 |
| Louisiana | 440 | 1.0 | 111 | 1.2 | 1,191 | 1.7 |
| Oklahoma | 420 | 0.9 | 104 | 1.1 | 878 | 1.3 |
| Texas | 2,640 | 5.8 | 522 | 5.6 | 5,578 | 8.0 |
| **West** | 11,800 | 26.1 | 2,315 | 24.8 | 16,344 | 23.5 |
| **Mountain** | 2,663 | 6.0 | 518 | 5.5 | 4,637 | 6.7 |
| Arizona | 586 | 1.3 | 125 | 1.3 | 1,278 | 1.8 |
| Colorado | 855 | 1.9 | 138 | 1.5 | 1,016 | 1.5 |
| Idaho | 164 | 0.4 | 42 | 0.5 | 352 | 0.5 |
| Montana | 201 | 0.4 | 57 | 0.6 | 229 | 0.3 |
| Nevada | 174 | 0.4 | 37 | 0.4 | 443 | 0.6 |
| New Mexico | 360 | 0.8 | 58 | 0.6 | 499 | 0.7 |
| Utah | 208 | 0.5 | 29 | 0.3 | 688 | 1.0 |
| Wyoming | 115 | 0.3 | 32 | 0.3 | 132 | 0.2 |
| **Pacific** | 9,137 | 20.1 | 1,797 | 19.3 | 11,707 | 16.8 |
| Alaska | 217 | 0.5 | 37 | 0.4 | 188 | 0.3 |
| California | 6,632 | 14.6 | 1,217 | 13.1 | 8,952 | 12.9 |
| Hawaii | 234 | 0.5 | 40 | 0.4 | 302 | 0.4 |
| Oregon | 787 | 1.7 | 152 | 1.6 | 811 | 1.2 |
| Washington | 1,267 | 2.8 | 351 | 3.8 | 1,454 | 2.1 |

*Source:* Nonprofit data from the Urban Institute, NCCS 1998 Core Files; population data from the U.S. Bureau of the Census, Statistical Abstract of the United States, 1998, table 33.

Figure 1.1 *Nonprofit Services for Children, by Type of Service*

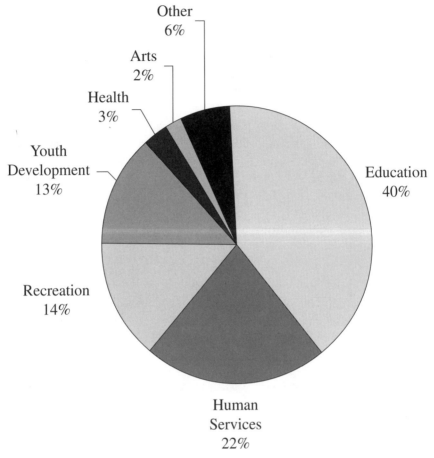

Other
6%

Arts
2%

Health
3%

Youth
Development
13%

Education
40%

Recreation
14%

Human
Services
22%

Source: The Urban Institute, NCCS 1998 Core Files.
Note: Number of observations = 45,354.

report that their primary activity is related to education. Such services include preschool and early childhood development programs, elementary and secondary schools, libraries, Parent-Teacher Associations, dropout prevention services, and more. They do not include higher education and adult education programs.

Human services were the second most-prevalent activity. Such organizations account for 22 percent of nonprofit services for children and include a broad spectrum of groups, including those working on adoption and foster care, YMCAs, YWCAs, teen pregnancy prevention programs, parenting skills, counseling programs, and more.

Recreation programs (14 percent) and youth development services (13 percent) are the next most frequently named activities. These programs include parks and groups sponsoring playground activities, sports clubs, Little Leagues, soccer leagues, Boys Clubs, Girls Clubs, scouting organizations, Junior Achievement, 4-H Clubs, and adult-child mentoring programs, such as Big Brothers, Big Sisters, and Foster Grandparents.

The remaining 11 percent of nonprofit service providers cover a wide range of services, including children's health programs, arts and cultural groups, housing, inner-city activities, and other miscellaneous programs.

Determining the focus of the 501(c)(4) organizations is more difficult because they are classified not by NTEE codes but by IRS activity codes. The IRS activity codes allow nonprofit organizations to describe the nature of their work and/or their substantive areas of interest, but these codes do not always provide a complete picture. For example, one in four organizations in the study lists legislative, political, and advocacy activities as a major activity but does not indicate the work's substantive area, so we do not know whether these organizations focus on one specific area or on many issues. In contrast, about 20 percent of the groups described themselves as schools or educational programs, and another 20 percent listed sports and youth activities as their area of focus, but neither group indicated whether they engage in any type of advocacy activity. The remaining 501(c)(4) organizations in the study report a wide range of other program and activity areas. Although the (c)(4) designation suggests that these groups act as advocates, they do not necessarily describe their activities in this way.

A review of the organizations in this study reveal other difficulties in defining and measuring the extent of advocacy activities in the sector.[6] As Sally Covington notes in "In the Midst of Plenty: Foundation Funding for Child Advocacy Organizations in the 1990s," conceptual and definitional issues can affect the portrait of child advocacy organizations. In our study, roughly 470 veterans' groups and almost 450 women's clubs (such as the American Association of University Women, the Women's Club in various cities, and the League of Women Voters) indicated that they focus on issues concerning children and youth. Under a very restrictive definition of child advocacy, these groups might not be counted as child advocates.

Table 1.4 *Distribution of Child-Focused Nonprofit Organizations that Report Advocacy Activity, by Region, 1997*

| Region | 501(c)(3) Groups | | (h) Electors | | Groups with Lobby Expenses | |
|---|---|---|---|---|---|---|
| | Number | Percent | Number | Percent | Number | Percent |
| United States | 45,354 | 100 | 886 | 100 | 513 | 100 |
| Northeast | 9,921 | 22 | 194 | 22 | 115 | 22 |
| Midwest | 10,324 | 23 | 235 | 27 | 144 | 28 |
| South | 13,309 | 29 | 236 | 27 | 126 | 25 |
| West | 11,800 | 26 | 221 | 25 | 128 | 25 |

*Source:* The Urban Institute, NCCS 1998 Core Files.
*Note:* Numbers and percentages may not sum to totals because of rounding.

## 501(h) Electors

Organizations that take the 501(h) election are easy to identify in the IRS database because they complete Schedule A of Form 990. This information provides one of the few indicators of the number and types of (c)(3) groups engaging in direct lobbying (face-to-face) or grassroots lobbying (urging the public to lobby).

For nonprofit groups that wish to lobby, the 501(h) election provides clear administrative and regulatory guidelines. Nonetheless, only a handful of organizations have taken the election. According to Form 990 returns filed with the IRS in 1998, about 2 percent of the nonprofit groups that focus on children (885 organizations) took the 501(h) election. Although this proportion appears small given the apparent benefits of the (h) election, it is in line with findings for the nonprofit sector as a whole, according to researchers at Charity Lobbying in the Public Interest (1999).

Geographically, the distribution of 501(h) electors closely resembles that of all child-focused 501(c)(3) groups (see table 1.4). The Midwest had a slightly higher share of child-focused (h) electors, but the difference was not significant. Within regions, however, several hubs of activity emerged (see table 1.5). In the Northeast, for example, New York State had 64 child-focused nonprofits that chose to take the (h) election—more than the number of child-focused (h) electors in all of New England. In the Midwest, Illinois had the largest number of (h) electors (40 organizations),

Table 1.5  *Child-Focused Nonprofit Organizations Reporting Lobbying Activities, by State and Region*

| Location | Number of Nonprofits Reporting | |
|---|---|---|
| | *501(h) Election* | *Lobbying Expenses* |
| **United States** | 885 | 513 |
| **Northeast Region** | 194 | 115 |
| **New England** | 63 | 42 |
| Connecticut | 9 | 12 |
| Maine | 5 | 5 |
| Massachusetts | 33 | 19 |
| New Hampshire | 2 | 0 |
| Rhode Island | 7 | 4 |
| Vermont | 7 | 2 |
| **Middle Atlantic** | 131 | 73 |
| New Jersey | 23 | 11 |
| New York | 64 | 42 |
| Pennsylvania | 44 | 20 |
| **Midwest Region** | 235 | 144 |
| **East North Central** | 140 | 90 |
| Illinois | 40 | 28 |
| Indiana | 19 | 5 |
| Michigan | 29 | 24 |
| Ohio | 31 | 29 |
| Wisconsin | 21 | 4 |
| **West North Central** | 95 | 54 |
| Iowa | 16 | 6 |
| Kansas | 16 | 6 |
| Minnesota | 24 | 23 |
| Missouri | 18 | 11 |
| Nebraska | 11 | 6 |
| North Dakota | 3 | 0 |
| South Dakota | 7 | 2 |
| **South Region** | 236 | 126 |
| **South Atlantic** | 142 | 86 |
| Delaware | 2 | 2 |
| District of Columbia | 34 | 26 |
| Florida | 25 | 13 |
| Georgia | 18 | 8 |
| Maryland | 13 | 7 |

Table 1.5  *Child-Focused Nonprofit Organizations Reporting Lobbying Activities by State and Region (Continued)*

| Location | 501(h) Election | Lobbying Expenses |
|---|---|---|
| | *Number of Nonprofits Reporting* | |
| North Carolina | 19 | 13 |
| South Carolina | 8 | 1 |
| Virginia | 19 | 12 |
| West Virginia | 4 | 4 |
| **East South Central** | 37 | 8 |
| Alabama | 14 | 3 |
| Kentucky | 9 | 1 |
| Mississippi | 6 | 1 |
| Tennessee | 8 | 3 |
| **West South Central** | 57 | 32 |
| Arkansas | 3 | 1 |
| Louisiana | 5 | 1 |
| Oklahoma | 9 | 1 |
| Texas | 40 | 29 |
| **West Region** | 220 | 128 |
| **Mountain** | 62 | 37 |
| Arizona | 10 | 8 |
| Colorado | 21 | 12 |
| Idaho | 4 | 2 |
| Montana | 8 | 3 |
| Nevada | 1 | 3 |
| New Mexico | 17 | 6 |
| Utah | 1 | 2 |
| Wyoming | 0 | 1 |
| **Pacific** | 158 | 91 |
| Alaska | 5 | 4 |
| California | 98 | 52 |
| Hawaii | 6 | 0 |
| Oregon | 17 | 11 |
| Washington | 32 | 24 |

*Source:* The Urban Institute, NCCS 1998 Core Files.

followed closely by Ohio (31), Michigan (29), and Minnesota (24). In the South, Texas had the most (h) electors (40), followed by the District of Columbia (34) and Florida (25). Forty-five percent of the (h) electors in the West were in California (98 organizations), while Washington (32), Colorado (21), and Oregon (17) also had a fair number of (h) electors.

Human service organizations were the most likely to be (h) electors (see figure 1.2). Of the 885 child-focused groups that chose the (h) election, nearly 30 percent were in the human services field. The second-largest group of (h) electors were nonprofit health organizations. While health organizations made up only 3 percent of all child-oriented (c)(3) organizations, they represented 26 percent of (h) electors. In contrast, nonprofits in the educational field constituted 40 percent of children's public charities but only 19 percent of (h) electors. Combined, these three types of organizations—human services, health, and education—represented three-quarters of all child-focused nonprofit groups that took the (h) election. Youth development organizations, responsible for 14 percent of all children's nonprofit electors, ranked a distant fourth.

Given the advantage of choosing the 501(h) election, it is curious that so few child-focused nonprofits have done so. Some groups may simply be misinformed about the usefulness of taking the election. Others may fear that becoming an (h) elector marks them as targets for an IRS audit.

It is important to note, however, that taking the (h) election is not a firm indicator of continual or substantial lobbying activity. Some groups may take the (h) election for advocacy pertaining to specific legislation and may continue under the election even after the lobbying effort is completed. Others may take the election as a protective measure in case they decide to lobby in the future. A somewhat better measure of lobbying activity is the group's actual lobbying expenditures as reported on IRS Form 990.

## Expenditures on Lobbying

Although 2 percent of child-focused nonprofit groups took the (h) election, only 1 percent actually reported lobbying expenses.[7] A total of 513 child-oriented nonprofit organizations reported non-zero values for lobbying expenses in their 1998 Form 990; as table 1.6 shows, these groups tended to be relatively large organizations. Average revenues for child-oriented (h) electors in 1997 were more than $7.5 million, while

Figure 1.2  *Distribution of (h) Electors and Types of Child-Focused Nonprofits*

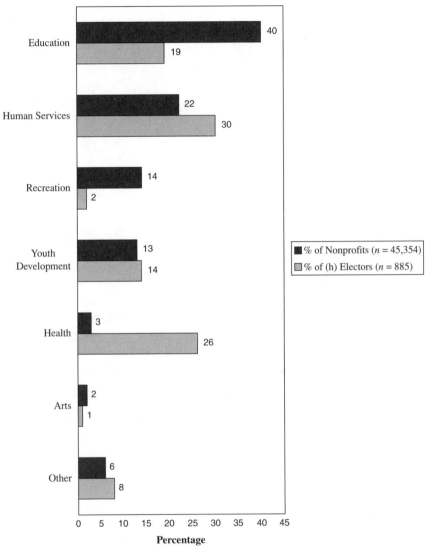

*Source:* The Urban Institute, NCCS 1998 Core Files.

Table 1.6  *Finances by Type of Nonprofit Organization, 1997*
*(Dollars in thousands)*

| Type of organization | Number | Average Revenues | Average Expenses | Average Assets | Average Lobbying Expenses |
|---|---|---|---|---|---|
| All 501(c)(3) | 218,649 | $5,024 | $3,052 | $6,182 | — |
| Child-oriented 501(c)(3) | 45,354 | 1,538 | 1,011 | 1,891 | — |
| With (h) election | 886 | 7,595 | 5,563 | 8,578 | $15 |
| With lobbying expenses | 513 | 29,001 | 14,033 | 33,604 | 37 |

Source: The Urban Institute, NCCS 1998 Core Files.

groups that reported lobbying expenses above zero had revenues averaging $29 million. Similar patterns emerged for average expenditures and assets. Compared with (h) electors, child-oriented nonprofits that reported lobbying expenses had, on average, three to four times more revenues, assets, and expenditures. They also had substantially more financial resources than the typical child-focused nonprofit in the study, which averaged less than $2 million in revenues, assets, and expenditures.

Because only direct lobbying expenses and grassroots lobbying expenses must be reported to the IRS, the actual amount spent on lobbying activities appears to be fairly small. On average, child-focused (h) electors reported $15,000 in lobbying expenses in 1997, while child-focused groups overall, regardless of (h) status, reported spending roughly $37,000 on lobbying activities. By these measures, direct and grassroots lobbying expenses account for less than 1 percent of these organizations' overall revenues. Other types of advocacy work, such as public education or voter registration, are not reported on Form 990.

The types of child-focused organizations that report lobbying expenses are far different from those that take the (h) election (see figure 1.3). Whereas human services groups were most likely to be (h) electors, health and education organizations were most likely to report lobbying expenses, regardless of their status as (h) electors. Two out of every three child-focused groups that reported lobbying expenses in 1997 were in the health and education fields. Human service providers ranked third, with fewer than one in five groups reporting any lobbying expenditures.

The amount spent on lobbying varied significantly, however, by type of provider. In the aggregate, child-oriented nonprofits reported more than

Figure 1.3  *Distribution of Nonprofits Reporting Lobbying Expenses and Dollars Spent, by Type of Child-Focused Nonprofit*

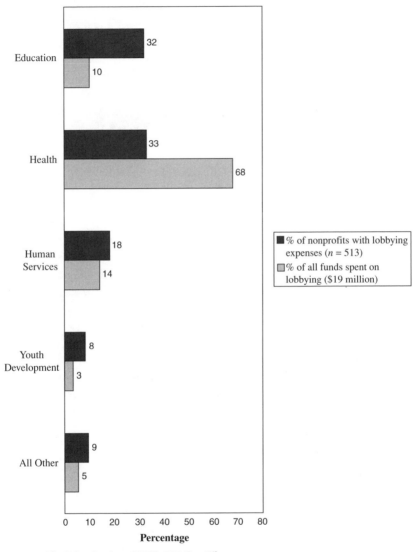

*Source:* The Urban Institute, NCCS 1998 Core Files.

$19 million in lobbying expenses in 1997. As figure 1.3 shows, more than two-thirds of this amount (nearly $13 million) was spent by health organizations. Legislative debates over the State Children's Health Insurance Program (SCHIP) and the distribution of funds from the legal settlement with the tobacco industry no doubt helped fuel this spending pattern. Lobbying expenditures by human service and education groups added roughly $4 million to the total spent in 1997 to further children's issues. Although these data provide only a small piece of the advocacy puzzle, they strongly suggest that larger children's organizations are more likely than smaller, more modestly funded groups to find a seat at the political table.

## Looking beyond Form 990: Profiles of Two Leading Child Advocacy Organizations

While statistics can shed some light on the issue of who is speaking for America's children, they cannot tell the whole story. As this chapter shows, there are considerable difficulties and ambiguities involved in using IRS data to define and measure nonprofit advocacy. A great deal of child advocacy work is accomplished through activities that are not even reported to the IRS, such as public education and community capacity building. A closer look at two child advocacy organizations—the Children's Defense Fund and the National Association of Child Advocates—reveals that these two groups engage in a broad range of activities in addition to lobbying. The histories and organizational structures of these two groups also provide important insights into the different paths for advancing an agenda for children.

### The Children's Defense Fund

The origins of the Children's Defense Fund (CDF) are closely tied to the civil rights movement of the 1960s. The Fund began in 1968, when Marian Wright received a fellowship from the Field Foundation of New York to research how to establish an effective voice for poor and minority citizens in the District of Columbia. Wright subsequently founded the Washington Research Project (WRP), a public interest law firm, to monitor federal civil rights and antipoverty legislation. WRP served as counsel and legislative liaison for the Poor People's Campaign begun by Dr. Martin Luther King, Jr. Jobs, education, health care, and nutrition were among the priority issues under WRP review.

WRP began to focus on children's issues in 1969, when it investigated whether programs under the federal Title I of the Elementary and Secondary Education Act of 1965 were actually helping poor children. The organization discovered that federal funds were being grossly misused by states and local entities. Although their findings did not immediately induce Congress to take corrective action, other advocacy groups began to champion the cause. That same year, WRP formally incorporated itself as a 501(c)(3) nonprofit and created the WRP Action Council, a separate (c)(4) lobbying arm. In essence, this dual structure allowed the WRP to work on issues from two perspectives: a research and public education strategy under WRP, and a direct lobbying strategy through the Action Council.

A year later, WRP and the Action Council sought to protect the Head Start program from state attacks by folding it into a comprehensive bill, the Child Development Act of 1971. Drafted by a broad coalition convened by WRP, the act was designed to make quality child care available to all children. The landmark, bipartisan bill was passed by Congress in less than a year, but President Nixon vetoed it just before his first trip to China. Although WRP was unable to mobilize an override of the veto, the intense experience convinced WRP to focus its activities solely on children. Within two years, the organization had changed its name to the Children's Defense Fund and opened field offices in Cambridge, Massachusetts, and Jackson, Mississippi. The New World and Field Foundations provided startup funds for the new CDF.

Over the last three decades, CDF has remained a strong national voice for children. Still led by Marian Wright Edelman, it continues to work for children in the areas of health, education, child care, special needs, and poverty. Today, CDF is arguably the most well-known child advocacy organization in the country. With a budget of nearly $26 million, it is also one of the largest.

As it did during its infancy and like many other activist groups, CDF struggles with the issue of advocating for universal versus targeted programs for "the most vulnerable children" (CDF 1999, 12). CDF's history shows that it often does both by supporting targeted programs while working toward universal goals. Its mission, as stated on the CDF Web site, is to "leave no child behind and to ensure every child a Healthy Start, a Head Start, a Fair Start, a Safe Start, and a Moral Start in life and successful passage to adulthood with the help of caring families and communities" (CDF 2001).

Because the political and social environments have changed greatly since the late 1960s, CDF has had to adapt as well. During the 1960s, it was acceptable, even expected, for nonprofit organizations to be politically active in the policy-making process. CDF's activities were very much in line with this expectation: The group drafted and lobbied for federal legislation, acted as a "watchdog" on regulations, filed lawsuits when investigations showed lack of compliance, and mobilized broad-based coalitions to fight for new comprehensive programs. Since most major children's issues were playing out at the national level, being headquartered in Washington, D.C., placed CDF near the seat of federal power.

But over time, the words "political" and "advocacy" became associated with "dishonest" and "self-interested." Nonprofit organizations found that advocating through less direct, or "softer" vehicles, such as public education and capacity building, garnered more acceptance among foundations, the public, and even government itself. Indeed, CDF's advocacy efforts are now centered on public education rather than on direct lobbying of legislators. CDF proudly notes in its materials that it has "never taken government funds" (CDF 2000) and that "less than 10 percent of the Children's Defense Fund's resources . . . are devoted to legislative lobbying" (CDF 1999, 11). According to its 1998 IRS Form 990, CDF spent $1.8 million on public education and an additional $2.6 million on publications and conferences. In contrast, CDF spent $175,000 for direct lobbying activities—only 1 percent of its budget. This amount was well below CDF's legal limit of $937,000 under the 501(h) election.

CDF's activities and funds are still centralized in Washington, D.C., but devolution has encouraged the group to create more local offices. CDF now has offices in California, Minnesota, Mississippi, New York, Ohio, South Carolina, and Texas. These offices conduct their own fundraising and have their own budgets, but they operate under the fiscal agency and governance of the national headquarters. For the most part, the local offices work at the state level to achieve the same goals sought by the national CDF: increasing "awareness about the needs of children and their families and encourag[ing] preventive investment before they get sick, drop out of school, get into trouble, or suffer family breakdown" (CDF-Minnesota 2001). CDF also facilitates community-based child advocacy through financial support of Stand for Children, a spin-off group that helps grassroots children's activists build Children's Action Teams.

As policymaking on children's issues shifts toward state and local levels of government, CDF is having to alter its centralized structure and traditional focus on federal legislation in order to work with a new decision-making locus. CDF's staff increasingly monitors proposed legislation and initiatives in the states, and provides comparative information that can be used by local advocates. Activities such as Stand for Children help mobilize local activists and provide them with technical assistance. CDF's central work, however, is still identified with federal policymaking, and its national reputation continues to make CDF a strong voice for all the nation's children rather than just those in a particular state or region.

## The National Association of Child Advocates

Like CDF, the National Association of Child Advocates (NACA) was conceived and spearheaded by a single individual, but its development has followed a very different course. These differences reflect both the social and political context in which NACA was founded and the philosophy that shaped the organization. Unlike CDF's direct focus on children's issues and federal legislation, NACA focuses on building an organizational infrastructure across the country that can speak for children.

In the late 1960s and early 1970s, community activists around the country were working for systematic changes at the state level for children in need. This work, often done by one or two volunteers, was not coordinated, widely recognized, or well funded. The California Children's Lobby, Kentucky Youth Advocates, and the Florida Center for Children were a few of the pioneers trying to make legislators aware of and accountable for the needs of children in their states.

Jim Lardie, who created the Institute for Child Advocacy in Ohio in 1976, felt isolated from other advocates who were doing similar work in other regions of the country. Motivated by a need to brainstorm with fellow children's activists as well as by the knowledge that "broad mobilization was necessary to create meaningful social change for children" (NACA 2000, 8), Lardie circulated a white paper in 1978 that proposed forming a national multi-issue institute for child advocacy. This idea was met with interest by the Edna McConnell Clark Foundation in New York, which subsequently provided funding for a meeting of child advocates from around the country and which also offered seed money to help Lardie support advocates in Illinois and Missouri.

In 1981, Lardie and advocates from 13 other states convened in Cleveland, Ohio, to share stories, ideas, and inspiration. The group continued to meet annually for the next three years, and the number of members grew significantly. Bolstered by the support they received at these annual gatherings and convinced that their effectiveness as advocates would benefit from more regular communication, the informal network of child advocates officially incorporated in late 1984 as the Association of State-Based Child Advocacy Organizations (ACA) and became a 501(c)(3) nonprofit organization.

ACA came into being in the early 1980s, when President Reagan's block-granting efforts and cuts in federal programs for the poor were at their peak. The political tide was shifting toward greater decision-making at the state and local levels and less oversight by federal authorities. In response to this environment, the ACA organizers charged the association with "increasing the number of independent state-based child advocacy organizations and enhancing their effectiveness" (NACA 2000, 9). Rather than lobbying for or against federal programs targeting children, ACA's mission was to nurture the strong voice of advocates in the states by facilitating their communication and mutual support. The association established its headquarters in Ohio and ran it with a very small staff.

By the early 1990s, ACA membership had grown in size and sophistication and included city and regional advocacy organizations as well as state organizations. In 1991, Jim Lardie stepped down, and Eva Brooks became the head of ACA. A year later, the organization changed its name to the National Association of Child Advocates and moved its headquarters to Washington, D.C. Despite the move to the nation's capital and its name change, NACA continued to concentrate on the role of activist groups at the state level. Brooks's decision to relocate was simply a recognition that a "Washington presence would . . . give NACA's members access to more information about policy and practice" (NACA 2000, 10).

In the late 1980s and early 1990s, foundations began to show a renewed interest in the child advocacy movement, with initiatives such as Annie E. Casey's national KIDS COUNT that "strengthened the ability of state-based child advocacy organizations to produce hard data in support of their positions" (NACA 2000, 11). Major grantmakers began to fund NACA and its activities. These new funds helped expand NACA's staff, allowing the organization to provide technical assistance on formulating policy responses and developing organizational strategy to member organizations.

By 1996, when Congress passed welfare reform legislation, the NACA network was well established within the states, allowing the group to monitor these reforms and to advocate for children in state legislatures and governors' offices. Tamara Lucas Copeland, NACA's current president, joined the organization in 1997, just as the first effects of welfare reform were being assessed.

NACA's current membership totals 63 member organizations in 48 states and 11 cities and communities. NACA requires its members to be nonprofit child advocacy organizations (either 501[c][3] or [c][4] status), independent, state- or community-based, and professionally run, answering to no one but the children they represent. They must be multi-issue organizations that "view the child as a whole, knowing that children need all the pieces of the puzzle—food, shelter, security, education, health care—to grow up strong and productive" (NACA 2000). Finally, members must be advocates in the broadest sense, not single-issue lobbyists or direct service providers.

NACA and its member organizations rely on advocacy tools such as public education and community empowerment to improve the lives of American children. Unlike the Children's Defense Fund, NACA reports no lobbying expenses.

Compared with CDF, NACA is a relatively small organization, with $2 million in revenue—about 10 percent of CDF's budget. However, because of its bottom-up structure, NACA has had significant influence on how child advocacy is conducted across the country. As policies affecting poor families are shaped and implemented at the state and local levels, NACA and it state-based members are well positioned to play a major role in advocating for America's children.

## Conclusions

During a time of relative wealth and prosperity, many of America's children are still being left behind. Nearly one child in six is growing up in poverty, and the gap between rich and poor remains wide. To address these concerns, child advocates are finding that they can no longer operate at the federal level alone; they must also take their case to the states and to numerous localities. Responding to new conditions and developing a stronger voice for children's issues requires crafting a clear message and building a stronger organizational infrastructure to carry out the agenda. The results of this study point to three conclusions that should help guide child advocates as they build and strengthen the organizational infrastructure of all groups.

1. **APPROACHES WILL NEED TO VARY FROM STATE TO STATE.** Because devolution has placed the focus of policymaking on state and local governments, a one-size-fits-all strategy to promoting the well-being of children is unlikely to yield satisfactory results. Not only will the issues vary from state to state, but the organizational resources that can be mustered to identify, track, and lobby for critical children's needs will also vary.

Assessing the geographic locations and capacities of child advocacy organizations can be a first step in understanding the strengths and gaps in the existing nonprofit advocacy landscape. In some states, an abundance of well-established and well-organized groups can be mobilized to take action on behalf of children. In other states, the organizational infrastructure may need to be built and nurtured. New groups may spring from grassroots concerns, but these new efforts, like those that have preceded them, are likely to turn to private foundations for support. Giving these groups guidance and resources to build an advocacy infrastructure will be an important step in developing an expanded and coordinated advocacy effort.

2. **LARGER ORGANIZATIONS ARE MORE LIKELY THAN SMALL ONES TO HAVE THE INSTITUTIONAL CAPACITY TO LOBBY.** The data in this study are a reminder that large amounts of money are needed to engage in legislative lobbying. Although smaller organizations can be effective in educating their members, clients, and the general public about the need for supporting particular children's issues, they are unlikely to have the human or financial resources to take part fully in the legislative process. Effective lobbying is a skill and an art. It requires building and maintaining relationships with legislators and their staffs and constantly monitoring issues. Larger nonprofit organizations are far more likely than smaller ones to have the institutional capacity to conduct a sustained campaign for children's issues.

3. **MEASURING THE SCOPE OF CHILD ADVOCACY WILL REMAIN DIFFICULT BECAUSE IRS REPORTING REQUIREMENTS DO NOT CAPTURE MANY ADVOCACY ACTIVITIES.** While the IRS database is the most comprehensive and systematic source of information on nonprofit organizations, it falls short of providing a complete and detailed picture of nonprofit advocacy activities. The IRS collects information on only one aspect of advocacy: legislative lobbying. Public education, arguably the most common form of nonprofit advocacy, is not included in the IRS reporting require-

ments. Because legislative lobbying is undertaken by a small percentage of child advocacy organizations, the extent and influence of their activities escape simple descriptive statistics.

Changing IRS reporting requirements to include more forms of advocacy would not necessarily clarify the issue. Such a proposal is likely to meet resistance from nonprofit groups, not only because it would be burdensome, but also because it would encroach on their role as voices for citizen action, particularly if similar regulations were not placed on for-profit organizations. The sheer breadth of activities that can be construed as advocacy would make regulations very difficult to write. More important, the activities are not always discrete or mutually exclusive. Activities that could be defined as advocacy in one context may be viewed as programmatic activities in another context. For example, disentangling the costs of public education from a nonprofit's overall budget is likely to provide only a gross "guesstimate" of those advocacy expenditures rather than accurate data. Ultimately, an effort to redefine IRS reporting requirements is likely to benefit the attorneys who would draft and debate the proposed regulations more than the children who need to be heard.

The real question in finding an effective voice for children is not how to encourage *more* nonprofit groups to advocate for children, but how to strengthen the organizational capacity of existing child-focused nonprofits. In some cases, enhancing the organizational infrastructure may mean increasing the number of groups that engage in advocacy. In other cases, it may involve building strong coalitions among existing groups, developing persuasive messages, or using resources more effectively.

The history and experience of child advocacy organizations provide valuable insights into how groups form and flourish. Extensive case studies of organizations' shared experiences and divergent paths can shed light on the factors that lead to effective advocacy. When and why were the organizations founded? Why did the organizations choose a particular tax status—that is, 501(c)(3) versus 501(c)(4)? At what point did the organizations begin focusing on children's issues? What motivated the organizations' leaders to choose a single-issue or multi-issue advocacy strategy? How have the organizations responded to their political environment? How are the organizations structured, and do they take part in a network of alliances or coalitions? How do the organizations generate resources, and how do different sources of support affect advocacy activities?

Investigating such questions can lead to the development of models that can be used by policymakers, child advocates, and foundation leaders to understand and shape the advocacy voice for children. In this era of devolution, child advocates will need to learn from one another—through state or regional networks, through good case practices, and through the adaptation of successful strategies to local environments. By building organizational capacity to speak out for children, communities will have a firmer platform for learning how children are faring.

## NOTES

1. The commonly cited "5 percent test" (5 percent of total budget) for determining what is a substantial level of lobbying has never been accepted by the Internal Revenue Service. The IRS reserves the right to define an absolute level of lobbying that is substantial—as measured by dollars, time, public prominence, success, or importance to the nonprofit. Because the IRS has never defined what constitutes substantial lobbying, an organization that has not taken the 501(h) election has no way of determining whether it has exceeded the legal lobbying limits (Charity Lobbying in the Public Interest 1999).

2. The NCCS database identified almost 6,500 labor unions classified as 501(c)(5) organizations. Although these organizations have often been strong advocates for children's issues, they focus primarily on their members and on labor issues. Because the data cannot be separated by issue area, labor unions were omitted from the analysis.

3. The NCCS cleans, classifies, and codes the annual Form 990 returns to make the data more reliable and user-friendly. As part of its data-cleaning procedures, NCCS cross-checks the Core files with information from the IRS Statistics of Income (SOI) files and reconciles discrepancies. The SOI, a stratified sample of approximately 11,000 tax-exempt public charities, is meticulously checked for errors and categorized by the IRS. Most of the SOI file comprises U.S. nonprofit organizations with assets of $10 million or more.

4. The NTEE is a mixed-notation classification system that consists of 10 major group categories and 475 subdivisions. The codes reflect the types of activities conducted by nonprofit organizations. Several organizations, such as the Foundation Center, the AAFRC Trust for Philanthropy, and Philanthropic Research, Inc., use NTEE in their reports and publications to make their data collection systems comparable. For more information on the construction of the NTEE system, see Stevenson, Pollak, and Lampkin (1997).

5. In 1999, the IRS Activity Code used for classifying organizations was replaced with the NTEE code.

6. There appears to be some inconsistency in the designation of nonprofit organizations as either 501(c)(3) or 501(c)(4). For example, approximately 130 PTA organizations have obtained 501(c)(4) status, while more than 7,000 PTAs have received 501(c)(3) status. Similarly, about 350 youth service clubs, including Key Clubs, Circle K International, and Links, Inc., had obtained (c)(4) status, but more than 4,500 scouting organizations, 4-H Clubs, and other close counterparts had (c)(3) status. Determining why one group seeks (c)(3) status while a counterpart seeks (c)(4) status is beyond the scope of this paper. This

problem, nevertheless, highlights the difficulties of measuring the extent and variation in advocacy activities among nonprofit organizations in the IRS database.

7. Taking the (h) election and reporting lobbying expenses are mutually exclusive events. Some nonprofit organizations that report lobbying expenses are not (h) electors, and (h) electors may not have lobbying expenses to report in a given year.

# REFERENCES

Bremner, Robert H. 1988. *American Philanthropy.* Chicago: The University of Chicago Press.

Charity Lobbying in the Public Interest. 1999. Http://www.independentsector.org.

Children's Defense Fund (CDF). 2000. "About Us." Http://www.childrensdefense.org.

———. 1999. *A Chronology of the Children's Defense Fund.* Washington, D.C.: Children's Defense Fund.

CDF-Minnesota. 2001. Top page. Http://www.cdf-mn.org.

Hall, Peter Dobkin. 1987. "A Historical Overview of the Private Nonprofit Sector." In *The Nonprofit Sector: A Research Handbook,* edited by Walter W. Powell (3-26). New Haven: Yale University Press.

Harmon, Gail. 1996. *Regulations of Advocacy Activities of Nonprofits That Receive Federal Grants.* Washington, D.C.: Alliance for Justice. Information downloaded from Http://www.afj.org/fai/regulation.html.

Hopkins, Bruce. 1992. *Charity, Advocacy, and the Law.* New York: John Wiley and Sons.

National Association of Child Advocates (NACA). 2000. "An Introduction to NACA," September. Http://www.childadvocacy.org.

———. 2000. *Voices for America's Children: The Progress and the Promise.* Washington, D.C.: National Association of Child Advocates.

OMB Watch. 1996. "Core Elements of Anti-Advocacy Proposals during the 104th Congress," February 22. Http://www.ombwatch.org/las/1996/istook.html.

Stengel, Nicholas A. J. 1997. "Lobbying by Public Charities: A Legislative, Administrative, and Judicial History." Unpublished paper.

Stevenson, David R., Thomas H. Pollak, and Linda M. Lampkin. 1997. *State Nonprofit Almanac 1997: Profiles of Charitable Organizations.* Washington, D.C.: The Urban Institute Press.

U.S. Bureau of the Census. 2001. "Historical Poverty Tables." Http://www.census.gov.

———. 2000. *Statistical Abstract of the United States, 2000* (120th ed.) Washington, D.C.: U.S. Government Printing Office.

U.S. Centers for Disease Control and Prevention, National Center for Health Statistics. 2001. "Births: Final Data for 1999," *National Vital Statistics Reports* 49 (1, April 17).

———. 2000. "Deaths: Final Data for 1998," *National Vital Statistics Reports,* vol. 48 (11, July 24).

U.S. Congress. 1976. House Committee on Ways and Means. *Committee Print: Summary of Issues on Lobbying by Charities.* 94th cong., 2d sess. H.R. 13500. Washington, D.C.: U.S. Government Printing Office, May 18. p. 4.

Appendix 1.A: *NTEE Codes Used in Constructing the Dataset on Child-Focused Nonprofit Organizations*

| NTEE-CC | Description |
|---|---|
| **NTEE Codes Used** | |
| A52 | Children's Museums |
| B20 | Elementary, Secondary Education, K–12 |
| B21 | Kindergarten, Preschool, Nursery School, Early Admissions |
| B24 | Primary, Elementary Schools |
| B25 | Secondary, High School |
| B28 | Special Education Institutions, Programs |
| B90 | Educational Services and Schools/Other |
| B92 | Remedial Reading, Reading Encouragement Programs |
| B94 | Parent/Teacher Group |
| E40 | Reproductive Health Care Facilities, Allied Services |
| E42 | Family Planning Centers |
| G20 | Birth Defects, Genetic Diseases |
| G25 | Down Syndrome |
| G98 | Pediatrics |
| H20 | Birth Defects, Genetic Diseases Research |
| H25 | Down Syndrome Research |
| H98 | Pediatrics Research |
| I21 | Delinquency Prevention |
| I72 | Child Abuse, Prevention of |
| O20 | Youth Centers, Clubs, Multipurpose |
| O21 | Boys Clubs |
| O22 | Girls Clubs |
| O23 | Boys and Girls Clubs (Combined) |
| O30 | Adult, Child Matching Programs |
| O31 | Big Brothers, Big Sisters |
| O40 | Scouting Organizations |
| O41 | Boy Scouts of America |
| O42 | Girl Scouts of America |
| O43 | Camp Fire |
| O50 | Youth Development Programs, Other |
| O51 | Youth Community Service Clubs |
| O52 | Youth Development–Agricultural |
| O53 | Youth Development–Business |
| O54 | Youth Development–Citizenship Programs |
| O55 | Youth Development–Religious Leadership |
| O99 | Youth Development–Not Elsewhere Classified |

Appendix 1.A:  *NTEE Codes Used in Constructing the Dataset on Child-Focused Nonprofit Organizations* (*Continued*)

| NTEE-CC | Description |
| --- | --- |
| P30 | Children's Youth Services |
| P31 | Adoption |
| P32 | Foster Care |
| P33 | Child Day Care |
| P45 | Family Services, Adolescent Parents |
| R61 | Reproductive Rights |
| R62 | Right to Life |

**NTEE Codes Reviewed for Appropriateness**

| | |
| --- | --- |
| A65 | Theater |
| A69 | Symphony Orchestra |
| B99 | Education, Not Elsewhere Classified |
| E24 | Hospital, Specialty |
| E86 | Patient Services–Entertainment, Recreation |
| F33 | Group Home, Residential Treatment Facility–Mental Health Related |
| N20 | Recreational, Sporting Camps |
| N60 | Amateur Sports Clubs, Leagues |
| N62 | Basketball |
| N63 | Baseball, Softball |
| N64 | Soccer Clubs, Leagues |
| N65 | Football Clubs, Leagues |
| N67 | Swimming, Water Recreation |
| N68 | Winter Sports (Snow and Ice) |
| P20 | Human Service Organizations–Multipurpose |
| P27 | Young Men's or Women's Associations |
| P40 | Family Services |
| P46 | Family Counseling |
| P70 | Residential, Custodial Care |
| P73 | Group Home, Long Term |
| P82 | Developmentally Disabled Centers, Services |
| X20 | Christian |

*Source:* The Urban Institute, NCCS 1998 Core Files.

# 2

# In the Midst of Plenty: Foundation Funding of Child Advocacy Organizations in the 1990s

*Sally Covington*

This chapter examines the role of philanthropy in supporting child advocacy organizations that are working to improve children's well-being in American society. Its fundamental premise is that philanthropy ought to support *public* interest advocacy organizations as well as other nonprofit groups dedicated to addressing the political, social, and economic marginalization of historically disenfranchised constituencies. Indeed, as argued by Tom Asher more than 20 years ago, without greater efforts to organize and advance the interests of "broad, non-commercially oriented citizen constituencies . . . public needs will be neither defined nor met in a democratic fashion" (Asher 1977, 1072). America's well-documented inequalities regarding democratic participation and the growing influence of money on politics makes this warning all the more pertinent today (Verba, Schlozman, and Brady 1995).

Despite the importance of public interest advocacy in promoting underrepresented interests, scholars of philanthropy in American society have generally arrived at four discouraging conclusions. First, private giving tends to either benefit already comfortable groups or have no clear distributional consequences (Margo 1992; Odendahl 1990). Second, most foundations avoid public policy grantmaking (McIlnay 1997). Third, organized philanthropy exhibits a strong top-down approach and a professional bias, with the bulk of funding going to professionals in service and research occupations rather than to the activities or institutions that promote citizen participation (Johnson 1988; Smith 1989). Fourth, exceedingly few dollars support progressive social movement organizations or advocacy activities (Jenkins 1998; Jenkins and Halcli 1996).

Quantitative and qualitative data gathered for this study support these conclusions. The findings draw on three types of analysis: a review of the recent literature on foundation grantmaking for children, youth, and families; a comparison of grants to selected national and state-based child advocacy organizations in 1991 and 1996; and interviews with child advocates. The analysis reveals that

1. Child advocacy organizations receive only a tiny fraction of the total funds that foundations spend on basic and applied research, social services, and other nonadvocacy activities related to children and youth. In an era of continued reliance on state governments to finance and deliver a host of services for children, state-based child advocacy organizations remain particularly underfunded.

2. When foundations do make investments in child advocacy organizations, they are far more likely to fund softer advocacy activities, such as data collection or media outreach, than to fund more direct activities, such as grassroots mobilization, allowable political lobbying, membership development, and coalition-building. Scholars and practitioners agree that direct activities are necessary for the children's movement to develop greater political strength. Foundations did, however, increase their support of leadership development, advocacy training, and constituency-building between 1991 and 1996, from $795,000 to $5.9 million.

3. Foundations award far more grant money to specific projects, single-issue organizations, and advocacy efforts on relatively non-controversial issues such as reducing childhood tobacco use or preventing child abuse. Although poverty itself is a major factor in determining children's overall well-being and has been closely linked to other social problems, foundations and child advocates do not appear to be attacking poverty in any direct, aggressive way.

4. Child advocates express profound dissatisfaction over the ways foundations choose to operate. Activists believe that less money is going to advocacy and that the growing trend is for foundations to design and direct their own program initiatives. Rarely do advocates say that foundations give them the full opportunity and freedom to craft and implement their own program strategies and initiatives.

## Tracking Foundation Support of Child Advocacy: Methodological and Conceptual Issues

Several data constraints make it difficult, if not impossible, to determine accurately how much philanthropic foundations have invested in child advocacy nationally. Foundations do not report grantmaking activities in a way that allows for easy identification of grants to organizations engaged in child advocacy. Although most of the larger foundations do publish annual reports, they are not required to do so, and full grant information may not be disclosed. Reported data among corporate foundations can be particularly spotty. In annual reports, grant awards are typically listed by broad program area, such as education or the arts, rather than by program strategies or type of activities. The same is true for foundation reporting of grantmaking activities to the IRS. Few foundations structure and report on grantmaking programs according to strategic approaches, such as leadership development, community organizing, public policy advocacy, or media/public education.

Conceptual and definitional issues surrounding child advocacy also make it difficult to "map" the child advocacy community and, therefore, to assess its level of philanthropic support (see De Vita, Mosher-Williams, and Stengel, this volume). What constitutes advocacy for children, and how does it differ from family advocacy? Should advocacy organizations focus primarily on economic security issues, such as family or minimum-wage legislation? Should low-income housing developers be considered part of the children's advocacy community? Do nonprofits that primarily engage in the collection and analysis of data on children's well-being belong on the map? What about nonprofit agencies that primarily, if not exclusively, deliver social services to children, youth, and families? Or professional associations that weigh in on particular policy issues that address children's as well as their members' needs, such as the American Academy of Pediatrics? Are government or government-linked entities—such as big-city school districts or the National Governors Association—acting as child advocates when they engage in public education campaigns or in child-related administrative or legislative lobbying? And how do community-organizing groups that advocate for low-income families through issue campaigns figure into the picture?

The issues at stake are thrown into further relief when one considers the approach to advocacy adopted by many conservative think tanks and policy organizations. Conservative political activists have tended to operate in strategically different ways than liberal ones, engaging less in advocacy for children and more in advocacy to establish broad national policy priorities (Covington 1997). Family issues are often invoked both to advance a larger agenda that is attentive to advancing fiscal and economic policies based on notions of limited government and to establish the structural rules of the policy game (e.g., term limits or balanced budget amendments).

Because many of the activities that emerged under the "child advocacy" label in the late 1960s and early 1970s were supported by federal agencies, conservatives, in fact, reacted by forming a variety of institutions and networks to defend parents' rights, promote traditional family values, and advance limited government objectives, especially at the federal level.[1] Organizations such as Focus on the Family and the Family Research Council emerged (alongside many other conservative policy organizations) to push for government retrenchment, devolution of power to the states, privatization of key government services, and deregulation of industry. Often, these policy approaches have been woven together into a morally based narrative arguing that government expansion has imposed unreasonable tax burdens on hard-working American families and suppressed the problem-solving initiative of individuals, households, and communities.[2] Thus, no strong tradition of child advocacy has taken root among political conservatives. Rather, children's issues are brought up as they relate to larger ideological or policy principles (e.g., privatization through school vouchers, or teen pregnancy reduction through abstinence education).

## Methodology

This chapter attempts to identify national and state-based child advocacy organizations whose primary mission is to improve children's social and economic well-being through one or more of the following activities: government and legislative monitoring, administrative negotiation, legislative lobbying (direct and grassroots), class-action litigation, public and media education, applied policy research and development, and community organizing. This definition generally excludes nonprofit agencies that deliver social services under government funding or contracting arrangements. This restriction is important because, as Smith and Lipsky (1993) note, when publicly funded nonprofit organizations engage in political advocacy, they do so knowing that their fate as organizations is at risk. It is the material interest of nonprofit organizations under contract that "tends to reduce the ideological character of [their] political advocacy and shift it to technical issues relating to rates, funding levels, and regulations" (187).

The study design also excludes research centers—whether university-based or independent—that engage primarily in data collection and analysis. Research plays an important role in the policy process, but the use of tossing every type of organization and activity, without distinction, into the advocacy bin is questionable. What is needed is greater analytical precision about the specific contributions, limitations, and activities of different types of organizations and a greater understanding of which types of organizations and activities get funded and which do not. This agenda is consistent with the view that political power fundamentally determines how and for what purposes public resources are mobilized and deployed (see, for example, Majone 1988 and Minkler 1999). From this vantage point, technical expertise, hard data, and moral argument may be important components of political action, but they cannot be a substitute for it.[3]

Given these parameters, a multistep approach was employed to identify 156 nonprofit organizations thought to be engaged primarily in child advocacy. (See the appendix for a listing of these organizations.)[4] First, organizations were identified using the organizational contacts and membership lists of national groups such as the National Association of Child Advocates, the Children's Defense Fund, and the Coalition for America's Children. Internet searches for the organizations meeting the criteria outlined above supplemented these lists. The Foundation Center's grants information-retrieval database was also helpful in identifying organizations that were internally cross-coded both as "alliance" (e.g., advocacy) organizations and as organizations serving children and youth; all organizational names that did not duplicate current entries were added to the list.

The Foundation Center, which systematically tracks and analyzes foundation grantmaking, then conducted a search through its *Foundation Grants Index* database to identify all grants awarded to these organizations in 1991 and 1996. The search yielded a total of 692 grants awarded to 103 of the 156 child advocacy organizations originally identified. Information about these grants was then entered into a database for further analysis, including examination of type of grant support awarded, issue areas funded, and type of activities supported.

To supplement the grants data, telephone interviews were conducted with 12 child advocates around the country. These interviews delved into the following areas: (1) organizational history, mission, activities and accomplishments; (2) views on the components of effective advocacy, the intersection or overlap between child and family issues, and the strengths and weaknesses of the children's movement; and (3) perspectives on and experiences with the foundation community. A review of the relevant literature, including several recent analyses of foundation grantmaking to children and youth, was also conducted.

## Limitations of the Data

Beyond the decision to narrow the definition of child advocacy in the ways described (e.g., exclusion of nonprofits engaged primarily in service delivery and university-based or independent applied policy research), certain limitations to the data should be acknowledged. First, the analysis excludes most local child advocacy organizations because of the difficulty of developing a comprehensive list of the advocacy organizations seeking to improve child well-being at the neighborhood, city, or county levels. Although including these organizations would certainly provide a richer and more detailed funding picture, many of these groups likely function as hybrid institutions, combining service delivery with occasional or tightly focused advocacy related to their specific institutional interests or those of their clients.[5] As noted earlier, service-based advocacy has certain limitations that can reduce the vigor or narrow the focus of advocacy efforts.

Second, the analysis excludes grants of less than $10,000 that were awarded to the 103 organizations in the database. It also excludes grants awarded by smaller foundations. The Foundation Center's database contains information on between 800 and 1,000 of the nation's larger foundations, as well as information on grants of $10,000 or more, and includes all of the major national, regional, and local funders with name recognition (and many without). Although the foundations in the database represent only about 2 percent of the approximately 42,000 foundations in the country, they control more than 65 percent of assets and allocate 50 percent or more of all grants.

Finally, private grantmaking foundations are not the only source of revenue for child advocacy organizations. Child advocates also seek support through individual donations, membership fees, fundraising events, and, to a more limited extent, aid from the public sector.[6] The grants data thus reflect only a portion of the operating budgets of the child advocacy organizations included in the analysis. Still, the children's movement relies far more heavily on the support of philanthropic foundations than do other social movements, and it is likely that child advocates will continue to require an infusion of outside resources to support their work (Richart 1997).

The remainder of this chapter is divided into five sections. The first section seeks to establish a broader social, economic, and political context for discussing philanthropy's current and potential role in improving children's well-being in American society. Toward that end, it briefly reviews some of the major policy trends of the past two decades and examines their impact on children, youth, and families. The second section considers the historical and contemporary record of philanthropic foundations in addressing critical social issues and public needs, especially among children. The third section reports and elaborates on key findings, providing specific information on grants awarded to child advocacy organizations in the years examined. It also reviews and comments on what we know about child advocacy funding in previous decades. The fourth section discusses contemporary issues in child advocacy and explores the links between the perceived weaknesses in the child advocacy movement and philanthropic approaches to improvements in child welfare.

## The Changing Political and Policy Landscape

Those who document children's status in American society rarely acknowledge the *political* causes of child poverty. Surprisingly, for all of the socioeconomic data collected on children, few observers have discussed how public policy decisions (or the lack thereof) have exacerbated child poverty and contributed to poor social, educational, and health outcomes for children. A pattern of steady federal and state government disinvestment in cities, for example, has contributed to rising child poverty rates. The federal and state aid component of central city expenditures declined from a high of 44 percent in 1977 to less than 23 percent in 1999 (U.S. Bureau of the Census 2000). Federal disinvestment policies were particularly prominent between 1981 and 1993, when the funding of community-development block grants, urban-development action grants, general revenue sharing, mass transportation aid, and other discretionary programs fell by 66 percent in real dollar terms (Paget 1998). In Detroit, where the child poverty rate exceeds 40 percent, federal funds declined as a percentage of general city revenues from about 28 percent in 1976 to less than 6 percent just 12 years later.

Other federal policies—some that came about well before the 1980s—have also helped create the high concentration of low-income families and children in inner-city communities. Federal housing, tax, and development policies since World War II, for example, have geographically constructed and reinforced "ghetto" neighborhoods. These policies not only have created the conditions for a downward economic spiral in such communities, but also have made it difficult to construct broad-based political coalitions to address urban problems at the required level or scale (Massey and Denton 1993; Halpern 1995). The impact of these and other policy (and economic) trends on child welfare has been significant.[7] According to the Annie E. Casey Foundation's *City KIDS COUNT* (1997), the child poverty rate in the nation's 50 largest cities increased between 1969 and 1989 from 18 to 27 percent. In 11 states and the District of Columbia, a quarter or more of children in 1996 were growing up poor, with the percentage as high as 30 percent in Mississippi, Louisiana, and West Virginia, and 36 percent in Washington, D.C. (Annie E. Casey Foundation 2000). In the midst of plenty, the U.S. child poverty rate in 1999 was 17 percent, 3 percentage points above its level in 1969 (U.S. Bureau of the Census 2000). These figures are all the more remarkable given that in the 1990s, the United States experienced the longest peacetime economic expansion in history.

Considerable variation in state policy commitments also helps explain the extent and severity of child poverty. One recent study, for example, found that state spending per poor child in the highest-spending states was more than 9 times the amount spent in the lowest-spending states for Medicaid, more than 20 times for the (now-abolished) Aid to Families with Dependent Children, and more than 11 times for all these programs combined (Orland and Cohen 1995). Even where federal entitlement and discretionary programs exist to address or ameliorate child poverty and related social problems, they are rarely taken full advantage of. Approximately 3.2 million children under the age of six who are eligible for Medicaid were not enrolled in the program in 1994, and low-income student participation in the federal School Breakfast Program was just 39 percent in 1994 (Foster and Srivastava 1996).

Cross-national comparisons also reveal that children in the United States are far poorer than their counterparts in most other western democracies. A recent study found that the child poverty rate in the United States was not only the highest among 17 selected countries, but also 50 percent greater than the next-highest rate (Annie E. Casey Foundation 2000). To a large extent, such differences reflect the more generous social welfare policies enacted by Western European countries and Canada. Sadly, our nation tolerates a much higher level of child poverty than other industrialized democracies. The United States is the only advanced western economy that has no family allowance, no universal health insurance for children and adults, and limited support for early childhood programs (Schorr 1997). Given these and other failures of collective political will, it should not surprise anyone that children, who make up about 25 percent of the U.S. population, account for nearly 40 percent of those living in poverty.

Changing national and state policy priorities—and their negative impact on children—reflect both the political isolation of American cities and, more broadly, the disequalizing political effects of the nation's growing wealth and income gap (Paget 1998; Verba, Schlozman, and Brady 1995). As Verba, Schlozman, and Brady so closely document, there is a "systematic bias in representation through participation," with participatory input "tilted in the direction of the more advantaged groups in society" (512). Their findings are consistent with decades of research on American political participation—research that has found that patterns of political participation are deeply embedded in the American social structure. One study of the interest group universe, for example, concludes that "the heavenly choir of American interests sings with an upper-class accent" (Schattschneider 1960, 160).

With the 30-year decline in electoral participation and the pronounced class bias in both national and state electorates, it is no surprise that public benefits flow most heavily to those who need them the least. Myron Orfield's analysis of major metropolitan regions, for example, has found that the wealthiest suburbs—not working-class suburbs or impoverished inner-city communities—derive the greatest benefit from public expenditures (Orfield 1997).

The nation's growing wealth and income gap and the increasing geographic segregation of rich and poor make it difficult to generate political support for "other people's children." Without attention to these broader policy trends and political realities, the status and well-being of children is unlikely to improve substantially, especially for the 20 million poor and near-poor children living in the country's most impoverished communities.[8]

## Private Philanthropy and Public Needs

Although an increasing number of foundations are engaged in advocacy grantmaking, the funding patterns observed in this analysis are consistent with much that has been previously observed about philanthropy's reluctant stance toward independent, citizen-based advocacy organizations. Going back to the late 1960s and early 1970s, critics have enumerated a long list of complaints about the failure of foundations to respond to the nation's most critical public needs, including advocacy for children.

In a paper prepared for the Commission on Private Philanthropy and Public Needs (known informally as the Filer Commission), Carey (1977) described foundations as "permanent bureaucracies whose well-paid staffs attempt to impose their ideas of what the problems are . . . ; they are faddist and won't stick with the tough ongoing issues that plague society; they measure progress and success by newspaper stories, sometimes creating issues through grantees that manipulate the press and believing them solved simply because they have become the subject of public debate" (1111). Carey also noted "the strong academic bent of foundations, and their willingness to make vast expenditures on new entities—often foundation-created—with big boards, high overhead, well-paid staff, and designed to deal with broad, rather ill-defined problems like the 'urban crisis' or 'drug abuse' without dealing with the underlying causes or political realities" (1112).

Since the time of the Filer Commission, a small but growing number of scholars and public interest advocates have focused needed attention on philanthropy's role as a catalyst for social progress and democratic engagement. Their work has shed collective light on philanthropic foundations' general discomfort with professional advocacy and grassroots citizen action, particularly when these efforts enable and support the participation of low-income constituencies in the political process. Foundations that have chosen to engage in public-policy grantmaking most often exert their influence by developing an "infrastructure of expertise." In his historical review of foundations' public policy impact, James Allen Smith identified the four principal ways foundations have sought to alter the public-policy environment. They have (1) created and financed institutions that bring applied knowledge to bear on public problems; (2) catalyzed changes in professional training and development; (3) organized and supported forums for the exchange of information and ideas; and (4) promoted the idea of the social sciences as a valuable tool for policy decisionmaking (1989).[9]

When it comes to the support of progressive social movement organizations, Jenkins (1998) and Jenkins and Halcli (1996) have shown that an expanding circle of foundations had begun funding advocacy and related activities by the 1980s. Still, relative to the number of grantmaking foundations (estimated to exceed 42,000 today), the circle of 146 social movement grantmakers that Jenkins has identified remains small, with only a tiny fraction of foundation grants directed to social movement organizations.

Between 1953 and 1980, for example, Jenkins found that the high point of foundation grantmaking came in 1977, when foundations awarded less than 1 percent of their grants to social movement organizations. After updating the analysis with data up to 1990, Jenkins and Halcli found a slight increase in foundation giving to social movement organizations; foundations awarded just over 1 percent ($88 million) of their 1990 grants to support any "organized attempts to bring about institutional change by organizing or representing the collective interests of some disadvantaged or underrepresented group" (1996, 4). More recently, the National Network of Grantmakers conducted its own study of social change grantmaking, reporting that foundations awarded an annual total of $336 million, or roughly 2 percent, to nonprofit organizations (National Network of Grantmakers 1998).

Regarding children and youth in particular, researchers have suggested that significantly more needs to be done in the realm of constituency-building and antipoverty initiatives. A recent paper commissioned by the Early Childhood Funders Collaborative examined the steps that foundations might take to advance a quality agenda in early childhood care and education. The common thread in the authors' interview data was the need for "a more strategic, more forceful, better-informed advocacy effort," with more than half of the 70 interviewees identifying this goal as important (Mitchell and Shore 1998). The authors also outlined key challenges that they believe funders and child advocates must confront in order to advance an early childhood agenda. Among the challenges was the need to stimulate increased public-sector investment in children through more active constituency-building efforts and to address finance issues by introducing greater realism into public debates about the cost of quality care. In addition, the authors found that more needs to be done to transform public awareness into public engagement.

In another paper, Takanishi (1998) took foundations to task on several counts for their approach to child poverty. First, she argued, philanthropy has tended to ignore the structural causes of poverty. Second, philanthropy has taken reactive stances to critical social policy trends. For example, foundations have exhibited far greater willingness to track the effects of the 1996 welfare-reform legislation than to support active efforts to develop and promote needed policy alternatives. And third, foundations lack a coherent vision of poverty reduction, with foundations taking pieces of the solution, such as early childhood care and education or childhood immunization, rather than adopting a coordinated approach to child poverty and related social issues.

Weiss and Lopez (1998) also examined current grantmaking for children and youth. Based on a series of interviews with the leaders or program officers of major foundations, they reported optimistically that foundations are reconsidering their approaches and are developing promising new strategies. Included among the new strategies are an increased emphasis on "multi-component, often place-based initiatives" and the development of national initiatives with "complex field-building, policy change, and reform goals designed to improve the status of children and youth" (6). The authors also reported a reduced emphasis on early childhood care and education (for children up to the age of five), relatively few state-level investments, and expanded interest in asset-based youth development.

What is perhaps most interesting about Weiss and Lopez's analysis, however, is that a very high percentage of the grant allocations of major national and regional funders is awarded to grantees to implement foundation-designed initiatives. Of 18 major foundations, 9 distribute 60 percent or more of their grant allocations via staff-initiated programs or solicited proposals, including, at the high end, the Eugene and Marion Kauffman Foundation (98 percent), the Annie E. Casey Foundation (95 percent), the DeWitt Wallace-Reader's Digest Fund (95 percent), the Edna McConnell Clark Foundation (95 percent), the Heinz Endowment (90 percent), and the Rockefeller Foundation (90 percent).

Weiss and Lopez regard these new foundation initiatives on behalf of children as a qualitatively different form of grantmaking that moves beyond earlier funding of multiple, categorical services toward the development of an integrated infrastructure. This integrated approach combines "service delivery with education and knowledge development, evaluation and continuous learning, leadership and professional capacity development, communication and dissemination, and public engagement" (19).

Weiss and Lopez's panoramic overview of funding strategies for children and youth does not, however, probe the implications of foundations' decisions to design and implement their own initiatives. In many respects, the new strategic grantmaking that Weiss and Lopez discern has an historical analogue in the "medical," or "scientific," model of philanthropy practiced by foundations earlier in the 20th century. That model has been called a top-down, measured, deliberate, professional, and technocratic approach to social improvement, usually involving problem identification, the establishment of objectives by which to measure progress, the design and implementation of a plan to accomplish these objectives, and assessment of results.

More important, Weiss and Lopez do not consider any of the limitations of place-based initiatives (usually neighborhood-level programs) in solving the social isolation and economic devastation of inner-city communities, where so many of the nation's poor children reside (Halpern 1995). To appreciate these limitations, one needs only to note the strong role that federal housing, tax, and urban-renewal policies have played over the past 50 years in concentrating poverty within certain areas and in isolating the poor. Federal highway programs have destroyed communities by running highways through minority neighborhoods. Urban-renewal policies have led to a net decrease in low-income housing stock by destroying four low-income housing units for every one created (Halpern 1995). And public housing programs have helped to ensure the social and economic isolation of poor people by selecting sites in areas with no job base and little commercial activity.

Now, under conditions of continued federal (and state) neglect, there is a persistent tendency to ask the most marginalized communities to solve problems not of their own making. As Halpern (1995) notes, place-based initiatives today reflect many of the same premises and pitfalls of earlier decades, including the tendency to locate the causes of urban poverty and social disadvantage "in the people who are experiencing them, to interpret [the causes] in terms that do not require adjustment by those who live outside the inner city" (221). Currently, few attempts are being funded to address the political isolation of cities and the need to build bridges between inner-city communities, working class suburbs, and middle-income communities in support of broader reform agendas at the state and national level.

## Philanthropic Support of Child Advocacy Organizations: Key Findings

For the conceptual and methodological reasons described, it is difficult to track overall foundation giving to children and youth. It is more difficult to determine the amounts that individual foundations invest in child advocacy organizations. Foundations themselves do not report their grants by beneficiary group, so grants benefiting children may be spread across multiple areas, such as health, education, and human services.

Still, data compiled by the Foundation Center provide a rough indication of grant dollars awarded to children and youth. According to the 1998 edition of *Grants for Children and Youth,* foundations invested $2.1 billion to benefit infants, children, and youth, mostly in 1996 and 1997 (Foundation Center 1998).[10] Assuming that these grants were fairly evenly distributed across these two years, just over $1 billion was invested in 1996 by 896 of the foundations for which the Foundation Center maintains grants data. Compare this with data from Kaplan (1997), which reported that total giving by private and corporate foundations in 1996 was $20.3 billion. Weiss and Lopez (1998) provide an alternative number in their recent examination of grantmaking strategies for children and youth. Based on estimates provided by 19 major national foundations, Weiss and Lopez report that approximately $569.0 million was invested to benefit children and youth in 1996, roughly half of the amount reported by the Foundation Center.

### Snapshots of Giving in the 1990s

Relative to these figures, grantmaking foundations directed only a small percentage of their funds to national and state-based child advocacy organizations in the two years for which grant information was developed. The data show that foundations awarded a total of $24.0 million in 1991 and $57.5 million in 1996 to 103 of the 156 child advocacy organizations identified for inclusion in the analysis (see table 2.1). The 1996 figure, however, was greatly inflated by a $19.5 million grant awarded by the Robert Wood Johnson Foundation to the National Center for Tobacco-Free Kids. If this grant is excluded from the analysis, giving to national and state-based child advocacy organizations in 1996 totaled $38.0 million. This amount is less than 4 percent of the $1.1 billion that foundations provided in that year to benefit infants, children, and youth, and is roughly 7 percent of the total estimated amount that just 19 major foundations awarded to child and youth-serving entities.[11]

When examined from the vantage points of issue focus, type of beneficiary organization, national versus local investments, grant type awarded, and range of activities supported, the funding picture is even more troubling. According to the 1996 grants analysis,[12] for example, the foundations that did invest in child advocacy organizations showed a preference for funding relatively noncontroversial issues (e.g., tobacco-use reduction or child-abuse prevention), national child advocacy organizations, and single-issue (or single-strategy) organizations.

## FUNDING BY ISSUE AREA

Tobacco-use prevention was the issue receiving the most foundation support, owing to an exceptionally large $19.5 million grant to the National Center for Tobacco-Free Kids. The reform of elementary and secondary education received the second-highest support, with foundations awarding $8.2 million in grants for this purpose; most of that money was directed to organizations whose primary mission focused on K-12 education rather than to child advocacy organizations working on multiple issues at the national or state levels. Education reform was followed by child protection and systems reform ($5.8 million) and health care ($1.7 million). Welfare reform ($880,600), child care ($732,000), and budget advocacy ($667,500) received far less support.

## TYPE OF RECIPIENT

The grants analysis also revealed a funding preference either for national child advocates or for single-issue or single-strategy organizations, both at the state and national levels. Of the 103 recipient organizations, 27 national organizations received $39.5 million, or 69 percent of the total amount invested by foundations in 1996. If the $19.5 million grant

(*text continues on page 59*)

Table 2.1 *Nonprofit Organizations That Received Grants in 1991 and 1996*

| Recipient Name | City | State | Total 1991 Grant Amount | Total 1991 Grants | Total 1996 Grant Amount | Total 1996 Grants |
|---|---|---|---|---|---|---|
| Action Alliance for Children | Oakland | CA | $0 | 0 | $10,000 | 1 |
| Action Alliance for Virginia's Children and Youth | Richmond | VA | 0 | 0 | 715,000 | 2 |
| Advocates for Children and Youth | Baltimore | MD | 321,000 | 5 | 145,100 | 5 |
| Advocates for Children of New York | Brooklyn | NY | 317,000 | 9 | 0 | 0 |
| Agenda for Children | New Orleans | LA | 0 | 0 | 17,100 | 2 |
| Alliance for Children's Rights | Los Angeles | CA | 0 | 0 | 190,825 | 7 |
| Alliance for South Carolina's Children | Columbia | SC | 0 | 0 | 32,000 | 1 |
| Alliance to End Childhood Lead Poisoning | Washington | DC | 35,000 | 2 | 30,000 | 1 |
| American Academy of Pediatrics | Elk Grove Village | IL | 819,587 | 3 | 977,617 | 8 |
| Arkansas Advocates for Children and Families | Little Rock | AR | 163,091 | 3 | 36,664 | 1 |
| Association for Children of New Jersey | Newark | NJ | 62,500 | 3 | 246,400 | 6 |
| California Partnership for Children | Sacramento | CA | 0 | 0 | 200,000 | 1 |
| Campaign for Fiscal Equity | NYC | NY | 0 | 0 | 1,010,000 | 5 |
| Campaign for Our Children | Baltimore | MD | 161,250 | 4 | 0 | 0 |
| Center for Education Reform | Washington | DC | 0 | 0 | 199,425 | 5 |
| Center for Law and Education | Washington | DC | 110,000 | 2 | 275,000 | 3 |
| Child Advocates | Indianapolis | IN | 0 | 0 | 45,000 | 2 |
| Child Advocates | Houston | TX | 112,000 | 5 | 443,000 | 11 |
| Child Advocates of Santa Clara and San Mateo Counties | San Jose | CA | 0 | 0 | 10,000 | 1 |
| Child and Family Policy Center | Des Moines | IA | 255,000 | 1 | 472,000 | 3 |
| Child Care Action Campaign | NYC | NY | 312,225 | 13 | 904,000 | 14 |

| Organization | City | State | | | | |
|---|---|---|---|---|---|---|
| Children at Risk | Houston | TX | 0 | 0 | 35,000 | 2 |
| Children First for Oregon | Beaverton | OR | 0 | 0 | 10,000 | 1 |
| Children Now | Santa Monica | CA | 267,500 | 4 | 0 | 0 |
| Children's Action Alliance | Phoenix | AZ | 477,524 | 9 | 565,000 | 7 |
| Children's Advocacy Institute - Child Welfare | San Diego | CA | 0 | 0 | 325,000 | 2 |
| Children's Alliance | Seattle | WA | 42,500 | 2 | 135,000 | 3 |
| Children's Alliance of New Hampshire | Concord | NH | 0 | 0 | 42,000 | 2 |
| Children's Defense Fund | Cincinatti | OH | 0 | 0 | 10,000 | 1 |
| Children's Defense Fund | NYC | NY | 57,500 | 2 | 365,000 | 8 |
| Children's Defense Fund | Houston | TX | 60,000 | 2 | 0 | 0 |
| Children's Defense Fund | Columbus | OH | 157,500 | 3 | 781,350 | 12 |
| Children's Defense Fund | Saint Paul | MN | 415,000 | 8 | 381,000 | 7 |
| Children's Defense Fund | Washington | DC | 6,296,087 | 39 | 5,171,425 | 35 |
| Children's Rights Project | NYC | NY | 0 | 0 | 231,000 | 5 |
| Children's Rights, Inc. | NYC | NY | 0 | 0 | 10,000 | 1 |
| Citizens Committee for Children of New York | NYC | NY | 400,400 | 15 | 337,000 | 17 |
| Citizens for Connecticuts Children and Youth | New Haven | CT | 0 | 0 | 160,000 | 2 |
| Citizens for Excellence in Education | Costa Mesa | CA | 0 | 0 | 10,000 | 1 |
| Citizens for Missouris Children | Saint Louis | MO | 10,000 | 1 | 105,000 | 2 |
| Coleman Advocates for Children and Youth | San Francisco | CA | 75,000 | 4 | 420,625 | 11 |
| Colorado Children's Campaign | Denver | CO | 95,150 | 4 | 455,000 | 7 |
| Connecticut Association for Human Services | Hartford | CT | 169,000 | 4 | 40,000 | 3 |
| Council for Children | Charlotte | NC | 0 | 0 | 22,000 | 1 |
| Designs for Change | Chicago | IL | 455,000 | 6 | 1,167,500 | 12 |
| Education Law Center | Philadelphia | PA | 50,000 | 3 | 65,000 | 2 |

(Continued)

Table 2.1 *Nonprofit Organizations That Received Grants in 1991 and 1996 (Continued)*

| Recipient Name | City | State | Total 1991 Grant Amount | Total 1991 Grants | Total 1996 Grant Amount | Total 1996 Grants |
|---|---|---|---|---|---|---|
| Education Law Center | Newark | NJ | $80,000 | 2 | $50,000 | 1 |
| Georgians for Children | Atlanta | GA | 337,500 | 2 | 335,000 | 4 |
| Human Development Center of Mississippi | Jackson | MS | 17,000 | 1 | 0 | 0 |
| Indiana Advocates for Children | Indianapolis | IN | 0 | 0 | 25,000 | 2 |
| Indiana Youth Institute | Indianapolis | IN | 3,504,650 | 3 | 1,146,265 | 2 |
| Institute for Educational Leadership | Washington | DC | 3,583,252 | 24 | 2,775,925 | 28 |
| Juvenile Law Center | Philadelphia | PA | 445,190 | 7 | 330,000 | 5 |
| Kansas Action for Children | Topeka | KS | 37,500 | 1 | 70,000 | 2 |
| Kentucky Youth Advocates | Louisville | KY | 170,000 | 1 | 84,000 | 2 |
| Kids in Common | San Jose | CA | 0 | 0 | 10,000 | 1 |
| Maine Children's Alliance | Augusta | ME | 0 | 0 | 25,000 | 1 |
| Maryland Committee for Children | Baltimore | MD | 204,000 | 4 | 13,500 | 2 |
| Massachuesetts Advocacy Center | Boston | MA | 105,000 | 3 | 0 | 0 |
| Massachusetts Committee for Children and Youth | Boston | MA | 27,000 | 2 | 0 | 0 |
| Michigan League for Human Services | Lansing | MI | 249,150 | 2 | 344,630 | 5 |
| Michigan's Children | Lansing | MI | 0 | 0 | 51,000 | 3 |
| Minnesota Advocates for Human Rights | Minneapolis | MN | 0 | 0 | 471,000 | 8 |
| Mississippi Forum on Children and Families | Jackson | MS | 0 | 0 | 225,000 | 7 |
| Mountain States Group | Boise | ID | 0 | 0 | 93,000 | 2 |
| National Association of Child Advocates | Washington | DC | 0 | 0 | 182,000 | 4 |
| National Association of Counsel for Children | Denver | CO | 0 | 0 | 12,000 | 1 |

| Organization | City | State | | | | |
|---|---|---|---|---|---|---|
| National Black Child Development Institute | Detroit | MI | 0 | 0 | 10,000 | 1 |
| National Black Child Development Institute | Durham | NC | 0 | 0 | 13,926 | 1 |
| National Black Child Development Institute | Washington | DC | 205,000 | 4 | 304,914 | 6 |
| National Center for Tobacco-Free Kids | Washington | DC | 0 | 0 | 19,930,110 | 4 |
| National Center for Youth Law | San Francisco | CA | 0 | 0 | 361,975 | 3 |
| National Coalition for Child Protection Reform | Cambridge | MA | 0 | 0 | 25,000 | 1 |
| National Coalition of Advocates for Students | Indianapolis | IN | 0 | 0 | 2,260,000 | 2 |
| National Coalition of Advocates for Students | Boston | MA | 375,000 | 4 | 430,000 | 4 |
| National Committee to Prevent Child Abuse | Chicago | IL | 0 | 0 | 3,310,030 | 17 |
| National Parenting Association | NYC | NY | 0 | 0 | 212,500 | 4 |
| New Mexico Advocates for Children and Families | Albuquerque | NM | 0 | 0 | 60,000 | 1 |
| North Carolina Child Advocacy Institute | Raleigh | NC | 287,500 | 5 | 230,000 | 4 |
| Parents Union for Public Schools in Philadlephia | Philadelphia | PA | 20,000 | 1 | 544,580 | 3 |
| Partnership for Children | Kansas City | MO | 0 | 0 | 75,000 | 2 |
| Pennsylvania Partnerships for Children | Harrisburg | PA | 0 | 0 | 717,138 | 4 |
| Philadelphia Citizens for Children and Youth | Philadelphia | PA | 484,500 | 5 | 939,725 | 10 |
| Prevent Child Abuse New Jersey | Newark | NJ | 0 | 0 | 40,000 | 1 |
| Pritchard Committee for Academic Excellence | Lexington | KY | 858,210 | 8 | 1,087,400 | 7 |
| Rochester Area Children's Collaborative | Rochester | NY | 0 | 0 | 10,000 | 1 |
| South Carolina Budget and Control Board | Columbia | NC | 200,000 | 1 | 60,000 | 1 |
| Stand for Children | Washington | DC | 0 | 0 | 262,000 | 5 |
| Statewide Youth Advocacy | Albany | NY | 0 | 0 | 140,000 | 4 |
| Statewide Youth Advocacy | Rochester | NY | 285,140 | 5 | 0 | 5 |
| Student Advocacy Center | Ann Arbor | MI | 0 | 0 | 150,000 | 1 |

*(Continued)*

Table 2.1 *Nonprofit Organizations That Received Grants in 1991 and 1996 (Continued)*

| Recipient Name | City | State | Total 1991 Grant Amount | Total Grants | Total 1996 Grant Amount | Total Grants |
|---|---|---|---|---|---|---|
| Support Center for Child Advocates | Philadelphia | PA | $40,000 | 3 | $132,500 | 4 |
| Tarrant County Youth Collaboration | Forth Worth | TX | 10,000 | 1 | 40,000 | 2 |
| Teach Michigan Education Fund | Lansing | MI | 60,000 | 2 | 170,000 | 5 |
| Tennessee Commission on Children and Youth | Nashville | TN | 0 | 0 | 60,000 | 1 |
| Voices for Alabama's Children | Montgomery | AL | 0 | 0 | 40,000 | 3 |
| Voices for Children in Nebraska | Omaha | NE | 0 | 0 | 30,000 | 1 |
| Voices for Illinois' Children | Chicago | IL | 139,000 | 6 | 693,000 | 12 |
| West Virginia Kids Count Fund | Charleston | WV | 0 | 0 | 47,500 | 1 |
| Wisconsin Council on Children and Families | Madison | WI | 0 | 0 | 220,000 | 2 |
| Youth Advocate Program | Harrisburg | PA | 0 | 0 | 50,000 | 1 |
| Youth Law Center | Washington | DC | 0 | 0 | 129,500 | 1 |
| Youth Law Center | San Francisco | CA | 285,000 | 4 | 1,701,969 | 12 |
| **TOTAL** | | | **$23,706,406** | **257** | **$57,535,118** | **435** |

*Source:* Author's tabulations based on the *Foundation Grants Index* database.

to the National Center for Tobacco-Free Kids is excluded, the percentage remains high, at 52 percent.

Of the $57.5 million foundations donated to child advocacy groups, $21.1 million (37 percent) was directed to multi-issue organizations using a mix of advocacy strategies to improve children's well-being. Of this amount, $12.3 million was awarded to 49 state-based child advocates (for an average of $251,000 per organization) and $8.8 million to national multi-issue organizations. Most of the remaining $36.4 million supported national groups focusing on a single issue area or working to affect child welfare primarily through litigation. Examples include the National Center for Tobacco-Free Kids ($19.9 million), the National Committee to Prevent Child Abuse ($3.3 million), and the Youth Law Center in San Francisco ($1.7 million).

GENERAL OPERATING VERSUS PROJECT-SPECIFIC SUPPORT

With respect to the types of grants awarded, foundations invested in child advocacy organizations mostly on a project-specific rather than general-support basis. Interestingly, foundations gave a significantly higher percentage of their grants as general operating support in 1991 than they did in 1996, at 29 percent and 8 percent, respectively. The same was true for organizational development grants, with foundations providing 11 percent of their 1991 grants and 6 percent of their 1996 grants to support such activities as strategic planning and staff development. Conversely, project-specific grantmaking increased from 50 percent in 1991 to 79 percent in 1996.

The decline in general operating and organizational development support may reflect what many perceive to be the increasing tendency of foundations to engage in "strategic grantmaking" through the design and implementation of their own program initiatives. The issue of general-operating versus project-specific support is important because it may hinder advocacy organizations' ability to adapt to shifting political or policy circumstances, to take advantage of new opportunities, or to make necessary institutional adjustments based on their own experience and learning curves.

TYPE OF ACTIVITIES FUNDED

The data also suggest that foundations appear to be far more comfortable funding what might be termed "soft" (e.g., general information dissemination) rather than "hard" (e.g., direct or grassroots lobbying)

forms of public-policy advocacy. A significant portion of grants (45 percent in 1991 and 20 percent in 1996) could not be coded by activity
because of insufficient information; of those coded, however, the data suggest that foundations have vastly increased their giving to public education
and media outreach projects. Funding for these two purposes rose from
$543,000 in 1991 to $22.6 million in 1996. Although the data do not reveal
whether these funding patterns more closely reflect the strategic priorities
of the foundations or those of the child advocates, there appears to be a
strong operating assumption that media work and other information dissemination strategies lead to effective public and legislative action.[13]

Foundations increased their giving in what advocates consider key—
but often underfunded—areas of advocacy activity. Support for leadership development and advocacy training, for example, increased from
$367,000 in 1991 to $2.6 million in 1996. Constituency-building efforts
were also funded at significantly higher levels, with only $60,000 provided
for this purpose in 1991 and $3.3 million in 1996. And government-
monitoring and policy-impact projects also received greater support,
increasing from $869,000 in 1991 to $1.5 million in 1996.

### GEOGRAPHIC DISTRIBUTION OF GRANTS

The grants data also show a high degree of geographic concentration. Of
the $24 million that foundations invested in child advocacy organizations
in 1991, $18 million, or 75 percent, was directed to organizations in just
five states (California, Illinois, Indiana, Pennsylvania, and New York) and
the District of Columbia. Even greater geographic concentration of grant
dollars was seen in 1996, with organizations in these same five states and
the District of Columbia receiving $48 million, or 83 percent, of the
$57.5 million invested overall.

### COMPARISON WITH DOCUMENTED DATA FOR PREVIOUS YEARS

Based on the available data, child advocacy organizations appear far
more reliant on foundation support today than in earlier decades.
Indeed, in the late 1960s and early 1970s, child advocacy was heavily,
and sometimes exclusively, government supported. According to Kahn,
Kamerman, and McGowan (1972), the federal Department of Health,
Education, and Welfare (HEW) was one of the single largest sources of
public support, spending more than $7.5 million on 64 advocacy pro-
grams in fiscal year 1972. The range of activities that Kahn, Kamerman,
and McGowan included under the child advocacy label was quite broad,

not only consisting of such traditional advocacy activities as lobbying, litigation, and administrative negotiating, but also encompassing community planning, neighborhood-based service interventions, and even individual client counseling and referral. Federal funding of these activities was entirely consistent with national urban policy, which placed resident participation, community action, and decentralized service delivery at the conceptual core of government antipoverty objectives.

While there has been little in-depth historical examination of philanthropic support of child advocacy organizations, one longitudinal study of social movement philanthropy found that child advocacy organizations received a total of $12.2 million in foundation grants between 1953 and 1980 (Jenkins and Halcli 1996). This amount represents 5 percent of the $245.5 million that foundations awarded to social movement organizations over the 28-year period examined. Jenkins and Halcli's data also show considerable fluctuation in child advocacy funding, with just over 1 percent of social movement grants awarded to child advocacy organizations in 1970, 8 percent awarded in 1980, and 4 percent in 1990.

## The Link between Perceived Weaknesses of the Children's Movement and Observed Funding Patterns

When one compares the criticisms of child advocacy—offered by scholars and practitioners alike—with the funding patterns and priorities described, it is not hard to draw at least some tentative conclusions about how foundations reinforce, if not create, some of the acknowledged weaknesses or limitations of the children's movement. What are those criticisms? They include the failure to develop a politically mobilized constituency for children, the lack of an overarching children's policy agenda, and relatively weak or unsophisticated efforts to target legislative leaders in the policy change process.

### Disconnection from Constituency

One consistent theme running through the literature and interview data is that the children's advocacy community lacks a politically mobilized constituency, with many observers suggesting that child advocates need to move from traditional to civic engagement models of advocacy. While those who articulate this point differ in their emphasis on *who* should be mobilized on behalf of children—parents, business and civic leaders, low-income or other historically disenfranchised groups—most agree that, in the absence of a defined constituency, professional advocates will be constrained in their ability to advance anything but the most incremental reforms.

In this volume, for example, Theda Skocpol and Jillian Dickert argue that the replacement of federated membership organizations with centrally managed and professionally run advocacy organizations has reduced prospects for the enactment of significant new national measures on behalf of children and families. Although they were class based and racially exclusionary, such old-line groups as the National Congress of Mothers and the General Federation of Women's Clubs were effective in social policy reform precisely because their structure as federated membership associations allowed them both to develop local memberships and to link them together across states and communities in a broader national movement for change. (See also Imig, this volume.)

The issue of constituency has, of course, been more generally discussed by those concerned about the ways that changes in America's civic and political landscape have influenced national policy priorities. In this sense, the absence of constituency, although a recognized problem for the child advocacy community, is not unique to it. Weir and Ganz (1997), for example, associate declining levels of citizen engagement with the changes in the structure and function of American political parties, the evolution of social movements into Washington-based lobbies, and the media's growing role in the political process. Not only have these developments weakened the ties between citizen constituencies and public policymakers, they have also significantly reduced opportunities for ordinary citizens—especially the poor—to participate in the process. Few observers seem to discuss what specific remedies are available to bring people back into politics. Social policy advocates generally agree, however, that a renewed national commitment to vulnerable populations, including children, will only emerge through organized efforts to link citizens together in larger networks capable of developing and implementing local, state, and national reform strategies.

## Lack of an Overarching Policy Agenda

Another key issue for the children's movement is the failure to develop a common policy vision or unified agenda capable of substantially improving the lives of America's children. As Weir and Ganz (1997) note, "From the 1970s on, advocacy organizations run by professional staff members at the state and national levels found that they could operate most effectively if they focused on single issues that could be addressed with specific insider strategies based on lobbying, litigation and fund raising" (160). The tendency—aptly demonstrated in this volume by Sara Rosenbaum and Colleen Sonosky's analysis of the State Children's Health Insurance Program—is to look at what is possible, or "winnable," not necessarily what is desirable. When nonprofit organizations perform both service delivery and advocacy, the tendency toward more technocratic and specialized approaches to policy reform can be even more pronounced. There are also significant pressures—fueled by fundraising imperatives—to find a niche in the policy marketplace and to demonstrate a measurable impact.

As with constituency-building, issue fragmentation and policy specialization are not unique to child advocacy. In his interesting analysis of "public interest liberalism," Michael McCann (1986) analyzes the conundrum in which environmental and consumer advocates find themselves when they pursue specific or narrowly based concerns. He argues that the public-interest movement has marginalized itself politically by staying "aloof from those traditional macroeconomic issues of income, wage, price, tax, debt, and investment management policies which concern most citizens" (157). For McCann, the public interest movement's "inherent narrowness of conceptual concern" has deprived it of an ability to speak to the concerns of most Americans and to develop or promote "a comprehensive program that specifies the actions necessary to provide welfare for all . . . . " (157). When political pragmatism is preferred to broad-based vision, the paradoxical result is an admirable ability to win important legislative or public policy battles within a more general political context of losing the war.

McCann's charge that public interest liberalism is little more than an amalgam of diverse and uncoordinated policy efforts can be almost equally applied to the children's movement. Indeed, in concentrating on a number of discrete, if crucial, policy issues—early childhood education, immunization campaigns, medical insurance, and the like—most child advocates have failed to articulate common analytic or moral principles on which to develop a unified social vision, guide action, or pursue broad-based reform. One result is that legislators do not sense that the child advocacy community is unified in its goals and objectives.

As Republican pollster John Deardourff remarked at a mid-1990s conference on constituency-building for children, legislative decision-makers typically say that they know what the American Association of Retired People wants, but they have little idea what constitutes a child and family policy agenda: "Children's hospitals in most states do a good job of going in and defending their budgets. So do a lot of the day-care providers, who have an association that pays for lobbyists. But overall there is no coalition that can give a legislator the kids' agenda for this year and the bills it will take to get them accomplished" (Children's Partnership 1996, 16). Hence, Deardourff concluded, legislators do not see that they pay a price for not engaging in child advocacy.

## Ineffective Legislative Advocacy

The lack of constituency and the failure to develop an overarching and more coherent policy approach to child well-being are both contributing factors to what some also observe to be weak legislative work by child advocates. Based on interviews with 177 state legislators, a report found that most of them seemed ill-informed about how well children and families were faring in their districts (State Legislative Leaders Foundation 1995). Legislators apparently hear little from their constituents on child and family policy matters, discern no clear legislative agenda for children and families, and hold a somewhat negative view of child advocates as "elitists." State legislative leaders also tend to view certain strategies pursued by child advocates as either counterproductive (e.g., long written reports) or ineffective (e.g., media campaigns).

Finally, and perhaps most important, the report concluded that child advocates are not provided with the training, funding, and flexibility essential to successful legislative advocacy. One of the report's central findings is that legislative advocacy is neither aggressively pursued nor effectively implemented as a major strategy largely because many, if not most, foundations place restrictions on the use of funds for such purposes. These restrictions may explain why almost two-thirds of the state-based child advocates in the study did not organize their supporters by legislative district or by the districts of key legislative committee chairs (State Legislative Leaders Foundation 1995).

Interestingly, a retrospective study of the Annie E. Casey Foundation's KIDS COUNT program found that while media coverage of children's issues had increased substantially and spawned a voluminous amount of reliable and user-friendly data, few of the KIDS COUNT grantees were actually able to cite concrete examples of improved program or policy decisions (Academy for Educational Development n.d.). In fact, grantees reported that, in the present political climate, positive change in their states and communities would be rare. One Indiana respondent admitted feeling ineffective at the state level, given the legislature's mood, while a Washington State grantee felt that the political climate in his state, which emphasized ideology over factual analysis, had prevented policy reforms. As seems to be the case for most KIDS COUNT grantees, this respondent felt that far more influence had been exerted in institutional arenas where agency staff had the discretion to make program or policy decisions.

## The Role of Foundations

All of these problems are exacerbated by how grantmaking foundations often direct their resources. Professionally driven activities, for example, are clearly the preferred route to policy change for most foundations that fund advocacy. According to Jenkins and Halcli (1996), foundations directed 78 percent of their child advocacy grant dollars to professional advocates and technical assistance intermediaries between 1953 and 1990, but only 14 percent to grassroots social-action groups.[14]

The data developed for this analysis also show a marked tendency among grantmakers to avoid grassroots constituency development activities in favor of more traditional advocacy operations, such as public education through media outreach, data collection and dissemination, and technical assistance provision to governmental and nonprofit child-serving entities. The $22.6 million provided in 1996 for public education and media outreach purposes, for example, far outstripped the amounts directed to supporting new leadership development, citizen-based advocacy, membership development, and direct or grassroots legislative lobbying.

Foundations have also likely reinforced the single-issue orientation of child advocacy groups by organizing grantmaking programs and allocating resources on a categorical (e.g., by program area) rather than a strategic (e.g., data generation and dissemination, constituency-building, policy development) basis. In addition to single-issue funding, foundations have tended to fund short-term projects, usually limiting their grants to one or two years; rarely does funding exceed three years. Such short-term funding commitments, along with the shifting program interests of many foundations, work against child advocates' ability to think and act with a long-term view. When foundations add their own program initiatives to the mix, child advocates are often left chasing after program dollars that may or may not fit within their own organizational priorities and longer-range goals.

Finally, another aspect of grantmaking that many argue reduces the effectiveness of advocacy organizations is foundations' propensity to fund projects rather than general operations. Ironically, such categorical funding may reinforce the kind of specialized thinking and fragmented approach that many foundations seek to counteract when they fund system-reform efforts that increase cross-agency coordination of services to children and their families. Foundations have also provided few resources that support strategic-planning processes or fundraising activities that could strengthen the institutional capacities of child advocacy organizations, assist these organizations in thinking long term, and develop a more integrated social vision.

## Practitioner Perspectives

Most of the 12 child advocates interviewed and quoted below were quite candid about what they perceived as the weaknesses of their own communities and the ways foundations feed into and reinforce those shortcomings. Although the interviews uncovered different strategic points of view, almost all the respondents acknowledged the failure of the children's movement to build broad-based constituencies for children. One practitioner linked this failure to the "aversion that the child advocacy community has to political action." In her view, child advocates had become

> . . . very seduced by slick public relations materials and advertising, much of which is brilliantly done. But who is reading it and what is it producing? There's also a lot of soft media work, a lot of "hug a kid today"–type stuff. I'm quite skeptical.

She added that effective advocacy also entails a willingness to challenge the status quo through public actions and events and to be able to use many different strategies in addition to media work, including political mailings, community mobilization, legislative hearings, and other activities.

Others agreed that while media work is important, it has often come to replace rather than support political action. One state-level advocate, for example, questioned the use of the media for policy change, asserting that, in the current media frenzy, some child advocates are constantly, almost reflexively, seeking attention.[15] "Sure it helps to raise consciousness," he said, "but raised consciousness is no guarantee of anything, and it shouldn't be confused with policy change."

Another advocate took a different tack, arguing that the strategic use of media was very important to constituency-building for children:

> Effective advocacy no doubt has several different components and properly sequenced steps. But absent media communications, few others will work. Without resources to buy media access, our recourse is to obtain media coverage of the issues through stories and op-eds. This is especially critical in our state because of the overlap that exists between media consumers and political activists. Politicians want to be associated with popular effective programs, and so we are targeting the politically active voters through our media efforts. This, coupled with other forms of public or community mobilization, is what we call strategic political reform.

At the same time, this advocate noted the difficulty of raising money from grantmaking foundations for deeply political, if nonpartisan, work on behalf of children. In fact, he explicitly emphasized not having sought the support of major foundations, in the interest of maintaining the maximum amount of strategic flexibility for his organization.

Another interviewee observed that child advocates tend to fall back on the things they do well, such as gathering data or writing reports, and one practitioner expressed the view that the growing pot of money available for data collection and analysis had encouraged more "careerists" to join the field. These professionals, he argued, bring "faith in data" as a primary mechanism for change, resulting in less emphasis on community mobilization and citizen-activation strategies.

While the child advocates interviewed demonstrated a clear willingness to examine and critique their own practices, they were also eager to discuss their frustrations with the foundation community. Common sentiments included the following: Foundations don't really understand or like to fund advocacy; grant-seeking organizations often have to twist and turn to fit into foundation priorities; little candor exists between those who fund and those who do the work; and foundations maintain unrealistic expectations about what advocates can produce in return for the relatively small amounts of money provided. In a particularly forceful statement, one child advocate said,

> Unless they themselves are doing it, foundations neither understand nor trust advocacy. They want to put their own programs together or to dictate how we

should do our work. It is so maddening because we have a long-term track record and can show impact and results in terms of changes in law and public policy, but we still don't get respect for our work.

Another said,

Foundations are stuck in a direct service or research mode. They don't understand or respect the nitty-gritty of advocacy. They say they want to build constituency, but they're not willing to acknowledge that effective constituency-building takes time and resources, especially when it involves those who should be at the table but often are not. We get rejections all the time for this aspect of our work. The grants we do get are small relative to the sums that foundations pour into service agencies and systems, yet it always seems like we're held to a higher standard and expected to produce so much more.

Other respondents expressed similar concerns that foundations exert undue influence over their choice of issues, strategies, and methods. Child advocates are clearly frustrated by foundation-designed programs and the perceived unwillingness of many foundations to let advocates determine how best to move an agenda forward:

Foundations develop funding initiatives, and we structure our programs to fit them. We all play this game, and it is a dangerous one. A good, candid dialogue needs to happen, with longer-term thinking about agendas and how to build toward them. Frankly, we survive by pretending that we are something that we're not. So many of the good things that we've done have happened in spite of, not because of, our funding.

Such statements are consistent not only with the grants data reported on earlier, but also with the views that many child advocates have expressed in other settings or through other reports. In *Building a Constituency for Children: A Discussion among Child Advocates,* for example, child advocates asserted that while constituency-building for children is valuable and even necessary, it is also time-consuming and expensive, requiring far more resources than most foundations are willing to provide (National Association of Child Advocates 1998).

Based on a national survey of organizations that advocate on children's behalf, the State Legislative Leaders Foundation (1995) concluded that foundations' unwillingness to support legislative advocacy is the biggest barrier to nonprofit organizations' ability to underwrite a sustained and aggressive legislative advocacy program for children. As Stephen Lakis, president of the foundation, said in his introductory remarks, "[T]he responsibility for getting state legislative leaders more involved will continue to rest with those organizations and individuals who are concerned about children and families. . . . The philanthropic community must revisit its reluctance to fund effective outreach and education to legislative leaders and those the leaders rely upon for information" (iii).

Survey research conducted on state-based child advocacy organizations in the late 1980s and early 1990s reveals how little financial and organizational capacity many of these groups have to address the issues that confront them, including the enormous challenge of building political clout for children. According to Richart and Bing (1991), the average budget of state-based child advocacy organizations in the early 1990s was $294,454. When the 5 largest organizations were excluded from the analysis, however, the average budget for the remaining 28 groups surveyed was only $178,779. Not surprisingly, these child advocacy organizations were severely constrained in their ability to hire both support and program staff. One-third had no full-time administrative staff, for example, while the average number of full-time professional staff was two.

Richart and Bing also note that almost all the child advocacy organizations surveyed have no hard revenue sources on which to rely, forcing their directors to spend significant time raising nonrecurring revenues year after year. This constant search for funding, in combination with short staffing arrangements, undercuts child advocacy organizations' ability to work up to their full potential. Since the early part of the decade, however, some progress has been made, at least with respect to the soft-money contributions of foundations and other donors.

A 1995 survey of 35 child advocacy groups affiliated with the National Association of Child Advocates found that the groups raised a total of $16.7 million to support their work. In an updated study, Richart (1997) found that the mean organizational budgets of child advocacy groups increased from $69,807 in 1985 ($n = 13$) to $478,571 in 1996 ($n = 35$). Given the considerable limitations imposed by scarce resources and by what many consider a difficult political climate, he says it is a wonder that child advocates have been able to accomplish as much as they have, not only in keeping children's issues in the public eye but also in protecting children's programs from being considered as potential candidates for the "chopping block."

## Conclusions

Although foundations increased their grants to child advocacy organizations through the 1990s, their record of support for child advocates is not strong. The 103 grantee organizations included in this analysis do not represent the entire child advocacy universe, but they make up much of its organizational core. This infrastructure can and should provide national and state leadership on questions of crucial importance to children, youth, and families; it should work to advance policies and programs capable of substantially addressing poverty and other social conditions that diminish children's lives. In 1996, the collective investment made by some of the nation's largest national, regional, and local funders was only $57.5 million (a figure greatly inflated by a single $19.5 million grant to the National Center for Tobacco-Free Kids). This amount is about 5 percent of the roughly $1.1 billion that foundations awarded that same year to institutions serving infants, children, and youth.

The grant analysis further shows that when foundations are willing to fund advocacy, they do so in ways that may weaken child advocacy organizations or detract from the ability to build broad-based political support for kids. In 1996, foundations directed only 8 percent of their 1996 grant awards to child advocacy organizations on a general-support basis and only 6 percent to help child advocates build their organizations through strategic planning, staff development, and resource development activities.

Foundations also continue to think and fund categorically, targeting a majority of their grant dollars either to single-issue, mostly national organizations or to single-issue projects of multi-issue organizations. In addition to single-issue approaches to funding, the data show that foundations also significantly engaged in single-strategy funding, awarding more than $22.6 million to support public education and media-outreach activities. While public and media outreach may prepare the groundwork for or complement more direct constituency-building and activation strategies, they cannot substitute for sustained efforts to cultivate a membership base, develop community leaders, train advocates, build alliances, and otherwise involve ordinary citizens in influencing key decisionmakers in matters of critical importance to children, youth, and families. But many practitioners suggest that these kinds of activities will be necessary if the children's movement is to develop the kind of political muscle it needs to reduce child poverty rates, improve child health and well-being, and rebuild the impoverished inner-city and rural communities in which so many of our nation's children reside.

# NOTES

1. In their baseline study, Kahn, Kamerman, and McGowan (1972) place the conceptual origins of child advocacy in government-sponsored efforts. They identify four institutional antecedents of the children's movement that, along with civil rights and antipoverty activism, helped to galvanize professional and lay advocacy on behalf of children: the 1969 Report of the Joint Commission on Mental Health of Children, the 1969 establishment of the Office of Child Development (OCD), the 1970 White House Conference on Children and Youth, and the 1971 formation of OCD's National Center for Child Advocacy.

2. In his analysis of the moral underpinnings of national politics, Lakoff (1996) writes, "Conservatives know that politics is not just about policy and interest groups and issue-by-issue debate. They have learned that politics is about family and morality, about myth and metaphor and emotional identification" (19).

3. In his examination of the role that persuasion plays in the political process, Majone (1988) argues that there are two different modes of policy analysis. The first he calls "analysis as maximization" because it focuses on how public resources can be most frequently distributed for maximum effect. This analytical mode is technocratic, and considers the relative costs and benefits of particular expenditures. The central concern of the second mode—"analysis as argument"—is how to improve the quality of public discourse and public reasoning processes. Where the former draws on formal methods of proof, rational choice theories, and macroeconomics, the latter sees argument—including the use of rhetoric, ethics, metaphors, values, and evidence—as central. Indeed, Majone argues that "in a democracy, where almost every aspect of public policy is a legitimate topic of debate, analysts who stick to the task of working out unique solutions to well-defined technical problems deny themselves any significant role in the policy process" (158).

4. Following a review of grant descriptions, 5 organizations were removed from the original list of 161 organizations: Aspira, Child Trends, the Child Welfare League, Urban Strategies Council, and We Can.

5. In the mid-1980s, the State Legislative Leaders Foundation surveyed 167 organizations thought to be multi-issue, nonprofit, citizen-based advocacy groups with little or no public funding. Of those organizations, only 52 percent reported advocacy as their primary mission. A full 26 percent of respondents identified their organizations as service providers. The remaining organizations reported their mission as education, health care, or data collection (State Legislative Leaders Foundation 1995).

6. A survey of state-based child advocacy organizations affiliated with the National Association of Child Advocates found that federal funding accounted for 6.7 percent of all funding to these organizations (Richart 1997).

7. Certainly, economic globalization and the shift in the nation's employment base from manufacturing to services (and from cities to suburbs) have also undermined wages for many families. Between 1979 and 1993, real family incomes fell for families in the bottom three-fifths of the income distribution.

8. According to a new report (Collins, Leondar-Wright, and Sklar 1999) jointly released by the Economic Policy Institute and United for a Fair Economy, most households now have a lower net worth than they did in 1983, notwithstanding the stock market's record-breaking growth over the past two decades. That growth has concentrated both wealth and income among an astonishingly small portion of the population: The top 1 percent of households now own more wealth than the entire bottom 95 percent of the population. Meanwhile, the weekly wages of the average worker, as measured in inflation-adjusted dollars, were actually lower 1998 than in 1973.

9. In her study of foundations' public policy influence, Colwell (1993) also concludes that foundation approaches to change rest on pervasive assumptions of democratic elitism. Conceptually dividing the nonprofit sector into two distinct levels (high and low), she notes that high-level policy organizations and other elite institutions receive the bulk of foundation grants.

10. This figure covers foundation grants made to support the following areas: services and activities for infants, children, and youth to age 18; neonatal care; child welfare, including adoption, foster care, and prevention of child abuse; child development; prevention and rehabilitation for juvenile delinquency; pregnancy counseling and prevention programs; adolescent parent services; pediatrics and children's hospitals; and children's museums. Also included are youth development services, youth centers and clubs, adult/child matching programs, scouting organizations, and various youth development organizations (Foundation Center 1998, iii).

11. An additional $3.3 million in 1991 grants and $7.1 million in 1996 grants were awarded to four national organizations providing relevant information resources to national and state-based child advocates across the country: the Center on Budget and Policy Priorities, the Center for Law and Social Policy, the Food Research and Action Center, and the Welfare Law Center.

12. The analysis that follows concentrates largely on the 1996 grants data; because of insufficient information, 50 percent of the 1991 grants data could not be coded by issue area. Based on this information, the two most heavily funded issues in 1991 were K-12 education reform ($2.4 million) and child-abuse prevention and systems reform ($2.4 million). As in 1996, welfare reform and child care issues received far less support.

13. To a certain extent, public education and media outreach appear to be funded as a proxy for constituency-building, with little strategic or analytic recognition that media, public, governmental, and electoral issue agendas are "only loosely connected to each other and that each is governed by their own incentive structures, processes, and gatekeepers" (McCarthy, Smith, and Zald 1996, 293).

14. Jenkins (1998), however, does not believe that the funding of professional movement organizations has been an unmitigated disaster. On the contrary, he views professionalization as having consolidated the social movement gains of the 1960s and 1970s by ensuring stronger enforcement or implementation of civil rights laws and other legislation won through grassroots efforts. Still, as Jenkins notes, professionalization contributes little to grassroots participation, and funders' professional biases may have reduced the incentives for constituency-building among national and state reform leaders.

15. State legislative leaders also report that the media do not dominate the legislative process for child and family policy issues; they do concede, however, that where media

coverage influences public opinion, it can encourage legislators to act on child and family issues (State Legislative Leaders Foundation 1995, 13).

## REFERENCES

Academy for Educational Development. n.d. *KIDS COUNT: Retrospective Study.* New York: Academy for Educational Development.

Annie E. Casey Foundation. 1997. *City KIDS COUNT: Data on the Well-Being of Children in Large Cities.* Baltimore, Md.: The Annie E. Casey Foundation.

———. 2000. *KIDS COUNT Data Book: State Profiles of Child Well-Being.* Baltimore, Md.: The Annie E. Casey Foundation.

Asher, Thomas R. 1977. "Public Needs, Public Policy, and Philanthropy: An Analysis of the Basic Issues and Their Treatment by the Commission on Private Philanthropy and Public Needs." In *Research Papers, Volume II Philanthropic Fields of Interest: Part II—Additional Perspectives* (1069–92). Washington, D.C.: Department of the Treasury.

Carey, Sarah C. 1977. *"Philanthropy and the Powerless."* In Research Papers, Volume II *Philanthropic Fields of Interest: Part II—Additional Perspectives* (1109–64). Washington, D.C.: Department of the Treasury.

Children's Partnership. 1996. *Building a Constituency for Children: Community and National Strategies.* Wingspread Conference Summary and Highlights (February 8–10). Washington, D.C.: The Children's Partnership.

Collins, Chuck, Betsy Leondar-Wright, and Holly Sklar. 1999. *Shifting Fortunes: The Perils of the Growing American Wealth Gap.* Boston: United for a Fair Economy.

Colwell, Mary Anne Culleton. 1993. *Private Foundations and Public Policy: The Political Role of Philanthropy.* New York: Garland Publishing, Inc.

Covington, Sally. 1997. *Moving a Public Policy Agenda: The Strategic Philanthropy of Conservative Foundations.* Washington, D.C.: National Committee for Responsive Philanthropy.

Foster, Catherine Crystal, and Anjali Srivastava. 1996. *Forging the Links: How Advocates Connect Kids and Public Benefits.* Washington, D.C.: National Association of Child Advocates.

Foundation Center. 1998. *Grants for Children and Youth.* New York: The Foundation Center.

Halpern, Robert. 1995. *Rebuilding the Inner City: A History of Neighborhood Initiatives to Address Poverty in the United States.* New York: Columbia University Press.

Jenkins, Craig J. 1998. "Channeling Social Protest: Foundation Patronage of Contemporary Social Movements." In *Private Action and the Public Good,* edited by Walter W. Powell and Elisabeth S. Clemens (206–16). New Haven: Yale University Press.

Jenkins, Craig J., and Abigail Halcli. 1996. "Grassrooting the System? The Development and Impact of Social Movement Philanthropy, 1953–1990." Paper presented at the Conference on Philanthropic Foundations in History: Needs and Opportunities, New York University, New York, November 14–15.

Johnson, Robert Matthews. 1988. *The First Charity: How Philanthropy Can Contribute to Democracy in America.* Cabin John, Md.: Seven Locks Press.

Kahn, Alfred J., Sheila B. Kamerman, and Brenda G. McGowan. 1972. *Child Advocacy: Report of a National Baseline Study.* Washington, D.C.: U.S. Department of Health, Education, and Welfare, Office of Child Development, Children's Bureau.

Kaplan, Ann E. 1997. *Giving U.S.A.* Indianapolis: American Association of Fundraising Council's Trust for Philanthropy.

Lakoff, George. 1996. *Moral Politics: What Conservatives Know That Liberals Don't.* Chicago: University of Chicago Press.

Majone, Giandomenico. 1988. "Policy Analysis and Public Deliberation." In *The Power of Public Ideas,* edited by Robert B. Reich (157–78). Cambridge, Mass.: Harvard University Press.

Margo, Robert A. 1992. "Foundations." In *Who Benefits from the Nonprofit Sector?* edited by Charles T. Clotfelter (207–34). Chicago: University of Chicago Press.

Massey, Douglas S., and Nancy A. Denton. 1993. *American Apartheid: Segregation and the Making of the Underclass.* Cambridge, Mass.: Harvard University Press.

McCann, Michael W. 1986. *Taking Reform Seriously: Perspectives on Public Interest Liberalism.* Ithaca, N.Y.: Cornell University Press.

McCarthy, John D., Jackie Smith, and Mayer N. Zald. 1996. "Accessing Public, Media, Electoral, and Governmental Agendas." In *Comparative Perspectives on Social Movements: Political Opportunities, Mobilizing Structures, and Cultural Framings,* edited by Doug McAdam, John D. McCarthy, and Mayer N. Zald (312–37). New York: Cambridge University Press.

McIlnay, Dennis. 1997. "The Public/Private Balancing Act." *Foundation News and Commentary* 39 (3): 25–30.

Minkler, Meredith. 1999. "Introduction and Overview." In *Community Organizing and Community Building for Health,* edited by Meredith Minkler (3–19). New Brunswick, N.J.: Rutgers University Press.

Mitchell, Anne, and Rima Shore. 1998. "Next Steps toward Quality in Early Care and Education: A Report Commissioned by the Early Childhood Funders Collaborative." White Plains, N.Y.: A.L. Mailman Family Foundation.

National Association of Child Advocates. 1998. *Building a Constituency for Children: A Discussion among Child Advocate: Executive Summary.* A report on a meeting held May 18–19 in Kansas City to assist Kansas Action for Children in its planning process. Washington, D.C.: National Association of Child Advocates.

National Network of Grantmakers. 1998. "Social Change Grantmaking in the United States: The Mid-1990s." San Diego: National Network of Grantmakers.

Odendahl, Teresa. 1990. *Charity Begins at Home: Generosity and Self-Interest among the Philanthropic Elite.* New York: Basic Books, HarperCollins.

Orfield, Myron. 1997. *Metropolitics: A Regional Agenda for Community and Stability.* Washington, D.C.: Brookings Institution Press.

Orland, Martin E., and Carol E. Cohen. 1995. *State Investments in Education and Other Children's Services: The Fiscal Challenges Ahead.* Washington, D.C.: The Finance Project.

Paget, Karen. 1998. "Can Cities Escape Political Isolation?" *The American Prospect: A Journal for the Liberal Imagination* 36 (January-February): 54–62.

Richard, David W. 1997. "Other People's Children and U.S. Politics: A Comparison of Social Movements and the Field of Child Advocacy as a Consensus Movement and the Contexts in Which This Field Functions." Ph.D. diss., The Union Institute.

Richart, David W., and Stephen R. Bing. 1991. *State Voices for Children: A Survey of Selected State-Based Child Advocacy Organizations.* Child Advocacy Resource Center, a project of The National Institute on Children, Youth, and Families, Inc. Louisville, Ky.: Kentucky Youth Advocates.

Schattschneider, E. E. 1960. *The Semi-Sovereign People: A Realist's View of Democracy in America.* New York: Holt, Rinehart and Winston.

Schorr, Lisbeth B. 1997. *Common Purpose: Strengthening Families and Neighborhoods to Rebuild America.* New York: Anchor Books, Doubleday.

Smith, James Allen. 1989. "The Evolving Role of Foundations." In *The Future of the Nonprofit Sector: Challenges, Changes and Policy Considerations,* edited by Virginia A. Hodgkinson, Richard W. Lyman, and associates (61–74). San Francisco: Jossey-Bass Publishers.

Smith, Steven Rathgeb, and Michael Lipsky. 1993. *Nonprofits for Hire: The Welfare State in the Age of Contracting.* Cambridge, Mass.: Harvard University Press.

State Legislative Leaders Foundation. 1995. *State Legislative Leaders: Keys to Effective Legislation for Children and Families: A Report.* Centerville, Mass.: State Legislative Leaders Foundation.

Takanishi, Ruby. 1998. "Children in Poverty: Reflections on the Roles of Philanthropy and Public Policy." In *The Future of Philanthropy in a Changing America,* vol. 2, edited by Charles Clotfelter and Thomas Ehrlich. Los Angeles: The Getty Center.

U.S. Bureau of the Census. 2000. Historical Poverty Table 3, "Poverty Status of People, by Age, Race, and Hispanic Origin: 1959 to 1999." Http://www.census.gov/hhes/poverty/histpov/hstpov3.html.

Verba, Sidney, Kay Lehman Schlozman, and Henry E. Brady. 1995. *Voice and Equality: Civic Voluntarism in American Politics.* Cambridge, Mass.: Harvard University Press.

Weir, Margaret, and Marshall Ganz. 1997. "Reconnecting People and Politics." In *The New Majority: Toward a Popular Progressive Politics,* edited by Stanley B. Greenberg and Theda Skocpol (149–71). New Haven, Conn.: Yale University Press.

Weiss, Heather B., and M. Elena Lopez. 1998. "New Strategies in Foundation Grantmaking for Children and Youth." Cambridge, Mass.: Harvard Family Research Project, mimeo.

## Appendix 2.A: *U.S. Child Advocacy Groups*

| Organization | City | State |
|---|---|---|
| 1. A Vision for Children Center | San Antonio | TX |
| 2. Action Alliance for Children | Oakland | CA |
| 3. Action Alliance for Virginia's Children and Youth | Richmond | VA |
| 4. Action for Alaska's Children | Anchorage | AK |
| 5. Advocates for Children and Youth | Baltimore | MD |
| 6. Advocates for Children of New York | Long Island City | NY |
| 7. Advocates for Justice and Education | Washington | DC |
| 8. Agenda for Children | New Orleans | LA |
| 9. Alliance for Children's Educational Excellence | Sparks | NV |
| 10. Alliance for Children's Rights | Los Angeles | CA |
| 11. Alliance for South Carolina's Children | Columbia | SC |
| 12. Alliance to End Childhood Lead Poisoning | Washington | DC |
| 13. American Academy of Pediatrics | Elk Grove Village | IL |
| 14. Arkansas Advocates for Children and Families | Little Rock | AR |
| 15. Association for Children of New Jersey | Newark | NJ |
| 16. Association of Maternal and Child Health Programs | Washington | DC |
| 17. Black Children's Institute of Tennessee | Nashville | TN |
| 18. Campaign for Fiscal Equity | New York | NY |
| 19. Campaign for Our Children | Baltimore | MD |
| 20. Campaign for Tobacco-Free Kids | Washington | DC |
| 21. Center for Florida's Children | Tallahassee | FL |
| 22. Center for Education Reform | Washington | DC |
| 23. Center for Law and Education | Washington | DC |
| 24. Center for Law and Social Policy | Washington | DC |
| 25. Center on Budget and Policy Priorities | Washington | DC |
| 26. Child Abuse Advocates of Tarrant County | Forth Worth | TX |
| 27. Child Advocates | Houston | TX |
| 28. Child Advocates of Santa Clara & San Mateo Counties | San Jose | CA |
| 29. Child and Family Policy Center | Des Moines | IA |
| 30. Child Care Action Campaign | New York | NY |
| 31. Children at Risk | Houston | TX |
| 32. Children First in Oregon | Portland | OR |
| 33. Children Now | Oakland | CA |
| 34. Children's Action Alliance | Phoenix | AZ |
| 35. Children's Advocacy Institute-Child Welfare | San Diego | CA |

## Appendix 2.A: *U.S. Child Advocacy Groups (Continued)*

| Organization | City | State |
|---|---|---|
| 36. Children's Alliance | Seattle | WA |
| 37. Children's Alliance of New Hampshire | Concord | NH |
| 38. Children's Defense Fund | Washington | DC |
| 39. Children's Defense Fund | St. Paul | MN |
| 40. Children's Defense Fund | Columbus | OH |
| 41. The Children's Partnership | Washington | DC |
| 42. Citizens Coalition for Children of New York State | Ithaca | NY |
| 43. Citizens' Committee for Children of New York | New York | NY |
| 44. Citizens for Connecticut's Children and Youth | New Haven | CT |
| 45. Citizens for Educational Freedom | Arlington | VA |
| 46. Citizens for Excellence in Education | Costa Mesa | CA |
| 47. Citizens for Missouri's Children | St. Louis | MO |
| 48. Citizens for Responsible Education Reform | McLean | VA |
| 49. Coalition for American's Children | Washington | DC |
| 50. Coalition for Asian American Children and Families | New York | NY |
| 51. Coleman Advocates for Children and Youth | San Francisco | CA |
| 52. Colorado Children's Campaign | Denver | CO |
| 53. Committee for Oklahoma Educational Reform | Oklahoma City | OK |
| 54. Congregations Concerned for Children | St. Paul | MN |
| 55. Connecticut Association of Human Services | Hartford | CT |
| 56. Connecticut Voices for Children | New Haven | CT |
| 57. Coordinated Campaign for Learning Disabilities | Washington | DC |
| 58. Council for Children | Atlanta | GA |
| 59. Council on Children and Families of New York State | Albany | NY |
| 60. DC Action for Children | Washington | DC |
| 61. Designs for Change | Chicago | IL |
| 62. Education Law Center | Philadelphia | PA |
| 63. Education Law Center | Newark | NJ |
| 64. Education Policy Institute | Washington | DC |
| 65. Family First | Lincoln | NE |
| 66. Fight Crime: Invest in Kids | Washington | DC |
| 67. Florida Children's Campaign | Tallahassee | FL |
| 68. Floridians for School Choice | Miami | FL |
| 69. Focus on the Kids | Wilmington | DE |

(*Continued*)

## Appendix 2.A: *U.S. Child Advocacy Groups (Continued)*

| Organization | City | State |
|---|---|---|
| 70. Food Research and Action Center | Washington | DC |
| 71. For the Children | Cleveland | OH |
| 72. Georgia Alliance for Children | Atlanta | GA |
| 73. Georgians for Children | Atlanta | GA |
| 74. Georgians for Freedom in Education | Palmetto | GA |
| 75. Hawaii Kids Watch | Honolulu | HI |
| 76. Home School Legal Defense Association | Paeonian Springs | VA |
| 77. Human Development Center of Mississippi | Jackson | MS |
| 78. Indiana Advocates for Children | Indianapolis | IN |
| 79. Indiana Youth Institute | Indianapolis | IN |
| 80. Institute for Educational Leadership | Washington | DC |
| 81. Intercultural Development Research Association | San Antonio | TX |
| 82. Kansas Action for Children | Topeka | KS |
| 83. Kentucky United for Children and Families | Louisville | KY |
| 84. Kentucky Youth Advocates | Louisville | KY |
| 85. Kids In Common | San Jose | CA |
| 86. Maine Children's Alliance | Augusta | ME |
| 87. Maryland Association of Resources for Families and Youth | Baltimore | MD |
| 88. Maryland Committee for Children | Baltimore | MD |
| 89. Massachusetts Advocacy Center | Boston | MA |
| 90. Massachusetts Campaign for Children | Boston | MA |
| 91. Massachusetts Committee for Children and Youth | Boston | MA |
| 92. Michigan League for Human Services | Lansing | MI |
| 93. Michigan's Children | Lansing | MI |
| 94. Minnesota Advocates for Human Rights | Minneapolis | MN |
| 95. Mississippi Forum on Children and Families | Jackson | MS |
| 96. Mississippi Human Services Agenda | Jackson | MS |
| 97. Mountain States Group | Boise | ID |
| 98. Multicultural Education and Training and Advocacy | Somerville | MA |
| 99. National Association of Child Advocates | Washington | DC |
| 100. National Association of Counsel for Children | Denver | CO |
| 101. National Black Child Development Institute | Washington | DC |
| 102. National Center for Infants, Toddlers, and Families | Washington | DC |

## Appendix 2.A: *U.S. Child Advocacy Groups (Continued)*

| Organization | City | State |
|---|---|---|
| 103. National Coalition of Advocates for Children | Washington | DC |
| 104. National Coalition of Advocates for Students | Boston | MA |
| 105. National Committee to Prevent Child Abuse | Chicago | IL |
| 106. National Families in Action | Atlanta | GA |
| 107. National Institute for Children, Youth, and Families | Louisville | KY |
| 108. National Parenting Association | New York | NY |
| 109. National School-Age Child Care Alliance | Los Angeles | CA |
| 110. National Youth Advocate Program | Washington | DC |
| 111. New Mexico Advocates for Children and Families | Albuquerque | NM |
| 112. North Carolina Child Advocacy Institute | Raleigh | NC |
| 113. North Carolina Education and Law Project | Raleigh | NC |
| 114. Oklahoma Institute for Child Advocacy | Oklahoma City | OK |
| 115. Parents Union for Public Schools in Philadelphia | Philadelphia | PA |
| 116. Partnership for Children | Kansas City | MO |
| 117. Pennsylvania Family Institute | Harrisburg | PA |
| 118. Pennsylvania Partnerships for Children | Harrisburg | PA |
| 119. Pennsylvania School Reform Network | Harrisburg | PA |
| 120. Philadelphia Citizens for Children and Youth | Philadelphia | PA |
| 121. Prevent Child Abuse America | Chicago | IL |
| 122. Prevent Child Abuse New Jersey | Newark | NJ |
| 123. Prevent Child Abuse Texas | Austin | TX |
| 124. Prevent Child Abuse Virginia | Richmond | VA |
| 125. Pritchard Committee for Academic Excellence | Lexington | KY |
| 126. Putting Children First | Austin | TX |
| 127. Rhode Islands Kids Count | Providence | RI |
| 128. Rochester Area Children's Collaborative | Rochester | NY |
| 129. South Carolina Budget and Control Board | Columbia | SC |
| 130. South Dakota Coalition for Children | Sioux Falls | SD |
| 131. Spalding University | Louisville | KY |
| 132. Stand for Children | Washington | DC |
| 133. Statewide Parent Advocacy Network | Newark | NJ |
| 134. Statewide Youth Advocacy | Albany | NY |
| 135. Student Advocacy Center of Michigan | Ann Arbor | MI |
| 136. Support Center for Child Advocates | Philadelphia | PA |
| 137. Tarrant County Youth Collaboration | Forth Worth | TX |

(*Continued*)

Appendix 2.A: *U.S. Child Advocacy Groups (Continued)*

| Organization | City | State |
|---|---|---|
| 138. TEACH Michigan Education Fund | Lansing | MI |
| 139. Tennessee Commission on Children and Youth | Nashville | TN |
| 140. Texans Care for Children | Austin | TX |
| 141. Utah Children | Salt Lake City | UT |
| 142. Utah Coalition for Freedom in Education | Logan | UT |
| 143. Vermont Children's Forum | Montpelier | VT |
| 144. Voices for Alabama's Children | Montgomery | AL |
| 145. Voices for Children in Dade County | Miami | FL |
| 146. Voices for Children in Nebraska | Omaha | NE |
| 147. Voices for Illinois Children | Chicago | IL |
| 148. Welfare Law Center | New York | NY |
| 149. West Virginia Kids Count Fund | Charleston | WV |
| 150. West Virginia Task Force on Children, Youth & Families | Charleston | WV |
| 151. West Virginia Youth Coalition | Charleston | WV |
| 152. Westchester Children's Association | White Plains | NY |
| 153. Wisconsin Council on Children and Families | Madison | WI |
| 154. Wyoming Children's Action Alliance | Cheyenne | WY |
| 155. Wyoming PARENT | Cheyenne | WY |
| 156. Youth Advocate Program | Washington | DC |

*Source:* Compiled by author using organizational lists and Internet searches.

# 3

# Medicaid Reforms and SCHIP: Health Care Coverage and the Changing Policy Environment

*Sara Rosenbaum*
*Colleen A. Sonosky*

Over the past 20 years, two major federal legislative advances in public health financing for children have occurred. The first was the restructuring of Medicaid (Title XIX of the Social Security Act) to cover low-income children regardless of their eligibility for cash assistance. This restructuring was done through a series of incremental reforms during the 1980s, and resulted in the near-doubling of the program's pediatric coverage, from 10 million to about 20 million children. The second was the 1997 enactment of the State Children's Health Insurance Program (SCHIP) (Title XXI of the Social Security Act), which extended assistance to approximately 3.3 million children by September 2000 (HCFA 2001).

On the surface, the two initiatives appear similar. Both programs were a response to structural deficits in the American health care financing system. However, they differ fundamentally in their basic legal structure, the depth and scope of coverage for enrolled children, the financial protections against out-of-pocket health spending for low-income families, and the degree of discretion afforded states in overall program design.

Medicaid is a federal entitlement program that specifies minimum eligibility standards, guarantees eligible children coverage for extraordinarily broad and deep benefits, and provides coverage without cost-sharing requirements (Kaiser 1999a, b). By contrast, SCHIP entitles participating states, rather than children, to receive federal contributions for child health assistance. SCHIP programs have broad discretion to define applicable eligibility standards. The SCHIP programs can define the scope and depth of child health assistance in broad or narrow terms and can require families to contribute up to a relatively significant amount of money for the services provided to children. Furthermore, because SCHIP is not an entitlement for eligible children, a state program could, at its discretion, defer enrollment altogether.

One of the most fascinating aspects of the enactment of the Medicaid and SCHIP legislation was the advocacy that surrounded the two sets of initiatives and made their passage possible. Despite the length of time between the initial reforms to the Medicaid program and the enactment of SCHIP, both efforts involved essentially the same advocacy groups. Many of these groups had collaborated on a variety of reforms over a generation (with surprisingly few changes along the way in the individuals working for these organizations). But while the Medicaid reforms generated a basically unified advocacy front, the SCHIP effort generated a series of organizational disagreements not only about the structure of the legislation, but also about its basic strategic and practical value.

Many children's advocacy groups saw SCHIP as a way to improve state coverage of children by identifying common ground during one of the most contentious legislative periods in recent U.S. history. These organizations believed that the SCHIP legislation could be drafted to take advantage of its potential to advance the issue of coverage for children without undermining Medicaid for children or for others. Other child advocates, however, were concerned about the risks the SCHIP legislation posed to existing benefits. In their view, the federal funds made available under SCHIP already effectively existed within the Medicaid program itself, because states already had the option to extend Medicaid coverage to the very children targeted by the SCHIP program.

As a result, one of the central roles played by advocates for children during the SCHIP debate was ensuring that SCHIP would do no harm to Medicaid. Although it is too soon to know whether SCHIP's potential will be realized without its perceived shortcomings, the legislation's enactment presents an important case study in the kinds of issues that can arise within an advocacy community when the immediate needs of one population subgroup (in this case, low-income children) appear to conflict with the broader interests of the larger group (in this case, all low-income Medicaid-eligible persons).[1] This chapter explores the advocacy effort that surrounded the enactment of both programs and examines how advocacy dynamics shaped each program, particularly SCHIP.

The SCHIP and Medicaid advocacy efforts cannot be understood without some knowledge of the reforms themselves. The next section of this chapter describes the Medicaid reform efforts and SCHIP in some detail, placing each piece of legislation within a broader historical and political context. The chapter then compares the important role played by advocates in securing the legislative advances.

## Medicaid Reforms

Between 1984 and 1990, Congress implemented a series of incremental reforms that fundamentally restructured the Medicaid provisions relating to coverage of children. The events that set the stage for the Medicaid reform effort were the failure of the Carter administration's national health reform effort and the spending reductions of the Reagan administration.

The Carter administration's National Health Insurance proposal would have federalized Medicaid as a basic public program for persons without access to employer coverage. As part of its plan, the administration recommended a series of Medicaid reforms, including improved coverage for children.[2] As prospects for enactment of national health insurance faded, support for the pediatric Medicaid improvements became the focus of reform. However, the efforts between 1978 and 1980 to achieve enactment of these reforms (known collectively as the Child Health Assurance Plan [CHAP]) ultimately failed.[3]

In addition to the failed health reform efforts of the Carter administration, the social welfare spending reductions in the first year of the Reagan administration set the stage for a renewed (and bipartisan) interest in achieving reforms for the poor through Medicaid. The spending cuts, along with a deep recession in the early 1980s, resulted in a rapid rise in the number of low-income and uninsured families.

The Medicaid reforms were enacted through a series of incremental changes in Medicaid eligibility requirements. This incremental approach was necessary because neither Congress nor the federal government was willing to budget sufficient moneys in any single fiscal year to enact all the changes at once. Because of the entitlement nature of Medicaid and the high cost of health care, any modification to federal Medicaid policy has significant budget implications. Thus, policymakers took a piece-meal approach that broke a single advance (coverage of all low-income children) into a series of legislative "bites."

## Stages of Reform

The legislative advances in Medicaid coverage for children began with the enactment of the first reforms as part of the Deficit Reduction Act of 1984 (DRA). The basic purpose of these reforms was to "de-link" Medicaid eligibility for children from eligibility for cash welfare benefits under the Aid to Families with Dependent Children (AFDC) program.[4] Separating Medicaid and cash welfare eligibility criteria required several separate types of restructuring. First, family composition had to be eliminated as a Medicaid eligibility factor. Under AFDC, only dependent children (i.e., those with a parent who was absent, deceased, or incapacitated) could qualify for cash aid. However, the DRA mandated that Medicaid cover children under 19 who had welfare-level family incomes/resources and did not qualify for AFDC because of family composition factors.[5] The DRA also mandated coverage of most pregnant women based on family income alone.[6]

In the second stage of reform, the financial eligibility standards applicable to AFDC were eliminated from Medicaid in order to extend coverage to children with family incomes that were too high to qualify them for welfare but too low to make insurance affordable. This change, accomplished first as a state option in 1986, became a state mandate in 1989. The Omnibus Reconciliation Act of 1989 (OBRA 1989) mandated coverage for children born after September 30, 1983, with income at 133 percent of the federal poverty level, in the case of infants and children up to age 6, and with incomes up to 100 percent of the federal poverty level in the case of children ages 6 to 19.

In the third stage, the methodologies for evaluating family income and resources were altered so that working families applying for Medicaid for their children could receive more generous deductions and thus more easily qualify for coverage. Standards and methodologies for AFDC-related welfare eligibility assumed basically no earned income at the time of application and only limited earnings during the term of welfare enrollment. To reach a greater number of low-income working families, states had to be free to adopt more generous rules governing the treatment of earnings. This change was accomplished as a state option in the Medicare Catastrophic Coverage Act of 1988.

Finally, the reforms simplified the application process at locations other than welfare offices in order to ease program entry and to encourage applications from families that were otherwise unwilling to enroll their children in a welfare program. Federal rules governing the Medicaid eligibility and enrollment process always permitted applications to be brief and to occur in sites other than welfare offices. In the Omnibus Budget Reconciliation Act of 1990 (OBRA 1990), this flexibility was explicitly expanded through a new requirement mandating the use of "outstationed" enrollment sites and simplified applications as a condition of federal financial participation.

Taken together, the Medicaid reforms for children enacted by 1990 restructured the entitlement as a matter of federal law. In addition to mandating coverage of poverty-level children born after September 30, 1983, and under age 19, the reforms introduced enrollment opportunities in settings other than welfare offices. The law also gave states the option to significantly liberalize existing AFDC-related standards and methodologies to extend coverage to children in near-poverty and moderate-income working families. In short, as of 1990, states could provide Medicaid coverage to all poor and near-poor children. Indeed, states had the option of extending coverage to children in families whose incomes could be considered moderate by any standard, simply by granting generous deductions to working families applying for child health coverage.

## Reform Aftermath

The fact that Medicaid did—and does today—offer more liberal eligibility options than SCHIP is crucial in assessing the decisions made by SCHIP advocates. By the mid-1990s, only a small number of states had taken advantage of Medicaid's flexibility to extend coverage to children with family incomes above the federal poverty level. Most of the states that elected to provide more liberalized coverage for children did so not as a state plan option but as a component of a larger mandatory Medicaid managed care demonstration program (Rosenbaum and Darnell 1997).

By 1997, Medicaid was effectively "all dressed up with nowhere to go." It was a statute with extraordinary coverage possibilities for children, but few takers. According to many state officials and policymakers, Medicaid had proved too large, too costly, and too generous to provide a realistic platform for extending coverage to near-poor children. In the opinion of other state policymakers, the open-ended entitlement nature of the program (all eligible children who apply for medical assistance must be enrolled) provided justification for avoiding Medicaid, even though states themselves receive open-ended funding to support the cost of their programs.[7]

Once enrolled, the children covered by Medicaid are entitled—without any premiums or cost-sharing—to an unusually broad and deep array of medical assistance benefits, known collectively as Early and Periodic Screening, Diagnostic, and Treatment services (EPSDT). First added to Medicaid in 1967, EPSDT mandates coverage of a wide array of preventive, acute, and long-term medical and health care services for children, regardless of whether those services are covered for adults. Most EPSDT requirements were part of the original statute. In OBRA 1989, Congress broadened the scope of the statute to expand coverage mandates for children under the EPSDT program. These mandates had a particularly strong impact on coverage of services used by children with mental and developmental disabilities. The law also requires that coverage be provided in accordance with a special standard for measuring the medical necessity of care, which prohibits coverage limitations that would otherwise apply to adults (Rosenbaum et al. 1999).

Because of Medicaid's extraordinary eligibility and benefit possibilities, the program became a target for debate within Congress and among the nation's governors in the mid-1990s. For example, during the 1995–96 budget battles, controversy arose over the block granting of the Medicaid program. Throughout this debate, the EPSDT benefit and standards figured prominently in governors' objections to federal Medicaid requirements. Consequently, the Medicaid amendments contained in the Balanced Budget Act of 1997 (which also authorized SCHIP) contained provisions requiring the Secretary of Health and Human Services to undertake a study of EPSDT's costs.

In the end, the very strengths of the Medicaid statute—its eligibility options, broad coverage, open-ended financing, and entitlement nature—also became its weaknesses in the eyes of the state policymakers whose support was crucial to the program's success.

## SCHIP Legislation

The impetus behind the SCHIP legislation parallels that of the Medicaid reforms. The initiative was a reaction to the failure of the Health Security Act in 1994 and the ensuing desire to find an incremental pathway to reform. During the summer of 1996, Congress enacted the Health Insurance Portability and Accountability Act (HIPAA), which was designed to address some of the portability and access-to-coverage issues raised during the 1993–94 health reform debate. HIPAA limits the use of preexisting conditions and waiting periods in both group and individual insurance and employee health benefit plans, and establishes certain group-to-group and group-to-individual insurance enrollment and coverage rights. Companion legislation enacted in the final months of 1996 also bars insurers from setting arbitrary length-of-stay limits for newborns and mothers, as well as the use of differential dollar limits on annual and lifetime coverage of mental health benefits under group health plans (Rosenblatt, Law, and Rosenbaum 1997).

The bipartisan success of HIPAA (sponsored primarily by Senators Kennedy [D-MA] and Kassebaum [R-KS]), the rising number of uninsured children and adults, and the continuing interest in finding an area of legislative compromise around the fundamental issue of affordability all combined to create a legislative backdrop for SCHIP.

## A "Not Medicaid" Benefit

Although the development of SCHIP legislation initially began in a way similar to the Medicaid reforms, the legislation that ultimately emerged differed from Medicaid in nearly every respect. From a legal and structural viewpoint, SCHIP can best be defined as a "not Medicaid" law.

States that participate in SCHIP have the option to implement SCHIP in one of three ways: entirely as a Medicaid expansion, in which case all Medicaid requirements regarding entitlement, eligibility, coverage, cost sharing, and administration apply; as a separate program to create freestanding child health assistance programs; or as a combination of the two (Rosenbaum et al. 1998).

The potential differences between Medicaid and the freestanding SCHIP programs[8] underscore the controversy that has surrounded Medicaid in recent years. As discussed above, SCHIP differs from Medicaid in several basic respects. Essentially, Medicaid is a permanent, open-ended entitlement program that guarantees a comprehensive benefit package for all eligible children. In contrast, SCHIP is a block grant program legislated for a period of 10 years that allows the states discretion in the program's eligibility, design, and implementation. Table 3.1 summarizes the differences between the two statutes in their basic legal, structural, and operational requirements.

Table 3.1  A Comparison of Medicaid and SCHIP

| Program Features | Medicaid | SCHIP |
|---|---|---|
| Time Span | Permanent | Legislated for a term of 10 years |
| Federal Funding Provisions | Open-ended funding | States receive a sum certain ($40 billion over a 10-year period) |
| Extent of Coverage | Provides comprehensive defined benefit package for children | Specifies several broad areas of coverage, but mandates few defined benefits in freestanding programs (well-baby exams, well-child exams, and immunizations) |
| Entitlement Status | Entitles eligible children to coverage | Entitles states to funding but explicitly specifies that nothing in the federal law creates an individual entitlement to coverage[1] |
| Cost-Sharing Requirements | Prohibits virtually all cost sharing in the case of children | Allows states with freestanding programs to impose relatively significant cost-sharing requirements[2] |
| Income Limits | No upper income limits on families whose children are eligible, and no barriers to the enrollment of low-income children with insufficient health coverage | Caps the income level for state programs and prohibits the enrollment of children who have some, but inadequate, private insurance coverage |
| Discretion of Coverage | Establishes conditions of participation for providers, including managed-care entities and organizations | States have complete discretion over conditions of participation for providers and consumer protections |

[1]The earliest legislative version of SCHIP, introduced by Senators Kennedy and Hatch, eliminated an individual entitlement to coverage. S. 525 §2824(e) provided specifically that "nothing in this Title shall be construed as providing an individual with an entitlement to assistance under this Title." This stipulation means that, depending on how states implement SCHIP, eligible children may be denied assistance.

[2]Under SCHIP, the families of enrolled children in states with freestanding SCHIP programs can be charged up to 5 percent of family income in cost sharing and have no protections on expenditures for uncovered services. The law does not prohibit states from using a gross income test to measure families' cost-sharing exposure. As of 1999, no states appear to impose cost-sharing requirements that approach the 5 percent test for covered services, but no state measures families' cost-sharing exposure in terms of its out-of-pocket exposure for noncovered services. See Rosenbaum and Markus (1999).

## SCHIP's Link to Medicaid and Future Implications

One of SCHIP's central aspects is its statutory link to Medicaid. States that elect to implement SCHIP as a Medicaid expansion are bound by all Medicaid requirements, while freestanding SCHIP programs provide states with nearly unlimited discretion over how they use funds. However, except for a few very limited exceptions involving employer group coverage, federal law bars states from enrolling children who are eligible for any other form of coverage, including Medicaid, into a freestanding SCHIP program. This "firewall" between SCHIP and other forms of insurance serves two purposes. First, it prevents "crowd-out," a phenomenon in which public funds effectively substitute for available private coverage.[9] It also prevents any spillover of Medicaid-eligible children into SCHIP.

The bar against enrolling Medicaid children in freestanding SCHIP programs reflects two important goals: (1) ensuring that SCHIP funds reach children who otherwise would not qualify for Medicaid coverage, and (2) preventing states from moving eligible children from more generous Medicaid programs into less generous, nonentitlement SCHIP programs.

While the bar against enrolling Medicaid-eligible children in SCHIP has specific goals, it has created some controversy. State officials have protested the administrative burdens such a requirement creates, since all children who apply for SCHIP must first be screened for Medicaid eligibility. Officials are also concerned about the effect of freestanding SCHIP programs on Medicaid enrollment (many states' Medicaid rolls have swelled because of the screening requirement). Finally, many states express concern that low SCHIP enrollment is caused in part by families' reluctance to admit Medicaid need and their unwillingness to apply for SCHIP if it means first being screened for Medicaid. A number of states with freestanding programs have attempted to overcome this problem by integrating the two programs in both name and administration so that a family with an enrolled child has no way of knowing which source of funding—Medicaid or SCHIP—is subsidizing their child's coverage.

A major difference between the Medicaid reforms and the SCHIP legislation was the speed with which the reforms were put into place. The Medicaid reforms were enacted over several years because of budget constraints. The 1997 tobacco settlement[10] discussions, which coincided with SCHIP, created support for the enactment of a ready revenue pool to be used in designing a program that could be enacted immediately and implemented over time—something that the Medicaid reform advocates could have only dreamed about.

Ironically, the funding for the legislation helped create a false impression that full *implementation* could be achieved in SCHIP's first year. Thus, policymakers and legislators have spent much of the first years of SCHIP's life measuring the estimate of eligible children and the rate of enrollment, as well as arguing over who is to blame for the slow pace of implementation.[11]

Although it is linked to Medicaid, SCHIP is governed by distinctly different legal requirements. SCHIP is a remedial response to the problem of uninsured children; it also reflects widespread opposition to further Medicaid expansion among the conservative members of Congress and the nation's governors, many of whom would like to see an alternative to Medicaid. The extent of Medicaid restructuring before the enactment of SCHIP left little room to expand benefits; indeed, by 1997 states could cover not only all near-poor and moderate-income children, but also their parents (Schneider, Fennel, and Long 1998).

SCHIP's dual role—an insurer of children and a political alternative to Medicaid—helps explain why it, rather than an alternative built solely on Medicaid, was enacted. One alternative approach might have been to broaden states' discretion to extend more limited Medicaid benefits to near-poor children under a greater cost-sharing arrangement. Such an approach would have been consistent with the Clinton administration's use of its authority under §1115 of the Social Security Act to permit states to alter the structure of Medicaid for nontraditional eligible families and children upon demonstration of need (Rosenbaum and Darnell 1997).

Senators Rockefeller (D-WV) and Chafee (R-RI) did propose a Medicaid amendment in lieu of a separate SCHIP program, but the amendment was considered less desirable because it retained the Medicaid entitlement structure (Center on Budget and Policy Priorities 1997a). Ultimately, it was struck down by the Senate Finance Committee.[12] This loss suggests that many members of Congress were interested in using SCHIP to advance a new paradigm for the coverage of low-income families, rather than simply to improve existing coverage levels.

Other factors inherent in the legislative process itself help explain the defeat of the Medicaid amendment and the enactment of the SCHIP legislation. SCHIP originated in a measure introduced by Senators Kennedy (D-MA) and Hatch (R-UT) early in 1997 (S. 525, 105th Congress, 1st session), before the jurisdiction of the Senate Labor Committee had been foreclosed (the Senate Finance Committee controls Medicaid). Both Kennedy and Hatch are members of the Senate Labor Committee; only Senator Hatch enjoys membership in both the Finance and Labor Committees. Had the original Hatch-Kennedy bill been drafted as a legislative modification of Medicaid, it would have been referred immediately to the Senate Finance Committee. Because it proposed new law, however, the bill allowed the Labor Committee to argue, at least initially, for some level of jurisdiction over the consideration of the new program, although not necessarily over the tax base on which the program's financing would ultimately rest.[13]

SCHIP, in large part, reflects the 1996 welfare reform approach to social welfare programs, eschewing individual entitlements in favor of maximum state flexibility. Although SCHIP is inextricably linked to Medicaid, it also represents a complete departure from Medicaid. Indeed, the connection between SCHIP and Medicaid creates the potential for an ongoing tug-of-war between the two programs. In the future, states may embrace SCHIP and move away from Medicaid rather than expand and coordinate both programs.

## Differences in the Legislative and Political Contexts

As noted, both the Medicaid and SCHIP eras were born out of a failed national health reform effort, deep concerns about the rising number of uninsured, and a search for bipartisan agreement on incremental reforms. The length of time between the two initiatives, however, meant that the legislative and political contexts were quite different.

### The Political Climate

During both the Medicaid reform and SCHIP eras, presidential and congressional control was split politically. The original Medicaid reforms occurred under a Republican administration and a split Congress (Democratic House, Republican Senate). The SCHIP reforms occurred under a Democratic administration and Republican Congress. Some child advocates argue that one political mix is more conducive to certain types of reforms than the other. As noted below, however, SCHIP was not actively championed by the Democratic president, although President Clinton's support ultimately did help get the program enacted. A more important determinant than political control is whether enough federal policymakers see some value in governmental action to find areas of consensus.

The role of the states and governors has always influenced the political climate surrounding health reform. Many governors have complained about Medicaid for as long as it has existed. However, certain governors—particularly Governor Richard Riley of South Carolina (later Secretary of Education, 1993 to 2000)—were leading proponents of the Medicaid expansions of the 1980s. Yet by the late 1980s, after the overall reform effort had been achieved, the states' governors had adopted a formal position against any continuation of Medicaid reforms, and conservatives in Congress and the Reagan administration had begun exploring ways to amend the Federal Budget Act to prevent future reform. Thus, in reaction to the enacted reforms, some members of Congress, supported by state leaders, took measures to make it virtually impossible to achieve further mandatory reforms in Medicaid.

The influence of state governments was even more important during the SCHIP era. The governors' role in the political climate increased significantly because of both the 1992 election of President Clinton (Arkansas' governor for 12 years) and the 1994 midterm Congressional elections that gave the Republicans a majority in both Houses. In conjunction with the Republican Congress, the governors supported a full-fledged block granting of the Medicaid program in the 1995–96 period. In addition, the governors agreed to strongly support the 1997 SCHIP legislation only if the states had broad discretion in the program's design and implementation. Thus, the influence of the governors contributed to the final passage of SCHIP as "not Medicaid" legislation.

## Program Funding

The revenue from the tobacco industry's settlement with the federal government and Congressional leaders' willingness to consider a large tobacco tax shaped the SCHIP debates. In designing large-scale benefits spending, the presence of this financing opportunity no doubt influenced, if not dictated, the course of the ensuing advocacy. Advocates for SCHIP had an unprecedented opportunity to lock in tens of billions of dollars in child health funding. Advocates for Medicaid reform did not have this financing option.

Whether the tobacco tax money was as large a windfall as it appeared to be is questionable. The states might have received a similar level of federal funds for children's health coverage had they opted to expand Medicaid. Because Medicaid is funded on an open-ended basis, a state's federal Medicaid funding depends on how extensively the state enacts reforms that qualify for federal financial contributions. If all states enacted Medicaid expansions for children up to 200 percent of the federal poverty level, the 10-year value of the federal contribution for these reforms would likely provide states with as much federal funding as the SCHIP legislation. Even though SCHIP's financial contribution formula is more generous, Medicaid's entitlement nature, its broad benefit package, and its prohibition against cost sharing make Medicaid expansions for children relatively costly. The states would have thus received tens of billions of dollars in federal contributions as a result of reforms.

During the era of Medicaid reform, commentators focused less on the long-term financial implications of the expansions and more on the short-term costs of the coverage. This made it possible to overlook (some advocates would say downplay) the cumulative financial value of the Medicaid reforms. During debates over the SCHIP legislation, however, cost estimates were presented and discussed in their entirety. Indeed, advocates believed the program was justified by the 10-year projection of costs, which put federal funding for SCHIP at about the same level as federal funding would have been had the states enacted extensive Medicaid reform. Advocates saw a nonentitlement remedy as a worthwhile price for securing sufficient support to lock in the tobacco money and ensure health coverage for poor children.

## Political Supporters

Medicaid reform and SCHIP faced strikingly similar reactions from the presidential administrations. President Reagan lent no affirmative support to the Medicaid reforms, but he did not overtly oppose them. President George H. Bush actively campaigned on the issue of Medicaid reforms for children; his 1988 campaign materials expressly called for Medicaid expansions for low-income children and families. Initially, President Clinton's support for SCHIP was tepid at best; his own spending recommendations were modest, and his proposals were ill defined. President Clinton's fiscal year 1998 budget called for about $3 billion in new funding for children's health, and offered essentially no proposal regarding how the initiative would be shaped. Ultimately, pressure from congressional supporters and advocates, as well as the availability of tobacco funds, led to President Clinton's growing support of SCHIP.

Congressional support was, of course, critical to successful child health care legislation in the 1980s and the 1990s. Both the Medicaid reforms and SCHIP were championed by a few key members of Congress. While active supporters of Medicaid reform could be found in both houses, intense support for SCHIP resided almost exclusively in the Senate.

## The Medicaid and SCHIP Advocacy Efforts

Neither the Medicaid reforms nor the SCHIP legislation would have been enacted without the work of the advocacy community. In the area of children's health, the advocacy community has two highly related, yet distinct segments: groups that engage in advocacy primarily for children as a specific population, and groups concerned about issues of the poor more generally, with children representing a distinct subset of a larger constituency. The traditions and values of the two advocacy segments are very similar. Members of the two groups have similar backgrounds in social welfare research, client representation, and policy advocacy, and they share a common set of skills.

As these groups have found, advocacy tends to be most difficult when it involves the creation of new legislation, because the legislative process (particularly the process used by Congress to enact entitlement and mandated spending legislation) is complex and contains many hurdles. For the Medicaid reforms and SCHIP, advocates overcame the complexity and inherent inertia of the American federal legislative process and succeeded in creating new benefits. In their efforts, advocates demonstrated the four skills that are essential to a successful effort: (1) the ability to recognize a policy opening and overcome opposition; (2) the ability to design a saleable remedy; (3) the ability to marshal enough support and resources; and (4) perseverance.

### Ability to Recognize a Policy Opening and Overcome Opposition

The first skill is the ability to see a "policy opening" and recognize the potential for what the advocate defines as beneficial change. The Medicaid advocacy effort of the 1980s reflected a recognition of the opportunity to restructure Medicaid—over time and with a fair degree of patience—to loosen the program's ties to the welfare system and reposition it as a freestanding source of health insurance for low-income individuals who do not have access to employer coverage. Although the Medicaid reforms became controversial, they were at first welcomed as a triumph of bipartisanship and a sensible advance in public policy.

In the case of SCHIP, children's advocacy groups—most notably the Children's Defense Fund, the American Academy of Pediatrics, and the National Association of Children's Hospitals—saw a chance to generate major improvements in state coverage of children, using an infusion of new resources and new coverage options, and to forge common ground between lawmakers on both sides of the aisle. Advocacy groups believed that the SCHIP legislation could be drafted to advance coverage for children without undermining Medicaid eligibility either for children or for others. These organizations pointed to Medicaid's permitted coverage of lower-income children, knowing that states were resistant to increasing their Medicaid programs for any reason.

A contrary view was endorsed by groups such as the Center on Budget and Policy Priorities and Families USA. These groups, while committed to improving coverage for children, tended to evaluate social legislation from a broader, less age-specific perspective. Although they recognized SCHIP's possible benefits, these organizations were also concerned about its potential risks. In their view, the federal funds made available under SCHIP already existed, in effect, because Medicaid gave states the option of extending coverage to the very children targeted by the SCHIP program.

Moreover, critics saw SCHIP as a nonentitlement, legislative beachhead formed at a critical juncture in American social policy for the poor. Just a year before, the federal Medicaid entitlement had nearly been lost during the 1996 welfare reform battle. From this beachhead, critics believed, advocates of more limited governmental assistance to the poor would be able to establish an alternative to Medicaid coverage that would ultimately eliminate Medicaid's constitutionally protected benefits.

Because of concerns over the threat to existing benefits, child advocates made policy containment one of their central strategies during the SCHIP debate. As groups promoted the reforms, child and family advocates engaged in a concerted effort to prevent states from implementing SCHIP in ways that would undermine existing Medicaid coverage. In effect, advocacy groups viewed protecting Medicaid benefits and eligibility as one of their main responsibilities during the fight for SCHIP.

## Ability to Design a Saleable Remedy

The second skill is the ability to design a saleable remedy, which requires sufficient analytical, technical, and political skills to develop a workable approach that is attractive to enough people to make enactment possible. In both the reforms of the 1980s and the legislation enacted in the 1990s, advocates worked to design remedies that met these requirements. The nature of their solutions, however, distinguished the two efforts. The advocates of Medicaid reform never considered any other type of plan, nor were they faced with the need to grant significant concessions in order to gain the support of the main legislative sponsors, since key members of Congress supported Medicaid expansions for both philosophical and jurisdictional reasons. In addition, Medicaid advocates, recognizing the need to secure committee support for the proposed reforms, worked almost exclusively with the Senate and House committees with jurisdiction over Medicaid. Thus, no serious alternatives to Medicaid vehicles surfaced. The governors were not strong enough, nor was the opposition to Medicaid in Congress deep enough, to warrant the basic structural compromises ultimately reflected in SCHIP.

Advocates for SCHIP knew from the outset (as shown by the early Hatch-Kennedy legislation) that their ability to secure a vast sum of money for child health hinged largely on their willingness to support a remedy other than a Medicaid expansion. This condition created a powerful springboard for a legislative alternative to Medicaid—at least in the area of family coverage, if not for all populations.

Some advocates ascertained that they could secure passage of SCHIP without sacrificing Medicaid; indeed, SCHIP's link to Medicaid arguably has helped stem the loss of children from the Medicaid rolls. Other SCHIP proponents have admitted that they backed SCHIP simply because they did not support Medicaid.

## Ability to Marshal Enough Support and Resources

The third required skill is the ability to marshal sufficient resources to make enactment of the remedy possible. Both groups of advocates built strong coalitions and tapped media sources to foster support for their causes. Advocates for Medicaid reform and for SCHIP legislation used two different media messages to support their positions, however: The Medicaid advocates framed their message in terms of the relatively high rate of infant mortality at the time, while SCHIP advocates focused on the number of uninsured children in the mid-1990s—despite the fact that the rise in the number of uninsured Americans was just as steep in the 1990s as it was between 1979 and 1982.

Advocates' use of the media for SCHIP was far more sophisticated than that of advocates of the Medicaid reforms, reflecting mainly the time between the two initiatives and the growing sophistication of the advocacy world. However, the 1984 advertisement and editorial writing effort supporting the Medicaid expansions was also strong for its time.

The groups that Medicaid and SCHIP supporters turned to for support differed significantly. Medicaid advocates' single biggest fear was the recurrence of abortion riders attached to the various pieces of legislation, so advocates went out of their way to build faith-based support, particularly that of the National Conference of Catholic Bishops. The effort paid off, with leading Catholic legislators (most notably Henry Hyde [R-IL]) among the reforms' strongest supporters.

For SCHIP proponents, however, the anti-tobacco lobby was an important link. SCHIP became an example of what the government could accomplish with a tobacco tax, and helped policymakers justify both the levy and efforts to curb tobacco use. The two coalitions helped each other mightily, as evidenced, according to advocates, by the breadth of editorial writing surrounding the SCHIP debate.

*Perseverance*

A fourth and final required skill, which tends to be overlooked but appears to distinguish highly effective advocates, is perseverance. Both groups of advocates continue to demonstrate the tough skin that advocacy requires. The proponents of Medicaid have withstood years of attacks on the wisdom of the cumulative child health amendments, and they will likely face even more resistance. Antipathy toward Medicaid and welfare reform has increased the pressure on Medicaid enormously. Things could get worse as states press for loosening the ties between Medicaid and SCHIP and push for more coverage options under the newer legislation. Indeed, policymakers and researchers studying child health insurance patterns frequently express concern that SCHIP will eclipse Medicaid in importance.

SCHIP's proponents have also withstood significant criticism. As noted, some observers believe that support for a remedy other than

Medicaid may ultimately set the stage for Medicaid's demise. But SCHIP advocates argue that Medicaid garners such strong ill will that it is no longer a viable vehicle for reform. Medicaid advocates counter that a modified Medicaid program would have been more consistent with the §1115 demonstrations than the new legislation would, and arguably would have created less of a threat to the rest of Medicaid.

## Advocacy at Work for Medicaid and SCHIP

In discussions with Medicaid advocates, it is hard to detect an ounce of regret for a single effort undertaken to expand or save the program. This dedication reflects a virtually unshakable belief in the uniqueness of Medicaid. Supporters applaud its strength as a permanent and open-ended entitlement that provides generous and unparalleled coverage for poor and medically indigent persons and that protects beneficiaries from the burdens of health care costs. They tend to view the sum of Medicaid's structural and operational weaknesses—its welfare stigma, essentially uncontrollable financing structure, low provider participation rates, and grievous complexity (still an issue, even after years of reform)—as a small price to pay for a program of such importance to the American health care system.

Similarly, SCHIP's supporters remain unwavering in their commitment to the path they chose. The creation of SCHIP signaled an acceptance (at least by some advocates) of Medicaid's limits as a vehicle for change, in part because of its controversial image and the climate of child health advocacy in the late 1990s. SCHIP advocates concluded that an alternative to Medicaid was necessary in order for their efforts to create affordable, publicly funded health insurance for low-income children and adults to succeed. Furthermore, many SCHIP advocates envisioned the new program as a structure for enhancing, rather than eroding, the Medicaid program.

Like advocates of Medicaid reform, advocates for SCHIP tend to perceive its limitations—its lack of permanency, its failure to entitle children to health care assistance as a matter of federal law, and the discretion it gives states in limiting coverage and imposing cost-sharing rules—as a relatively small price to pay for a law that helps secure benefits for low-income children.

The debate within the advocacy world over SCHIP, however, continues to center on the feature that some see as a strength and others as a weakness. SCHIP's concessions to the entitlement and Medicaid program structure make it a more popular and viable program for implementing broader coverage. SCHIP's proponents willingly made these concessions to arrive at a workable vehicle for reform. On the other hand, SCHIP's design, according to some advocates, not only duplicates Medicaid benefits, but also may help critics justify ending Medicaid coverage for families with children.

It is too soon to know whether SCHIP's potential successes will be realized without some effect on other benefits. SCHIP appears to have achieved what the Medicaid options could not: a significant and renewed political interest in covering lower-income children and families at a time when access to private health insurance continues to erode and when Medicaid itself is being battered by the spillover effects of welfare reform (Rosenbaum and Maloy 1999). During the 2000 presidential campaign, health reform proposals by Al Gore (who would have extended SCHIP to parents) and George W. Bush (who argued for making SCHIP a more flexible block grant program) suggested that SCHIP may indeed reflect a long-term shift away from Medicaid as the basis of health care coverage for the poor.

## Conclusion

It is not possible to predict how things will turn out, or whether advocates should have made other choices in securing benefits for children. Should they have pursued Medicaid reforms more slowly and less as mandates? If they had approached reform in this way, would opposition to Medicaid be as strong? Was locking in the SCHIP money worth it, and if so, should Medicaid reforms have been more seriously pursued to head off further attacks on the entitlement? What is clear is that advocates need to carefully assess the social and political landscape, focusing not only on immediate gains but also on future consequences.

Analyzing the opportunities and outcomes may have been easier in the 1980s. After the Reagan administration cutbacks of 1981, the threat to Medicaid and opposition to reform were minimal. Everyone viewed Medicaid as the legislative vehicle for effecting policy changes that addressed children's access to health care. The Medicaid reforms were debated mainly in terms of who would receive benefits, rather than in relation to proposed alternatives. For example, after 1984, advocates annually debated the merits of child health reforms versus the value of reforms for elderly or disabled beneficiaries. In the end, this debate facilitated compromise, and advocates for various groups were able to work together closely.

Advocates in both periods were influenced by the strong likelihood of structural reform. As a result of this favorable outlook, debate over the long-term consequences for Medicaid and the possibility of ever-growing mandates tended to take a backseat to discussions of how to enact legislation, particularly in the case of SCHIP.

Assessing the opportunities and risks associated with SCHIP is more difficult. An unresolved issue is whether the gains realized by SCHIP were worth the added risks to Medicaid. Some critics argue that, in fact, the threat to Medicaid was not fully understood by most observers and policy experts during the SCHIP debate in the fall of 1996 (Rosenbaum and Maloy 1999). Advocates had won the block grant battle and saved Medicaid. Few expected another major Medicaid reduction proposal or were aware that broader welfare reform efforts might further erode support for Medicaid.

With time, Medicaid's precarious position has come more sharply into view. Arguably, the weakening support for entitlement benefits may increase the potential for political leaders eager to appease states and families to use SCHIP as a way to replace Medicaid altogether.

Ultimately, the Medicaid and SCHIP efforts may underscore the limitations of incremental reform, where each advance must overcome additional, unforeseeable rounds of opposition. The Medicaid reforms demonstrated an unprecedented commitment to health care financing for the poor, but they may have placed the responsibility of coverage on an unstable base of support: state governments. State leaders have come to view the seemingly vast entitlement nature of Medicaid as an overwhelming burden on their economies and political structures. SCHIP gives the states much discretion in extending coverage and keeps funding responsibility on the federal government, while creating a host of spillover dilemmas that may put previous gains for both children and adults at risk.

A critical issue for child advocacy funders is the extent to which children's organizations are expected to tailor their agendas to the broader needs and interests of their constituents, even if such accommodations result in the loss of potential short-term or targeted gains. Analyzing the course of SCHIP implementation and resulting changes to Medicaid will be an important investment for public and private funders concerned with American social policy. SCHIP may succeed in promoting coverage for low-income families in general without significantly sacrificing the quality or content of coverage, an outcome that would surely generate a rethinking of American health policy. Alternatively, SCHIP could pave the way for efforts to substitute some kinds of coverage for low-income children and, in turn, erode coverage for low-income Americans in general. Advocates must carefully monitor the course of SCHIP's progress not only for the future of child health coverage, but for that of health reform generally.

NOTES

1. An interesting recent example of this dilemma arose in November 1999, when members of Congress proposed funding Medicaid expansions for working disabled persons contained in the fiscal year 2000 budget through reductions in other human services for low-income individuals and families. Pat Wright of the Disability Rights and Education Defense Fund (DREDF) was quoted as saying, "We cannot support any legislation that would advance the lives of people with disabilities on the backs of poor and middle-class Americans" (Pear 1999).
2. The administration's national health insurance plan was collected in a series of background papers that describe the basic plan and the role of Medicaid in the plan. See U.S. Department of Health, Education and Welfare (1978).
3. The legislative proposals that were under consideration during the 95th Congress never were considered by the full House or Senate. In 1979, Congressman Henry Waxman succeeded in crafting a legislative package that reached the House floor, only to be overcome by "poison pill" amendments such as amendments to prohibit the expenditure of Medicaid funds for abortion. The Senate bill never reached the floor; indeed, it was never reported out of committee. It was in great part the CHAP experience that caused many policymakers favoring Medicaid reforms to conclude that such legislation would not be able to pass as freestanding legislation but would instead have to be enacted as part of much larger legislation. The Medicaid legislation subsequently enacted for children and others during the 1980s and 1990s (including SCHIP) was considered as part of much larger budget reconciliation vehicles. These massive spending reduction measures mandated under the federal Budget Act are essentially nonamendable and are thus legislatively far more "bulletproof" once a matter is included as an amendment.
4. AFDC was repealed in 1996 and replaced with the Temporary Assistance for Needy Families (TANF) program (Title I, Public Law 104–193).
5. The original Medicaid statute allowed states the option of covering these children, who were known as Ribicoff children after the Senate sponsor of the amendment creating the coverage option. Fewer than half of all states had done so by 1984 (Deficit Reduction Act of 1984, Pub. Law 98–369, §2361).
6. Consolidated Omnibus Budget Reconciliation Act of 1985 Public Law 99–272, § 9501(b). Prior to the DRA, states could extend coverage to all medically indigent

pregnant women with family income at or below state cash welfare levels. Most states did not opt to do so.

7. The October 10, 1999, message from Governor Gray Davis to the California State Senate vetoing Senate Bill No. 1047 ( a bill requiring a report to consolidate Medicaid, Healthy Families, and other programs into a single program and purchasing pool) stated, "I have repeatedly expressed my opposition to converting Healthy Families into an entitlement program. The Healthy Families program has enjoyed great success by allowing lower-income families the opportunity to purchase health care for their children with a low-cost premium, rather than enrolling them in MediCal without sharing any of the cost. The consolidation of these programs would inhibit efforts to enroll uninsured children in the Healthy Families program, negatively influence the program's continued success, and create a new entitlement program." See http://www.ca.gov/s/governor/199~.

8. According to fiscal year 2000 HCFA data, 33 states had elected in whole or in part to create freestanding programs through separate or combination arrangements (HCFA 2001).

9. For a discussion of crowd-out, see Cutler and Gruber (1996); Dubay and Kenney (1997); and Holahan (1997).

10. In June 1997, the attorneys general of 40 states and 5 tobacco manufacturers entered into a proposed national settlement of lawsuits brought by the states. The proposed settlement called for (1) a limitation on the civil liability of the manufacturers for damages and injuries caused by cigarette smoking; and (2) payments by the industry totaling $368.5 billion in "face value" over a 25-year period. For additional information, see Schneider and Thom (1998).

11. A great deal of time has been spent tallying the new SCHIP children, which is not easy to do given the law's intertwining with Medicaid and the simultaneous loss of Medicaid among children who lose or are barred from welfare. The estimates of SCHIP enrollment during its first full year—about a million children—seem consistent with what one might expect in a program targeted to reach 3 million to 5 million children, depending on the estimates being used.

12. For information on the proposals considered by the Senate Finance Committee, see Center on Budget and Policy Priorities (1997a–d).

13. This was not the first time that jurisdictional considerations in the Senate or the House figured heavily in the final shape of the legislation. But there are relatively few examples in which a program that so clearly parallels another existing program has been enacted into law.

# REFERENCES

Center on Budget and Policy Priorities. 1997a. "Assuring Health Care Coverage for Low-Income Children: Why the Chafee-Rockefeller Bill Is a Better Approach than the Roth Proposal." Washington, D.C.: Center on Budget and Policy Priorities (June 11). Http://www.cbpp.org.

———. 1997b. "Child Health Block Grant: Key Conference Issues." Washington, D.C.: Center on Budget and Policy Priorities (July 9).

————. 1997c. "Medicaid and Child Health Provisions of the Bipartisan Budget Agreement." Washington, D.C.: Center on Budget and Policy Priorities (May 28).

————. 1997d. "Options for Increasing Participation of Currently Eligible Children in the Medicaid Program." Washington, D.C.: Center on Budget and Policy Priorities (April 16).

Children's Defense Fund. 1998. "25 Years of Child Advocacy: Building a Legacy to Leave No Child Behind." *Special Report: CDF Reports.* Washington, D.C.: Children's Defense Fund (December).

————. 1997. "SCHIP: Advocates Forge Consensus on State Children's Health Insurance Program." *Special Report: CDF Reports.* Washington, D.C.: Children's Defense Fund (December).

Cutler, David, and Jonathan Gruber. 1996. "Does Public Insurance Crowd Out Private Insurance?" *Quarterly Journal of Economics* (May): 391–429.

Dubay, Lisa, and Genevieve Kenney. 1997. "Did Medicaid Expansions for Pregnant Women Crowd Out Private Coverage?" *Health Affairs* 16 (1): 185–93.

Health Care Financing Administration (HCFA). 2001. *State Children's Health Insurance Program Annual Enrollment Report, October 1, 1999–September 30, 2000.* Baltimore, Md.: Health Care Financing Administration.

Holahan, John. 1997. "Crowding Out: How Big a Problem?" *Health Affairs* 16 (1): 204–06.

Kaiser Commission on Medicaid and the Uninsured. 1999a. "Medicaid: A Primer." Washington, D.C.: The Henry J. Kaiser Family Foundation.

————. 1999b. "The Medicaid Program at a Glance." Washington, D.C.: The Henry J. Kaiser Family Foundation.

Pear, Robert. "Deal Is Struck on Restoring Medicare Aid." *New York Times.* November 11, 1999.

Rosenbaum, Sara, and Julie Darnell. 1997. "Analysis of Statewide Medicaid Managed Care Demonstrations: Implications for Federal Policy." Washington, D.C.: Kaiser Commission on Medicaid and the Uninsured.

Rosenbaum, Sara, and Anne Markus. 1999. "An Analysis of Implementation Issues Relating to SCHIP Cost-Sharing Provisions for Certain Targeted Low-Income Children." A report prepared by The George Washington University Medical Center, School of Public Health and Health Services, for the Health Resources and Services Administration and the Health Care Financing Administration.

Rosenbaum, Sara, Kay Johnson, Christopher DeGraw, Colleen Sonosky, and Anne Markus. 1998. "The Children's Hour: The State Children's Health Insurance Program." *Health Affairs* 17 (1): 75–89.

Rosenbaum, Sara, and Kathleen Maloy. 1999. "The Law of Unintended Consequences: The 1996 Personal Responsibility and Work Opportunity Act and Its Impact on Medicaid for Families with Children." *Ohio State Law Journal* 60 (4).

Rosenbaum, Sara, Colleen Sonosky, Karen Shaw, and Marcie Zakheim. 1999. *Negotiating the New Health System: A Nationwide Study of Medicaid Managed Care Contracts,* 3rd ed. Washington, D.C.: The George Washington University Medical Center, Center for Health Services Research and Policy. Http://www.gwhealthpolicy.org.

Rosenblatt, Rand, Sylvia Law, and Sara Rosenbaum. 1997. *Law and the American Health Care System* and *1999–2000 Supplement.* New York: Foundation Press.

Schneider, Andy, Kristen Fennel, and Peter Long. 1998. "Medicaid Eligibility for Families and Children." Washington, D.C.: The Henry J. Kaiser Family Foundation, Kaiser Commission on Medicaid and the Uninsured (September).

Schneider, Andy, and Sara Thom. 1998. "The Proposed National Tobacco Settlement and Recovery of Health Care Costs." Washington, D.C.: Center on Budget and Policy Priorities (February).

U.S. Department of Health, Education and Welfare. 1978. Carter Administration's National Health Insurance Working Papers.

## ADDITIONAL READINGS

Bureau of National Affairs. 2000. "Special Report: Campaign 2000: Health Care Issues and the Presidential Race." Health Care Policy Report. Washington, D.C.: Bureau of National Affairs (August 14).

Guyer, Jocelyn, and Cindy Mann. 1997. "The Commerce Committee Child Health Block Grant: Health Insurance for Children or Windfall for States?" Washington, D.C.: Center on Budget and Policy Priorities (June 24).

Health Care Financing Administration. 1999. "Supporting Families in Transition: A Guide to Expanding Health Coverage in the Post-Welfare Reform World." Baltimore, Md.: Health Care Financing Administration.

Johnson, Kay, Christopher DeGraw, Colleen Sonosky, Anne Markus, and Sara Rosenbaum. 1997. "1997 Budget Reconciliation Provisions. Special Issue: Children's Health Insurance." Health Policy and Child Health 4 (3): 2–9.

————. 1997. "Children's Health Insurance: A Comparison of Major Federal Legislation." Health Policy and Child Health 4 (2): 1–16.

Mann, Cindy, and Laura Cox. 1997. "The Medicaid Program Has Been the Program of Choice for Most States that Have Expanded Coverage for Uninsured Children." Washington, D.C.: Center on Budget and Policy Priorities (June 4).

Rosenbaum, Sara, and Barbara Smith. 2001. "State SCHIP Design and the Right to Coverage." Washington, D.C.: The George Washington University Center for Health Services Research and Policy. Http://www.gwhealthpolicy.org.

Sardell, Alice, and Kay Johnson. 1998. "The Politics of EPSDT in the 1990s: Policy Entrepreneurs, Political Streams, and Children's Health Benefits." The Milbank Quarterly 76 (2): 175–205.

Schneider, Andy. 1997. "Reducing the Number of Uninsured Children: Building upon Medicaid Coverage Is a Better Approach than Creating a New Block Grant to the States." Washington, D.C.: Center on Budget and Policy Priorities (June).

Schneider, Andy, and Rachel Garfield. 2000. "Medicaid Benefits." Washington, D.C.: The Henry J. Kaiser Family Foundation, Kaiser Commission on Medicaid and the Uninsured (July).

Stevens, Robert, and Rosemary Stevens. 1974. Welfare Medicine in America. New York: Free Press.

Ullman, Frank, Ian Hill, and Ruth Almeida. 1999. SCHIP: A Look at Emerging State Programs. Washington, D.C.: Urban Institute Assessing the New Federalism Policy Brief A-35.

# 4

# Building a Policy Voice for Children through the Nonprofit Sector

*Elizabeth Reid*

U nderstanding advocacy for children means understanding the organizations and people who speak for them. Advocates for children have a rich and varied legacy of advocacy in legislatures, courts, and in the media, and their efforts have led to real gains for children. Some problems, however, call for broader reforms that have been difficult to secure in the complex policy environments in which advocates work. For example, the availability of accessible, quality child care, health care, and education remains uneven across the United States.

Business and government institutions are important advocates for children, but nonprofit organizations—the focus of this chapter—play a unique role. Nonprofits offer citizens ways to address government and to shape social views on public expenditures, community roles, and parental responsibility for children. How nonprofit groups find resources, train leaders, apply research, organize civic action, and form coalitions determines their capacity to leverage public and political support for children's issues.

What, then, should child advocates consider as they adapt their organizational priorities and strategies to better shape and enact public policy reforms? Traditionally, examinations of such groups' role and activities in promoting policy change have drawn heavily on political science studies of how interest groups behave in a competitive, money-driven political system. This chapter enriches that information by drawing on insights from other academic disciplines to describe the opportunities and challenges faced by child advocates.

The first section of this chapter provides background information for examining nonprofit policy advocacy. The second section discusses the broader environmental context for organized action. The third section examines the challenges of building organizations to represent children and mobilize the public on children's behalf. The fourth section examines advocates' strategies for shaping institutional outcomes. The conclusion suggests future directions for building child advocacy organizations.

## Advocacy Organizations in American Democracy

There are nonprofit groups on nearly every side of a given issue, and children's health and well-being are no exception. American democracy's long tradition of engaging community and interest groups in politics rests on the constitutional rights to free speech and association. Together, these rights provide the basis for people to form organizations, express their ideas and interests, gather resources, and pursue common activities without involving government.

Children, however, have a unique place in American democracy. Their rights and political agency are not as absolute or direct as those of adults. Thus, children's voices must be heard through the organizations of parents and professionals who negotiate children's status in the courts and in the policy process. Advocacy for children is as much about the adults and the organizations that represent them as it is about the children themselves. In a recent survey of child advocacy groups, a respondent observed, "Our legislators, even the best of them, address children's issues in terms of the adult standing next to the child, not in terms of the need of the child" (State Legislative Leaders Foundation 1995).

Child advocacy groups use a wide range of activities to influence the decisions and practices of government, business, and society. Organizing public education and media activities, monitoring government programs, reporting findings to the public and to government officials, and lobbying and testifying all build public awareness and support for policy issues. In addition, advocates for children litigate disputed issues, serve on public commissions, and collaborate with agencies and other stakeholders to improve program services. Writing letters, volunteering, holding public meetings, demonstrating, and speaking in public forums are other types of advocacy activities that encourage political participation beyond the act of voting. Groups influence election outcomes and foster a more receptive political environment for their policy goals by registering voters, publishing and distributing officials' voting records, forming and using political action committees, and participating in political parties.

As the array of activities suggests, a nonprofit advocacy organization can follow a variety of models. While tax status may distinguish one advocacy group from another in law, political behavior distinguishes them in practice. Charitable groups, classified as 501(c)(3) organizations under IRS regulations, are the most common. There are 5 times as many charitable nonprofits working for children as 501(c)(4) social welfare advocacy groups (De Vita, Mosher-Williams, and Stengel, this volume). Many of these 501(c)(3)s are very small and are not required to report activities to the IRS. Some large advocacy organizations spin off loosely related exempt organizations to create tax advantages and facilitate political action.

Success in shaping policies for children depends largely on building strong organizations and coalitions with enough resources to exercise power in politics. Power is relational, situational, asymmetrical, and potentially unstable (Knoke 1994). Groups must strategically design and adjust their activities to persuade decisionmakers in a variety of situations. Advocates may provide information to alter the receivers' perceptions, preferences, or behaviors (Knoke 1994); engage the public in grassroots action to hold elected officials accountable to voter preferences; or use more coercive action, such as extending or withholding benefits. Everyday politics is filled with the push and shove of political clout, which may be exercised as personal favors, political donations, or threats to personal reputations or to the public's well-being.

The competition of ideas and organizations in the political bargaining process should create fairer policy outcomes, but groups, along with other players, often contribute to legislative stalemate and inequitable outcomes. Successful short-term strategies may prove divisive over the long term when groups with different ideologies, interests, policy approaches, and partisan preferences combine to gain favor over other interests. In the end, such diverse factions can lead to polarized political bargaining and few, if any, significant policy gains. Some groups are better represented in politics because of their greater resources, and policy outcomes often favor one group over another.

Some groups find ways to overcome this fragmentation and stalemate, but many others do not. In theory, cross-cutting coalitions should promote social and political cooperation, encouraging organizations to align to promote issue agendas, build legislative and electoral coalitions, and agree to tradeoffs with other stakeholders. In practice, however, building bridges among groups with different constituencies is difficult. Deliberation between elected leaders and citizens, and among citizens, emphasizes building public consensus and overcoming partisan gridlock. Organizations can be a place for people to exchange information and persuade policymakers and other individuals to adopt policy viewpoints. Such groups can help people share their experiences productively, allowing them to agree on approaches to social concerns.

Even when policy efforts falter, the trust and reciprocity that result from association are thought to provide positive benefits for democracy, such as tempered self-interest, opportunities for consensus-building prior to policy action, and reduced political opportunism in political bargaining (Putnam 2000). Many activists, however, are ambivalent about the value of social capital if it reinforces the social or political exclusiveness of existing social networks. They may also be skeptical of the utility of dialogue if it does not translate into influence in the policy process.

## Opportunities and Barriers to Action in the Policy Environment

The broader policy environment determines how child advocacy organizations grow and develop, how groups use advocacy to accomplish policy goals, and the difficulties in generating a public or institutional response to children's issues. This section gives an overview of the different factors that determine how an organization attempts to have reform enacted. These actions may occur in a variety of settings—in the legislatures, state agencies, and courts—and are shaped by a variety of conditions—including election campaigns, regulatory restrictions, and social and economic change.

Advocates often stress the need to push for more protection for vulnerable children wherever and whenever the political and judicial systems are responsive. However, the choice of how to pursue reform— through legislatures, agencies, courts, or private action—shapes prospects for future reforms, so any analysis of goals and opportunities should take into account how reform in one venue might affect community action in another.

## Steps in the Policymaking Process

Decisionmaking processes can be seen as a political opportunity structure in which groups have varying degrees of access and authority to influence policy outcomes. When groups advocate, they create new opportunities and take advantage of existing ones to advance their goals. Breaking the policymaking process down into stages and reviewing what happens at each point can help groups decide what strategies will be effective (Howlett and Ramesh 1995).

### SETTING THE AGENDA

The first stage in shaping policy is setting the agenda, which occurs as problems come to the public's attention. During this stage, advocacy groups must clearly articulate their positions and provide supporting research. Child advocates and other citizen groups at the national level have been adept at using research and staff interactions to get policy ideas into legislation (Berry 1999). Building a coherent message on children's policy is challenging, however, because there is no clearly discernable legislative agenda for children and families; rather, a multitude of individuals and organizations with different agendas are sending mixed messages about what is best for children (State Legislative Leaders Foundation 1995). Campaigns with overarching slogans and public messages can provide an umbrella for groups with diverse but complementary interests to coordinate their political demands.

### PASSING LEGISLATION

The second stage is getting legislation passed. At this point, competition increases, and groups must be prepared to intensify their efforts to reach policymakers and use the groups' political capital to promote their favored policy options. Connections to policymakers, the media, and parent groups and a constant presence both in the legislature and before the public are key.

### POLICY IMPLEMENTATION

After legislation is passed, advocacy groups may shift from the more adversarial positions they may have adopted while the legislation was being debated to doing more collaborative work with other organizations and government agencies to ensure that the policy serves their constituents as intended. Some programs are implemented in ways that give a range of stakeholders sufficient authority to make a difference, but groups are often frustrated by legislation that limits funding or hampers their ability to improve program design and service delivery. Close monitoring of policy implementation and social outcomes is important for groups that wish to shape subsequent policy.

The courts have also been a productive venue for advocacy, with individual case decisions shaping future public policy. Mnookin and Burt (1985), however, have raised questions about the influence appointed judges have on legislatures' power to establish policy for children and on the relative balance of power between the courts and other branches of government.

### Systemic versus Incremental Change

Groups may strive for either incremental or systemic change in the policy process. Systemic change, although it can secure a group's goals, requires sustained campaigns with greater resources and larger legislative and electoral majorities than many organizations have. By contrast, incremental policy change, which usually represents small gains and may include a number of low-level battles, such as waging yearly budget fights for children's services or tweaking public programs for better outcomes for children, often succeeds with more modest resources. Incremental change can be easier to attain, but limited policy improvements for children can frustrate child advocates and parents when conditions for children are slow to improve.

## Election Politics and Political Power

Groups use the election process and their relationships with elected officials and parties to create swings in partisanship. Politicians also turn to groups for resources and votes to enhance their chances of getting elected. However, the high-stakes political environment of elections makes groups and politicians wary of each other. Leaders interested in constructing winning majorities must address the issues that advocacy groups bring to the fore during elections. Advocacy groups' long-term issue campaigns can be weakened if the party favoring the groups' policy positions is forced out of power.

Some political leaders have made children their cause and have long-term, productive relationships with advocacy groups. Others attempt to limit groups' influence in congressional agendas and elections, and can fuel organizational divisiveness using "wedge" issues (such as immigration or abortion) to polarize debate and capture support during elections. Once elected, policymakers may favor groups that supported their campaigns and have compatible policy goals. For example, President George W. Bush's administration supports having faith-based organizations deliver social services, a policy that fits with the goals of many conservative religious leaders who have actively supported Republican candidates.

When party majorities are slim, politicians often use compromise legislation to offer partial solutions and divide fragile policy coalitions into camps for and against final passage of a law. Changes in legislatures lead many child advocacy groups to recast their public messages and revise their political strategies to include the values and preferences of new majorities. Advocacy groups have also had to adapt to the major changes in welfare policy, devolved policies and programs, and shifting majorities in Congress that have changed how federal and state governments address the needs of children.

Advocacy groups' relationship with political parties has consequences for nonprofit advocacy in general. Some observers suggest that the decline of the public's identification with political parties has resulted in stronger, more effective interest groups as people have sought alternative forms of representation on important issues. However, intense political party mobilization and highly competitive national elections tend to increase group activism (Skocpol 1997). In each case, groups and parties have adapted simultaneously to increase their effectiveness in candidate-centered, money-driven national elections (Herrnson 2000b).

In the current electoral environment, some groups have questioned the value of their involvement in partisan activity. Children's organizations are no exception, and it appears that many make a strategic decision to refrain from political advocacy altogether. Environmental groups, for example, had 16 national political action committees in 1999–2000, while children had 5 (Center for Responsive Politics 2001).

Nevertheless, groups with effective research, lobbying, and public relations operations can have an influential role in shaping the preferences and strategies of party elites. In some cases, advocacy groups lead factions inside parties that are instrumental in shaping party rules and activities. The Women's Caucus within the Democratic Party, for example, offers members an opportunity to promote a children's agenda among sympathetic party activists. However, without either broad-based coalitions of organizations or effective political parties, interest groups alone are unlikely to muster the influence to build the legislative and electoral majorities necessary to win passage of child policy reforms.

## Regulatory Constraints

Nonprofit organizations are subject to a variety of IRS regulations regarding permissible political activities and expenditures. The IRS limits the advocacy activities of charitable 501(c)(3) groups, which offer donors a tax deduction, on the grounds that tax dollars should not subsidize political expression and action.[1] These groups are subject to the most stringent restrictions on direct and grassroots lobbying activities and are prohibited from engaging in partisan activity.[2]

Although such restrictions apply only to some activities, overly complex rules and contradictory definitions of advocacy (General Accounting Office 1999) create a barrier to action, especially for small human service organizations that fear, often unnecessarily, that advocacy will jeopardize their charitable tax status. In one study, 80 percent of state-based children's groups reported that they were aware of restrictions on lobbying and that they eschewed most legislative activity because of IRS restrictions (State Legislative Leaders Foundation 1995). Anecdotal evidence suggests that legal advisors tend to give conservative and cautionary advice about the risks of undertaking advocacy, which further dampens participation.

Nonprofit advocacy organizations and professional associations that are not classified as 501(c)(3)s, can engage in a wider range of political activities. In general, these groups lobby frequently, are instrumental in shaping voter attitudes and increasing voter turnout during national elections, and are important sources of money and volunteers. Political action committees and parties can also engage in a full range of partisan activity.

Groups can use several strategies to overcome barriers created by the regulatory process. Innovative practices, such as issue advocacy, have emerged as a powerful political tool. By teaming up with less restricted groups such as unions or public interest groups, more restricted groups such as service providers may extend their political influence through the political activity of their partners. As De Vita et al. (this volume) describe, the 501(h) election has simplified reporting of advocacy activities, but nonprofits have been slow to take advantage of the new option. Groups can also expand their knowledge of advocacy practices by taking part in forums about the law and about models of effective organizational action and permissible activities.

## Social Conditions, Economic Trends, and Cultural Values

Groups must consider the social conditions and public values that shape policy alternatives, since public perceptions affect the willingness of politicians and the public to address the plight of children. The socioeconomic environment also influences the advocacy practices of those pursuing reforms for children.

Attitudes vary about whether children have sufficient legal standing or sufficient authority to manage their needs in schools, families, and other settings. New family and child research recognizes that parents and other adult advocates act as filters between children and the rest of the world, and strives to include children as legitimate, direct stakeholders whose attitudes and preferences have implications for policymaking. For example, the Families and Work Institute, a think tank that tracks workplace trends, asks children, rather than parents, about how they feel about living in families with working parents.

Different groups bring diverse values to community and educational institutions, forcing advocacy organizations either to reconcile divergent views or to back only their own values in the policy process. The "return to family values" as a moral and religious response to high divorce rates, nontraditional living arrangements, and increased personal freedoms, emerged as a strong political force in the 1980s and 1990s to challenge the dominance of liberal advocacy groups and government social policy. The ongoing social debate over private versus public responsibility has shaped recent policies aimed at children and families. But values from liberal social movements have continued to shape child advocacy and policy reform. The civil rights movement and the emergence of organizations built momentum for children's rights and poverty organizing. Community and environmental organizations, for example, teamed up with government and business to eradicate lead from homes and public buildings.

Income and education often help determine who steers the direction of policy. Organizations whose members have higher incomes and education generally have greater resources, skills, and opportunities. These individual assets lend legitimacy to political expression, make leadership more effective, and increase political access and opportunities (Verba, Schlozman, and Brady 1995). Skills acquired through education, work, and association give members and leaders a sense that they can affect the political process and lead to greater participation in politics (Berry, Portney, and Thomson 1993). Organizations with higher-income and relatively educated memberships can bring attention and action to children's issues with greater ease than can organizations in poverty-stricken neighborhoods, where adult advocates with such skills, resources, and organizations are in short supply.

In 1967, the richest people were three times as likely to be active members of organizations as the poorest; by 1990, the ratio was exactly the same (Schlozman, Brady, and Verba 1997). Low-income people have far fewer face-to-face contacts with government officials, vote less, and are generally excluded from a political system that grants wider access to political donors (Schlozman, Brady, and Verba 1997). Groups in low-income neighborhoods are often oriented toward service delivery more than to advocacy, and usually lack the resources for sustained policy action.

Demographic trends, particularly among women, have also affected the course of child advocacy. The high percentage of women in the workforce and welfare reform's work requirements have intensified the need and demand for high-quality, affordable child care (Salmon 1999). As women have risen to positions of authority at work and in government, they have promoted pro-family and pro-child policies. Labor and professional organizations report increased activity by women leaders on behalf of children (Waldman 1997).

Changes in volunteerism and the growing numbers of women professionals in social work and law have also affected advocacy. Before 1945, women volunteers and social workers helped shape programs to "save the child." As women volunteers began pursuing law careers, they joined social workers in expanding child advocacy through the courts and legislatures (McDonald 1993). Further, data from Rutgers University's Center for American Women in Politics confirm that both conservative and liberal female officials tend to compile more progressive records on social issues than do their male counterparts (Amidei 1993).

New technologies also influence how groups conduct political change. The power of the media and Internet communications have spawned new political resources and encouraged citizen action in the political arena. A recent study indicated that about 25 percent of adults involved in social causes participate through the Web. Internet activists want groups to be accountable to their donors and demonstrate progress toward their goals. The study, which suggests that these individuals are a new source of income and activism for groups, reports that "baby boomers [who] have not previously been, as a group, big contributors . . . are looking for ways to engage" (Raney 1999).

One example of an on-line advocacy group, the Benton Foundation, has launched Web-based resources for advocates on "Connect for Kids" (http://www.connectforkids.org). The site is a living laboratory for applying public interest communications strategies to children's issues. How anonymous cyberspace interactions will compare with the hands-on technical assistance of groups like the National Association of Child Advocates, or how well Internet-based groups will be able to mobilize political participation, remain open questions.

Finally, groups must assess the impact of economic change on their constituency's interests and activism. Shifts from manufacturing to service and knowledge economies have changed wage levels, working conditions, communities, and individual conditions, and have helped shape the policy process.

## Building Organizations for Child Advocacy

Groups interested in effectively advocating for children must acquire and manage the necessary resources, which involves securing adequate funding, forming strategies to overcome barriers, building strong organizational structures, and applying proper governance.

### Funding Nonprofit Advocacy

An organization's capacity for advocacy grows as it mobilizes resources from the broader environment and focuses on policy change through organizational activity. All nonprofits rely on varying amounts of institutional sponsorship or patronage from government, foundations, other institutions, and individuals. Eighty percent of politically active groups have emerged from existing occupational or professional communities, such as businesses, unions, trades associations, or public welfare-related organizations, with the other 20 percent growing out of social movements (Walker 1991).

## GOVERNMENT FUNDING

Service-oriented groups, while less active politically, often rely on government contracts to sustain their program services. Groups that maintain close funding ties to government through contracts and programs and that face legal constraints must balance their ties with the need for better funding and improved programs. They must also be able to cope with changes in the government's investment in social services. Kenneth N. Bickers (1996), looks at several programs to investigate whether block grants spark the development of active policy networks at the local level, finds that although block grants stimulate grassroots involvement in politics, the political impact of such advocacy takes many years to reach higher levels of government.

A few organizations reject government dollars because they believe such funds compromise their credibility in the public policy arena. Nonprofits in the human service field have found that some legislators and bureaucrats consider the groups' advocacy for program funding overly aggressive. Several studies indicate that the receipt of government funding has had a chilling effect on nonprofit participation in advocacy (Bernstein 1991; Grønbjerg 1993; Saidel and Harlan 1998). Other studies, however, show that the close link between government funding and nonprofits' provision of social services may lead to partnerships that foster greater government openness to nonprofit goals (Salamon 1999).

## FOUNDATION FUNDING

Foundations, while responsible for a smaller proportion of overall nonprofit funding, have nevertheless shaped how groups conduct their affairs. Craig Jenkins (1998) examines foundation support for social change organizations, and finds that foundations fund the moderate organizational wings of social movements and encourage groups to professionalize by developing routine, predictable ways of participating in government through regular political channels. Foundations are less concerned with strategies for mobilizing and enlarging public participation, preferring to fund organizations that try to eliminate the legal and institutional barriers to participation. Robert Bothwell's (forthcoming) research suggests that foundation funding strategies have led to the development of program-oriented projects at the expense of broader policy reform.

Foundations have been criticized for their reluctance to fund advocacy. According to Karen Paget (1990; 1999), foundation funding in the 1980s fostered competition, overspecialization, and issue fragmentation among groups. She notes that the depoliticizing effects of organizational professionalization, and the polarizing impact of funding competition, hurt progressive advocates' ability to respond to the conservative Congress's targeting of liberal advocacy through the Istook amendment.

On the other side of the political spectrum, conservative foundations have been credited with contributing to conservatives' policy successes in the 1990s (Covington 1997; this volume). Covington emphasizes the importance of funding for developing ideological and intellectual frameworks for policy action, but she also notes the foundation's important role in supporting operations. The general support foundations provide allows groups to build the infrastructure required to maintain a policy focus and enables them to concentrate other resources on policy strategies.

Foundations can play a positive role by assisting groups in using media and communications strategically, cultivating networks of intellectuals and policy leaders, and supporting multiple social change strategies that combine public education, leadership development, and mobilization for sustaining policy action (Center for Community Change 1998). However, foundations' program focuses partly reflect the IRS regulations that forbid foundations to fund direct and grassroots lobbying, although foundations are permitted to support groups that lobby. Foundations' reactions to these restrictions may become a barrier to nonprofit advocacy. A recent survey of small, state-level social service groups that focus on children's policy suggests that grantees perceive foundation funding as sending a restrictive message about advocacy activities (State Legislative Leaders Foundation 1995).

## INDIVIDUAL CONTRIBUTIONS

Social movement organizations and popular citizens groups have been able to assemble and organize a lot of individual support for advocacy and representation on policy issues (Zald and McCarthy 1987). As groups develop more formal organizational structures, they often use more sophisticated direct-mail techniques and door-to-door canvassing campaigns. They also tap into organizational networks, build up membership dues, and sponsor appeals in the media to solicit individual donations. Studies show that fundraising appeals can be effective when combined with policy information and persuasive messages aimed at getting more highly motivated voters to turn out (Herrnson 2000a). In addition, groups relying largely on private donations are better able to survive when government funding for social services drops.

## CORPORATE GIVING

Many advocacy organizations turn to the business community for support. The number of corporate foundations is growing, and direct donations from businesses are rising. As the fundraising track record of the Children's Defense Fund demonstrates, businesses are willing to partner with nonprofits to improve children's well-being. Partnerships with businesses have become more important as social service delivery has been privatized. Furthermore, many businesses support day care reforms to allow working mothers and fathers to balance the demands of work and home. Businesses also invest in education to build a future workforce. Further research is needed to determine whether partnerships with the business community tend to alter policy demands or advocacy strategies.

## *Overcoming Barriers to Collective Action*

Understanding obstacles to collective action can help groups design outreach strategies that motivate people to participate and that sustain participation by focusing on political goals. Advocacy activities are embedded in distinct organizational models that set participation boundaries for insiders and outsiders alike (Minkoff 1998). Institutional structures and routines affect organizations' flexibility and adaptability. Further, by operating in a number of different institutional environments, such as public agencies and legislatures, nonprofits can create contradictory expectations among clients, funders, policy leaders, and the public. Organizations may find themselves caught between demands for representation and the need to provide more services (Fletcher 1998).

Forming a nonprofit and organizing its activities entails costs. Some groups try to encourage new members to join by offering additional benefits, such as coupons, newsletters, inexpensive health insurance, or other goods. But the recent success of voluntary citizens' groups that offer no incentives and are supported largely through direct-mail donations suggests that values and ideas, rather than individual benefits or material self-interests, motivate many individuals to support nonprofits.

Sustaining collective action becomes more difficult when volunteers can join and leave an organization at little cost to themselves (Hirschmann 1970). Payroll deductions, which allow supporters to give money automatically, are a powerful way to secure regular allegiance and financial support. However, recent state ballot initiatives that propose separate permission requirements to allow such deductions have put such collection methods at risk.

Groups that shift from a services-only orientation to a greater focus on advocacy face unique challenges. Debra Minkoff (1998) describes several problems social service groups encounter when they try to shift from service delivery to advocacy. Service delivery systems often require large investments in technology and management building; workers within the organization may resist learning the new skills and practices required for advocacy. Dependence on external sponsorship and fees for service can create organizational inflexibility or vulnerability.

An organization may need to make changes in its mission in order to address political developments or new policy mandates. Groups' responsiveness to change varies, but older groups may be better able to withstand disruptions. In some instances, "rigidity of aging" develops in older organizations because the expectations of established members and sponsors prevent change. In contrast, Minkoff (1998) promotes the idea of "fluidity of aging," attributing older organizations' successful shifts between protest, advocacy, and service provision to their institutional stability and suggesting that flexible action strategies help such groups weather changes.

The Child Welfare League of America, a large federation founded in 1915, is an example of an older organization that successfully managed change. It underwent transitions in leadership and resources, as well as going through mergers, to become an important player in national policy. In 1986, it moved its operations to Washington, D.C.; increased its presence on Capitol Hill; and broadened its definition of child welfare to encompass new issues, such as AIDS, in its public agenda (Hiedemann 1997). Another established organization, the American Lung Association, shifted its organizational mission to inner-city health problems, including asthma, and to anti-tobacco initiatives after scientists found a cure for tuberculosis. Following this shift, organizational donations dropped and a field-office rebellion ensued, seriously hampering the organization's programs and advocacy (Langley 1999).

## Structuring and Governing Advocacy Organizations

An organization's governing procedures, formal and informal, define how the group relates to citizens, manages priorities and resources, and ensures organizational accountability. Eighty-nine percent of state-based child advocacy organizations encourage their boards to develop legislative contacts with district representatives, and 81 percent encourage staff to contact legislators (State Legislative Leaders Foundation 1995). However, encouragement may not always translate into action. Saidel and Harlan (1998), in a survey of more than 200 New York–based nonprofits, found that more than one-third were bystanders in the public policy process. These nonprofits did not use staff or boards to influence public policy or to assess a given policy's effect on nonprofit goals and priorities.

Advisory groups can be meaningful adjuncts to boards of directors, and sometimes act as surrogates for boards of directors for a variety of functions, including advocacy (Saidel 1998). The Children's Defense Fund has long used broad networks of advisors, rather than a membership base, to extend its reach (Rees 1998). Membership in a powerful association of organizations appears to increase staff and board participation in political advocacy. Staff involvement, in particular, rises, because staff members' professional ties are stronger across networks (Saidel 1993). In some cases, however, groups (especially the smaller ones) defer to state or national associations for lobbying and advocacy (Council of Community Services of New York State 1998).

When working with government, nonprofit boards and managers sometimes focus on the internal administration of nonprofit business at the expense of long-term challenges (Sparks 1997). Groups may lack the communication channels to accommodate effective advocacy and polling procedures to determine their members' preferences. When public policy work becomes divisive, organizations need mechanisms to reconcile the diverse views of membership, staff, and leadership and build legitimate organizational consensus. For example, in the 1990s the Sierra Club asked members to reevaluate the organization's neutral stance on immigration after discussion among organizational leaders had failed to yield an internal policy position on the matter. Member preferences indicated support for the organization's existing policy position of neutrality on immigration issues (Branigin 1998).

Organizations can increase their capacity for advocacy by structuring themselves strategically. Organizations with chapters or committees that parallel legislative districts can apply political pressure in targeted ways. For example, they can target organizational resources and public messages to districts with close election margins, strong challengers, and substantial membership in the organization. Nonetheless, a survey of state-based children's groups revealed that 67 percent did not organize grassroots action by legislative district or key committee chairs (State Legislative Leaders Foundation 1995). Many effective policy organizations use a complex system of tax-exempt structures that permit certain kinds of political activities. One popular model combines the charitable 501(c)(3) organization, which allows a group to pursue public education and some lobbying activities, with a 501(c)(4) organization, which allows more substantial lobbying efforts and partisan communications to members. Political action committees are sometimes added to permit the group to work on national election campaign activities. Although liberal child advocacy organizations do not typically use complex organizational structures, conservative family-centered political coalitions, such as the Campaign for Working Families and the Christian Coalition, often do.

## Accounting for Different Types of Organizations

Nonprofit advocacy on children's policy is shaped largely by legal, medical, social work, education, and other professional organizations acting on behalf of children, often basing their stances on their professional values. These organizations' predominance has implications for all organized action. These established groups bring tremendous resources, elite networks, and legitimacy to child advocacy. Their professional norms also shape their approaches to activism; for example, social workers' rationalistic casework approach to social problems has supplanted the social reform model of earlier social movements. Moreover, the rise of the legal profession has paralleled litigation's rise as a strategy for advocating social reform.

Groups consisting mainly of professionals also face their own internal challenges. Status and organizational prestige motivate professionals (DiMaggio and Powell 1983), who usually prefer to work with stable organizations that do not threaten their professional status. Members may fear that high-profile advocacy activities might affect their careers if groups get caught in political crossfire. Minkoff (1998) notes that even if professional groups can embrace lobbying as part of their organizational mission, decisionmakers' and the public's expectations about professionals may be slow to change unless accompanied by public messages and political action.

Large national groups may take center stage in well-publicized policy debates. But small local nonprofits, informal networks, and local chapters are the backbone of U.S. civic activity. A recent study of political participation found that 92 percent of political activity was connected to local groups. Among participants whose political activity included more than voting (e.g., volunteering, contacting potential voters, campaign donations, etc.), 8 percent participated exclusively in national politics, 51 percent participated exclusively in state or local politics, and 41 percent participated in combined activity (Verba, Schlozman, and Brady 1995).

Children's other allies at the national, state, and local levels include religious, labor, professional, and women's organizations. These groups fold children's issues into their broader policy agendas, which often encompass family well-being, income, health, education, and safety, and offer low- and moderate-income people opportunities to engage in political action. Unions that narrowly defend the interests of middle-income workers have lost members, while activist unions that have organized low-wage workers, served members' interests more directly, welcomed women into union leadership, and made children and family issues a high priority have built new memberships.

Religious organizations bring moral leadership, volunteers, and institutional resources to policy campaigns. The Children's Defense Fund and other children's organizations reach out to church leaders to build awareness and encourage action on policy for poor children. African-American churches, which have a strong tradition of activist leadership, play a critical role in mobilizing popular political support on community and national issues (Harris 1994). Organizations with a religious orientation often speak out on family policy and welfare reforms, because these issues have a strong moral dimension.

In the child advocacy arena, greater interorganizational coalitions would allow groups to divide tasks and use resources strategically. Coordination may be difficult for groups with little experience working with volunteers or with few bridges to politically active groups. Individual policy entrepreneurs with the organizational skills to navigate professional networks can sometimes bring together public and private institutional actors, such as agency officials, legislators and staff, researchers, business leaders, and nonprofit advocates in concerted policy action. Cross-cutting coalitions also bring together groups of people from different economic and cultural backgrounds. Such coalitions reduce divisiveness, encourage public consensus, and offset the strong voice of single-issue, political organizations.

When professional advocates, parents, and other organizations form coalitions, they provide much greater support for children's issues. An example from the 1930s illustrates the usefulness of building bridges with allies. After a long, frustrating campaign to increase the legal work age, reduce hours worked, and improve child labor conditions, reformers allied with other interests to achieve their goals. The outcome was passage of the Fair Labor Standards Act of 1938, which established minimum wages for workers and set child labor standards (Hawes 1991).

## Advocacy Strategies

The venues, timing, and advocacy methods used by nonprofits to institute change require strategic planning. Planning must take many factors into account, including the nature and magnitude of the desired reform, an assessment of the institutions best equipped to fill the need, the political channels available, and the nonprofit's capacity for advocacy.

Effective advocacy strategies often depend on the context and timing of reform, making it difficult to generalize success from one experience to another. Moreover, short-term success does not always ensure long-term, effective reform. Nonprofits must examine "how choices made at one point in time create institutions that generate recognizable patterns of constraints and opportunities at a later point" (Powell and DiMaggio 1991, 188).

### Collaborative and Confrontational Strategies

Collaboration is a useful strategy when advocates can agree on policy-making strategies and when nonprofits set up forums to exchange ideas about policy formulation. Collaboration with government is also impor-tant when nonprofits set a policy agenda. Such partnerships, however, can backfire if state agencies implement scaled-back policies and grant program leaders limited authority and budgets. In attempts to prevent weakened reform, advocates may employ confrontational strategies that publicize their cause and preempt efforts to undermine reform propos-als. Advocates may begin with confrontational strategies to ensure their positions are heard or to gain access to decisionmakers, but they ulti-mately rely on collaboration to implement change. John McCarthy and Jim Castelli (1994) note that community organizations may mix collab-oration and confrontation strategies to their advantage, selecting a target for protest and pressure and later turning the target into an ally. Public education and "insider" strategies tend to involve collaboration, while litigation and "outsider" strategies tend to rely on confrontation.

## Public Education Strategies

Advocacy organizations build research, data, and background information to increase the public's and policymakers' awareness of issues and to give decisionmakers the opportunity to weigh potential solutions. When converted into balanced, reliable information, research defining a policy problem can influence congressional leaders and can help mobilize and sustain grassroots activism. Decisionmakers are particularly interested in scientific information, and advocates have learned to use such information to promote their causes. For example, child advocates have buttressed calls for higher-quality early education and child care with scientific studies on brain development.

Nonprofit and advocacy groups have become increasingly adept at pursuing nonpartisan, public education strategies during elections. Issue advocacy has become a popular and powerful tool. Advocates are increasingly interested in using the campaign cycle to raise children's issues and create awareness among those legislators who make children a priority (National Association of Child Advocates 1999). Some foundations, such as the Benton Foundation, while avoiding crossing the line to partisan activity, offer informational tools to groups that plan to engage in election-related advocacy.

Experimental projects that test approaches to solving social problems in local settings can increase public awareness about children and develop policy designs for widespread application. Lisbeth Schorr (1997) has pointed out that many programs that have flourished as demonstration projects have not been institutionalized through broad policy reform. Agreement on the elements of successful programs does not translate easily into policy and practice. The main challenge of the modeling strategy is to find ways to replicate effective projects and improve service delivery so that success becomes commonplace.

## Insider and Outsider Strategies

In a study of interest group mobilization, Walker (1991) analyzed the political significance of insider and outsider strategies adopted by the for-profit and nonprofit sectors. Insider strategies emphasize political clout in leveraging capital and making connections with elected leadership and government staff. Outsider strategies include public demonstrations, media events, and other public mobilization strategies that do not necessarily require the support of public policy figures. Studies have shown that protest strategies that involve general messages directed against all lawmakers rarely succeed. By contrast, organizations that develop strong leadership and institutionalize protest messages before mobilizing the public tend to see better results (Baer and Bositis 1988).

Trade unions and environmental groups pursue both insider and outsider strategies. Boyle and Kearnes (1998) compared the research strategy of the Children's Defense Fund with the public mobilization strategy of the Family Research Council. Although the Children's Defense Fund has recently expanded its strategy to include greater community building, it has traditionally focused on building reliable policy information about the needs of poor, minority, and special-needs children. CDF also mobilizes elite networks to increase passage of desired legislation. The Family Research Council (FRC) has a more expressly political agenda that focuses on conservative family values, an issue that appeals to many white, middle-class voters. FRC mobilizes grassroots action through conservative religious networks. Conservative advocacy groups' proposed government solutions to children's issues often take the form of tax incentives to individual taxpayers.

## Litigation Strategies

In the past 20 years, advocates have increasingly used the legal system to challenge or uphold legislation, build case law, or free up logjams in the political process. Lawyers and other professionals have initiated sweeping welfare and juvenile justice changes by filing suits against court agencies or by serving as court-appointed special advocates, who represent clients within the system. When the state must intervene in children's lives, groups such as the American Civil Liberties Union, the Children's Rights Project, and the American Bar Association's Center on Children and the Law hold government accountable to statutory standards of fairness and due process.

Litigation, although a fairly narrow strategy, enables advocates to help constituencies that are often ignored by legislatures. Mnookin and Burt, commenting on the potential benefits of litigation and legislative strategies, write,

To be sure, courts can engage in tactics of evasion and delay, but no one can compel the legislature to deal with an issue. Certain groups under certain circumstance may possess sufficient political power to force legislatures to act, but foster parents and children are surely not among these groups. Courts, on the other hand, are not merely available to give answers; they are available to the otherwise powerless. This quality, it is true, has nothing to do with the wisdom of their answers, but there is little value in extolling the virtues of legislatures if there is no way to get them to listen (Mnookin and Burt 1985, 120).

## The Challenge of Assessing Advocacy

Assessing organizational effectiveness in policymaking is not easy. Nonprofits, advocacy groups, the public, and legislators all perceive effectiveness differently. Advocates are often interested in seeing stronger and more active political organizations, progress on policy goals, and improved social conditions and behaviors.

In a recent study, Rees (1998) examined 12 national organizations that members of Congress had rated "very influential" in selected issue areas. The study provides insight into organizational effectiveness and suggests areas in which child advocates should focus on building capacity. It also identifies characteristics of organizational effectiveness, including the following:

- A strong presence on Capitol Hill, and well-developed lobbying skills and strategies;
- Membership-based organizations;
- Sizable budgets;
- Organizational structures that allow for policy deliberation and debate and that give groups political flexibility (e.g., 501[c][4] entities);
- One or two priority issues, and strong, authoritative information;
- Members with political skills and information;
- Grassroots structures and policy work at the state level;
- Bipartisan outreach, bipartisan support, and broad coalitions; and
- Experience working with policymakers on research commissions.

Groups might define success as gaining access to social and political forums. Or they might claim victory only when favored legislation is introduced or enacted. Groups might view their advocacy efforts as successful when they see positive changes for children made from a combination of laws, court rulings, and successful programs. Electoral alliances are considered effective when they create government majorities more receptive to improving children's policy. Grassroots activism or use of the media to promote awareness on children's issues may be considered successful when they produce changes in public opinion.

## Strengthening Child Advocacy Groups

Children's issues are high on the public agenda, yet public attitudes about poverty and the political isolation of poor children are substantial obstacles for groups trying to improve children's lives. Nonprofit organizations can help overcome these barriers.

Child advocacy groups have great experience in public education, research, and lobbying, but they need to get politicians to act. Advocates go to great lengths to build public and legislative awareness, but their work does not always translate into political change. Children's groups might benefit from a better assessment of which organizations and which constituencies are best organized to advance policy change. For example, groups need to find ways to tap the potential of women and parents; better recruitment and action strategies could help engage these communities. Advocates must build awareness and interest about children's issues, link constituents' concerns to policy agendas, and organize strategic public responses to congressional decisions.

Child advocacy organizations should reexamine the trade associations' insider tactics to learn about practices that could benefit children, and should consider the benefits and drawbacks of participating in party and campaign activities to increase their leverage in policymaking. Groups whose structures allow them to pursue a wider range of political activities have more opportunities to influence policy. To open the political system to more competition and to inspire community activists interested in children's issues to run for county and state offices, child advocates should consider joining forces with campaign finance reformers. Litigation strategies that have brought widespread improvements for children in the past need to be combined with political strategies that help build policy consensus within legislatures.

Prospects for reform are tied to the robustness of social and organizational networks and information at the local level. National organizations cannot do the hard work of grassroots organizing, but they can support local efforts. Field organizing operations, in which national staff support state organizations and mobilize constituency action, are one effective model. National organizations should reexamine their communication and governance structures to determine ways to build membership diversity and enlarge the scope of their work. Locally, child advocates need to link information on local policy with national action. By collecting information across states, groups can compare public programs and outcomes at the state level, and thus base their calls for improvements on consistent, comparative data.

Social service groups would benefit from a hard look at how to build their capacity to organize and advocate, since they have valuable information about people's experiences and about constituencies that need representation. Groups that can bring poor parents and children into contact with decisionmakers increase the likelihood that policymakers will spend more time and resources serving low-income neighborhoods. Grassroots organizing and leadership training for low-income parents can offer poor families a way to end their political isolation. Polling and direct testimony by children can help raise visibility about the conditions of children in need.

Foundations, too, are an important source of support for groups faced with adapting their organizations to policy advocacy. Most importantly, foundations can play a leadership role in renewing interest in political action. They can also educate and prepare their boards to understand the potential liabilities in political action, and can provide general institutional support and fund projects that help groups overcome obstacles to advocacy. For example, foundations might fund political skills training among leaders to broaden their expertise as political entrepreneurs. Foundations can identify and support new constituency action and connect citizens to the resources they need to succeed. In the spirit of deliberative democracy, foundations can bring groups together to share strategies for managing the conflicting demands of the media, the legislature, government agencies, and other organizations—including foundations. Continued support that helps organizations form broader alliances and overarching messages enhances small groups' capacity to get access to information and develop the organizational tools for more effective political action.

Children's groups must also perfect the art of coalition-building. Collaboration among policy advocates, lawyers, community organizers, union leaders, and religious leaders can increase attention to children's policy issues. Lawyers, pediatricians, and social workers might work more strategically with nonprofessionals in public forums and policy-making. Advocates can improve the chances of successful child policy reform by joining forces with mainstream movements for low- and moderate-income voters, education reform, child care provisioning, health care, and family wages and benefits.

Faith-based organizations, another important ally to children's causes, are increasingly important for social service delivery systems. They bring moral authority to children's causes and motivate members to bring compassion and voluntarism to programs. Faith-based groups are among the few institutions that bring together low- and moderate-income people. Unions, too, often act in children's and families' interests. They have the political connections, organizational structures, and resources required to engage in national and state-based campaigns.

Foundations, academics, and practitioners must analyze their strategic and organizational assets and deficiencies to uncover areas where groups can build institutional capacity, political expertise, and operational strength. Foundations' and nonprofits' restructuring efforts will increase the likelihood that children's issues will have a permanent place on the public policy agenda.

Advocates for children are meeting new challenges with energy and enthusiasm. However, until elected officials—and government in general—show a strong commitment to children's issues, advocates will continually face an uphill battle. Ultimately, to ensure sustainable policy gains, child advocacy must not only improve conditions for children but also bring greater legitimacy and broader public support to children's organizations.


## NOTES

The author thanks Gail Weigl for preparing the background information for this paper.
1. *Regan v. Taxation with Representation of Washington,* 462 U.S. 540 (1983)
2. Most legislative and political action is unregulated. It is important that nonprofit staff and volunteers know what is and is not regulated. Consult INDEPENDENT SECTOR, Charity Lobbying in the Public Interest, or Alliance for Justice, in Washington, D.C., for help.


## REFERENCES

Amidei, Nancy. 1993. "Child Advocacy: Let's Get the Job Done." *Dissent* 40 (spring): 213–20.

Baer, Denise L., and David A. Bositis. 1988. *Elite Cadres and Party Coalitions: Representing the Public in Party Politics.* Westport, Conn.: Greenwood Press.

Bernstein, S. R. 1991. *Managing Contracted Services in the Nonprofit Agency: Administrative, Ethical, and Political Issues.* Philadelphia: Temple University Press.

Berry, Jeffrey. 1999. *The New Liberalism: The Rising Power of Citizen Groups.* Washington, D.C.: Brookings Institution Press.

Berry, Jeffrey, Kent Portney, and Ken Thomson. 1993. *The Rebirth of Urban Democracy.* Washington, D.C.: Brookings Institution.

Bickers, Kenneth N. 1996. "The Politics of Devolution and the Emergence of Policy Substitutions, with Implications for the Implementation of Welfare Reform." Paper presented at the Baker Conference, November 12.

Bothwell, Robert O. Forthcoming. "Philanthropic Funding of Social Change and the Diminution of Progressive Policymaking." In *Exploring the Organizations and Advocacy: Strategies and Finances* 1 (2), edited by E. J. Reid and M. Montilla. Washington, D.C.: The Urban Institute Press.

Boyle, Patrick, and Robert Kearnes. 1998. "CDF vs. FRC." *Youth Today* 7 (September 8): 51–56.

Branigin, William. 1998. "Sierra Club Votes for Neutrality on Immigration." *Washington Post.* April 26, A16.

Center for Community Change. 1998. "Moving the Debate: How Conservative Groups and Donors Used Their Money to Sell Their Ideas." Washington, D.C.: Center for Community Change.

Center for Responsive Politics. 2001. "Political Action Committees." Http://www.opensecrets.org/pacs/index.asp.

Council of Community Services of New York State and Nonprofit Coordinating Committee of New York. 1998. "Advocacy and Lobbying: What Charitable Nonprofits Know and Do in New York State." New York: Council of Community Services of New York State.

Covington, Sally. 1997. *Moving a Public Policy Agenda: The Strategic Philanthropy of Conservative Foundations.* Washington, D.C.: National Committee for Responsive Philanthropy.

DiMaggio, Paul J., and Walter W. Powell. 1983. "The Iron Cage Revisited: Institutional Isomorphism and Collective Rationality in Organizational Fields." *American Sociological Review* 48 (2): 147–60.

Fletcher, Michael A. 1998. "NAACP Caught Between Calls to Focus on Advocacy, Broader Services." *Washington Post.* July 12, A2.

Fox, Leslie, and Priya Helweg. 1997. "Advocacy Strategies for Civil Society: A Conceptual Framework and Practitioners Guide." Paper prepared for the Center for Democracy and Governance, USAID, April 31.

General Accounting Office. 1999. *Federal Lobbying: Differences in Lobbying Definitions and Their Impact.* Washington, D.C.: General Accounting Office.

Grønbjerg, Kirsten. 1993. *Understanding Nonprofit Funding: Managing Revenues in Social Services and Community Development Organizations.* San Francisco: Jossey-Bass Publishers.

Harris, Fredrick C. 1994. "Something Within: Religion as a Mobilizer of African-American Political Activism." *The Journal of Politics* 56 (1): 42–68.

Hawes, Joseph M. 1991. *The Children's Rights Movement: A History of Advocacy and Protection.* Boston: Twayne.

Herrnson, Paul S. 2000a. *Congressional Elections: Campaigning at Home and in Washington.* Washington, D.C.: Congressional Quarterly.

———. 2000b. "Political Parties, Interest Groups, and Congressional Elections." Paper presented at Nonprofit Advocacy and The Policy Process, A Seminar Series, Urban Institute. Washington, D.C., June 2.

Hiedemann, Stephanie L. 1997. "The Child Welfare League of America." Case Western Reserve University Mandel Center for Nonprofit Organizations, Cleveland, Ohio. Photocopy.

Hirschmann, Albert O. 1970. *Exit, Voice, and Loyalty: Responses to Decline in Firms, Organizations and States.* Cambridge, Mass.: Harvard University.

Howlett, Michael, and M. Ramesh. 1995. *Studying Public Policy: Policy Cycles and Policy Subsystems.* Ontario: Oxford University Press.

Jenkins, Craig. 1998. "Channeling Social Protest: Foundation Patronage of Contemporary Social Movements." *Private Action and the Public Good.* Walter W. Powell and Elizabeth S. Clemens. New Haven: Yale University Press.

Knoke, David. 1994. *Political Networks: The Structural Perspective.* Cambridge: Cambridge University Press.

Langley, Monica. 1999. "Waiting to Exhale: The Lung Association, Its Donations Waning, Casts about for a Cause." *Wall Street Journal.* April 14, A1.

McCarthy, John D., and Jim Castelli. 1994. *Working for Justice: The Campaign for Human Development and Poor Empowerment Groups.* Washington, D.C.: Life Cycle Institute, Catholic University of America.

McDonald, Mary Jean. 1993. "Citizens' Committees for Children in New York and the Evolution of Child Advocacy, 1945–1972." Ph.D. diss., New York University.

Minkoff, Deborah. 1998. "Organizational Barriers to Advocacy." Paper prepared for the Aspen Institute Nonprofit Strategy Group on Advocacy, November.

Mnookin, Robert H., and Robert A. Burt. 1985. *In the Interest of Children: Advocacy, Law Reform and Public Policy.* New York: W. H. Freeman.

National Association of Child Advocates. 1999. "Connecting Non-Partisan Politics to Children's Policy: The Florida Model." Washington, D.C.: National Association of Child Advocates.

Paget, Karen. 1999. "The Big Chill: Foundations and Political Passion." *American Prospect* 10 (44): 26–33.

———. 1990. "Citizen Organizing: Many Movements, No Majority." *American Prospect* 1 (2): 115–28.

Powell, Walter W., and Paul DiMaggio, eds. 1991. *The New Institutionalism in Organizational Analysis.* Chicago: University of Chicago Press.

Putnam, Robert D. 2000. *Bowling Alone.* New York: Simon and Schuster.

Raney, Rebecca F. 1999. "New Audience for Advocacy Groups on the Internet." NYTimes Cybertimes, September. Http://www.nytimes.com/library/tech/99/09/cyber/articles/14donate.html.

Rees, Susan. 1998. "Effective Nonprofit Advocacy." Washington, D.C.: Aspen Institute.

Saidel, Judith R. 1998. "Expanding the Governance Construct: Functions and Contributions of Nonprofit Advisory Groups." *Nonprofit and Voluntary Sector Quarterly* 27 (4): 421–436.

————. 1993. "The Board Role in Relation to Government: Alternative Models." In *Governing, Leading and Managing Nonprofit Organizations,* edited by Dennis R. Young, Robert M. Hollister, and Virginia A. Hodgkinson (32–49). San Francisco: Jossey-Bass Publishers.

Saidel, Judith R., and Sharon L. Harlan. 1998. "Contracting and Patterns of Nonprofit Governance." *Nonprofit Management and Leadership* 8 (3): 243–60.

Salamon, Lester. 1999. *America's Nonprofit Sector.* New York: The Foundation Center.

Salmon, Jacqueline. 1999. "For Many Children, Nowhere to Go; Low Wages Put the Squeeze on Child Care Providers." *Washington Post.* September 19, A1.

Schlozman, Kay Lehman, Henry E. Brady, and Sidney Verba. 1997. "The Big Tilt: Participatory Inequality in America." *American Prospect* 8 (32): 74–80.

Schorr, Lisbeth B. 1997. *Common Purpose: Strengthening Families and Neighborhoods to Rebuild America.* New York: Anchor Doubleday.

Skocpol, Theda. 1997. "Building Community Top Down or Bottom Up." *Brookings Review.* Fall.

Sparks, John D. 1997. *Lobbying, Advocacy, and Nonprofit Boards.* Washington, D.C.: National Center for Nonprofit Boards.

State Legislative Leaders Foundation. 1995. *Keys to Effective Legislation for Children and Families.* Centerville, Mass.: State Legislative Leaders Foundation.

Verba, Sidney, Kay Lehman Schlozman, and Henry E. Brady. 1995. *Voice and Equality: Civic Voluntarism in American Politics.* Cambridge, Mass.: Harvard University Press.

Waldman, Amy. 1997. "Labor's New Face: Women Renegotiate Their Role." *Nation* 265 (8): 11–16.

Walker, Jack. 1991. *Mobilizing Interest Groups in America.* Ann Arbor: University of Michigan.

Zald, Mayer, and John D. McCarthy. 1987. *Social Movements in an Organizational Society.* New Brunswick, N.J.: Transaction Books.

Appendix 4.A: *Practitioner's Checklist: Questions for Building Advocacy Capacity*

- Is advocacy included in the group's mission?
- What is the organization's structure, and how is it used for advocacy? Is the group a complex organization? What advocacy restrictions does it face because of tax status, government contracts, conflicts of interest, or state regulations?
- How is the group governed? Do leaders promote advocacy for the public good? Do leaders themselves engage in advocacy? Are leaders obstacles to advocacy? Is leadership training necessary?
- Does the group take policy positions on particular issues? Does it develop strategic plans with well-defined objectives for influencing the policy process?
- What kinds of skills do staff, leadership, members, and volunteers have that can be used for advocacy activities, such as research, lobbying, mobilization, political connections, or public communications?
- Does the organization have resources for political action? Are there restrictions on the type of activities for which monies can be used? Are there resources to sustain long-term policy work?
- Does the organization have strong links to other groups in its policy area and in cross-cutting coalitions? Can the organization work well with other organizations?
- Does the organization have a communications system and a method for constituency outreach and action?
- Can the group mount a campaign for policy change?
- Can the group build a broad public message for reform, use the media for policy ends, formulate specific policy options, and conduct credible research?
- Can the group build a plan of action that maps out the potential of policy players and events and opportunities for legislative and electoral work; weigh options and choose appropriate strategies; mobilize resources in the group and in society; and build alliances and divide tasks?
- Can the group lobby as well as partner with government and others to implement and monitor results and reformulate policy?

*Source:* Adapted from Fox and Hewleg (1997).

# SECTION TWO:
## Perspectives on
## Creating a Movement

Table 5.1  *Membership Associations Enrolling One Percent or More of American Adults in 1955 (Continued)*

| Name (Year Founded) | Membership | Percent of Adults Enrolled | Number of Local Units |
|---|---|---|---|
| Fraternal Order of Eagles (1898) | 760,007 | 1.5 (m) | 1,566 aeries |
| Women's International Bowling Congress (1916) | 706,193 | 1.3 (w) | 22,842 |
| Independent Order of Odd Fellows (1819) | 543,171 | 1.1 (m) | 7,572 lodges |
| American Red Cross (1881) | * | * | 3,713 chapters |
| March of Dimes (1938) | * | * | 3,090 chapters |

*Source:* Data are from the Civic Engagement Project, Harvard University.

*Notes:* (m) indicates men only; (w) indicates women only. (est.) indicates a best-available estimate. NA indicates data not available at this time.

* Membership data are not given for the Red Cross and March of Dimes because they include contributors as well as participants.

been instrumental in supporting governmental provision of services and benefits to citizens. Many citizens' associations have been involved in demanding and administering public social programs, and the associations often gained new members, resources, and energy as a result.

In the past, the needs of children or families were most visibly and consistently addressed by women's voluntary membership associations. White and African-American women addressed children's upbringing and the needs of families through church-connected groups, the female auxiliaries of unions and fraternal brotherhoods, and a wide variety of moral-reform crusades. The Woman's Christian Temperance Union (WCTU), founded in 1874 as a federation of local, state, and national unions, pursued a wide array of social and legislative goals deemed to be in the interest of women (Bordin 1981). Community and government measures to help children and families were also priorities for the local clubs and state federations of the General Federation of Women's Clubs, founded in 1890 (Wells 1953). The National Congress of Mothers (later the PTA) was established specifically to promote both educational reforms and the well-being of mothers and children.

Nationwide, independent associations led by women were able to foster local initiatives, such as the establishment of kindergartens, playgrounds, libraries, and maternal and child health programs. The associations also influenced legislative priorities across states and regions. Because their ideologies portrayed homemaking and child-rearing as important national concerns and because their federated structures fostered regular communication among women's clubs, these national organizations took the lead in advocating for mothers' pensions, child labor restrictions, the creation of the federal Children's Bureau, and the enactment of the Sheppard-Towner Act of 1921, which provided a system of subsidies for child and maternal health clinics (Skocpol 1992).

Other kinds of organizations—even those with missions that focused on more general issues—also advocated on behalf of children, young people, and families. Farmers' associations, such as the Grange and the American Farm Bureau Federation, recruited husbands, wives, and children to help with a range of community-related activities. Fraternal and veterans' groups openly championed the traditionally male role of economic provider, and emphasized the value of caring for families. Fraternal groups offered life insurance in the name of providing for family dependents. They also proudly supported recreational or health programs for children and subsidized institutions to care for orphans.

Many classic U.S. membership associations were visibly engaged with local public schools. Women's and men's groups alike undertook special fundraising efforts to build school facilities or provide instructional materials. Veterans' associations took a direct interest in citizenship training in the schools, and other groups sought to influence parts of the curriculum. Public schools existed in the same communities and on the same social scale as the local chapters of membership federations, and most people saw schools as centers for the training of children, in whom everyone had a stake.

The terms "charity" and "localism" have been applied to many family and children's programs promoted by male-led membership associations. But in many cases, the role of both male and female associations went beyond this narrow definition. For example, the American Legion—a conservative, national veterans' association—was key in bringing about one of the most comprehensive, generous pieces of pro-family social legislation ever enacted in the United States, the GI Bill of 1944 (Bennett 1996; Skocpol 1997). As World War II came to an end, about 16 million service personnel (97 percent of them men) returned to civilian life. While most of the nation was committed to meeting their health and economic needs, various groups disagreed on the scope of such benefits. For example, university leaders and New Deal political leaders envisaged a program of educational loans that would be extended for just one year to all returning veterans. After the year was up, educational aid would be delivered to a select group of perhaps 100,000 qualifying individuals. Such a system would have maintained America's restrictive, highly stratified system of higher education and kept the doors of opportunity closed to millions of young, child-raising families.

The American Legion, however, pushed forward a comprehensive system of educational grants, economic loans, and family benefits that enabled millions of returning veterans to both build brighter economic futures and invest in family formation. The Legion also activated its nationwide network of local "posts" to agitate on behalf of the GI Bill and helped overcome conservative resistance to such social spending.

Historically, classic U.S. membership associations functioned as advocates for child-raising families. Such advocacy was not a specialized, professional function, but was woven into the ideologies and the community-based modes of such groups' operations, even as their federated arrangements made it possible to influence larger public debates and legislative drives.

National, professional advocacy groups also existed in the United States in the late 19th and early 20th centuries; the National Consumers League led by Florence Kelley, for example, fought to outlaw child labor. But such groups tended to operate in close cooperation with large membership federations. Traditionally, professional reformers in the United States—especially women reformers working to improve conditions for children and families—knew they had to rely on everyday association members to shape public opinion and influence elected officials. More importantly, professional reformers knew that they *could* proceed in such alliances because an array of membership federations dominated civic life in America.

## A Transformed Civic World

During the 1950s and 1960s, many voluntary membership federations were at the center of U.S. public policy debates as well as local community life. In the mid-1960s, however, American politics, communities, and institutions began to change. First came the great social movements of the 1960s and 1970s—including the civil rights revolution, the emergence of the women's rights and feminist movements, and the spread of various public interest efforts, such as the new environmentalism. Following these movements, professionally run, nationally focused advocacy groups started to displace the locally rooted membership federations at the center of American public life.

Social movements have rarely been spearheaded by established associations or institutions, and that was certainly true in the United States during the 1960s and 1970s. Civil rights struggles, feminism, and the new environmentalism all bypassed preexisting membership federations—at least at first. New grassroots or cadre organizations took the lead in organizing protests and agitations (Dunlap and Mertig 1992; Gelb and Palley 1982; Morris 1984). Large numbers of American youths abandoned or avoided old-line membership associations, directing their efforts instead into protest movements and related organizations. Suddenly, the racism and the rigid gender segregation of America's classic civic world looked very out of date. Many locally rooted national federations appeared to be too cumbersome, ritualistic, and set in their ways to champion new public-interest causes.

As the social movements of the 1960s and 1970s began to subside, some old-line membership federations regained lost ground. For example, in the environmental movement, the Sierra Club and the National Wildlife Federation gained new purpose, energy, and hundreds of thousands of members. In addition, the National Association for the Advancement of Colored People greatly expanded during and after the civil rights movement. New feminist groups emerged, and some, such as the National Organization for Women, recruited relatively large memberships and established a nationwide network of chapters.

But for the most part, membership associations did not proliferate in post-1960s America, and the limited number of new membership associations that did emerge were usually not organized into chapters that held regular meetings. Perhaps most significant, almost all of the classic membership federations listed in table 5.1 went into steady decline (Skocpol 1999).

Meanwhile, hundreds of new organizations espousing public-interest causes that did not directly reflect the material interests of their supporters were created (Berry 1977; Berry 1999). In these groups, professional staffs began to engage in publicity, lobbying, and research to address such broad concerns as the health of the environment, campaign finance reform, and the well-being of children and the poor. Business and professional associations were already very active in national civic life. But from the 1970s through the 1990s, many existing groups set up new headquarters in Washington, D.C., to vie for influence with rights and public-interest advocacy groups (Berry 1997).

## A New Focus on Professional Advocacy Groups

Why did the center of American civic life shift from membership-focused associations to staff-led professional advocacy groups in the late 20th century? A number of factors converged to effect this transformation (for an in-depth examination of these factors, see Putnam 2000 and Skocpol 1999). New ideals of racial integration and changing roles for men and women in families and workplaces undermined the legitimacy of classic membership federations built around individuals' social identities. Defeat in the unpopular Vietnam War helped discredit the martial ideals that had been crucial in sustaining America's fraternal and veterans' associations. The expansion of higher education after 1940 created a large stratum of managers and professionals. Even today, these men and women have little inclination to attend weekly meetings, although they often donate money to advocacy groups led by skillful professionals like themselves.

The changing work patterns of American women also reduced interest in, and time available for, activity at chapter-based membership associations. In the 1950s, fewer than a third of American women were employed outside the home. By the 1990s, nearly two-thirds of women were employed outside the home, and most of the increase in paid employment after the late 1970s resulted from heightened financial pressures on working families (Putnam 2000). American women are not necessarily doing less in civic life, but their new allocations of effort affect all associations. Although today's employed women are actually *more* likely to give money and otherwise become engaged in formal political activities than stay-at-home women (Schlozman 2000), the changing schedules of both men and women have clearly made traditional membership activities—which focus on residential communities, rather than workplaces, and which demand regular blocks of time—less feasible for millions of Americans.

Traditionally, men's membership federations depended on female support. Women's federations required the highest level of skill and commitment from women (generally married) who remained outside the paid labor force for much of their lives. Before the 1960s, highly educated American women who did not pursue lifelong paid careers were the leading officers and supporters of multipurpose membership federations. Such women played a critical role in linking local community and family life to broader social and political endeavors. Today, however, most highly educated American women are in the workforce, and are more likely to channel their civic energies into giving money to advocacy groups and political campaigns, organizing one-time charitable projects, and participating in professional associations or other occupationally linked groups (see Wuthnow 1998 for descriptions of many of these activities).

New political opportunities for Washington, D.C.–based advocacy groups opened up in the 1970s, as social changes took the wind out of the sails of many locally based and socially segregated membership federations. Many movement activists began to recognize D.C. as the center of political action. Lawyers could bring court cases, while lobbyists and researchers could influence a largely liberal Democratic Congress and monitor the activities of executive agencies once new laws were enacted. As one set of groups set up shop in D.C., others had to follow suit or see their interests lose out. Even after the Republicans and conservative Democrats gained ground in national politics, advocacy groups remained in the nation's capital to monitor and fight for their causes.

Meanwhile, institutional and technological changes made it much easier for national associations to eliminate membership dues and face-to-face contacts both among members and between members and leaders. Historically, civic leaders in the United States took it for granted that, at least after the start-up stage, an association would need to rely on members for energy and financial support, so it made sense for national founders to travel widely, recruit a nationwide network of intermediate leaders, and rely on local chapters to raise dues and recruit and retain members.

But in recent decades, American civic entrepreneurs have found new ways to operate. They can rely on continuing grants from wealthy foundations or individuals (Walker 1991; Jenkins 1998; and Covington, this volume), they can use computerized mailings to solicit funds, or they can combine the two methods. As a result, most recently launched associations can proceed without members or can recruit adherents through the mail, the Internet, or the mass media. Such adherents usually do not meet with each other or elect leaders. Instead, they relate separately to the association in question, and receive information in exchange for occasional financial contributions.

Research shows that mailing-list members who occasionally write checks are likely to be fickle and highly sensitive to the specific "hot-button" issue being addressed by the national leadership of the advocacy group (Godwin and Mitchell 1984). The presence of so many intensely competitive advocacy groups dominating the new civic world creates a great deal of volatility. In addition, many incentives prompt professional leaders to select causes to champion through highly visible legislative maneuvers and national media campaigns. Expertise and the ability to respond quickly are key for accomplishing such tasks skillfully and successfully. Thus, national leaders today find little reason to develop membership chapters, and have little incentive to interact regularly with national networks of intermediate leaders and membership groups.

## The Modern Field of Child Advocacy

What do these civic changes mean for the people who set out to address the needs of children and families? The modern field of "child advocacy" emerged from the changes that rocked the advocacy universe in post-1960s America. In 1998, children and family associations that fall under the "social welfare" and "public affairs" categories made up a significant proportion of the 4,000 associations in the *Encyclopedia of Associations*. The vast majority of children and family associations, broadly defined,[1] were founded after 1960, for an overall growth rate of 1,216 percent since 1959 (table 5.2). Significantly, of those organizations formed in the 1960s, 1970s, and 1980s, about two-thirds (65 percent) have 1,000 members or less (table 5.3).

Although it is impossible to say that all of these recently created groups are engaged in explicit political or legislative advocacy, many of them clearly are. Most of the recently founded associations with few or no members do not seem to attempt to organize chapters or recruit large numbers of individual participants who pay dues. Historically, U.S. voluntary federations relying on membership dues recruited large membership bases very quickly, usually within one to two decades. We see few comparable trajectories since the 1950s, because newer organizations are

Table 5.2  *Growth in Number of National Children and Family Associations, 1959 to 1998*

| Selected Association Categories | Number of Associations By Database Year | | | |
| --- | --- | --- | --- | --- |
| | 1959 | 1980 | 1998 | Increase 1959–98 |
| Social Welfare | 56 | 191 | 846 | 1411% |
| Public Affairs | NA | 25 | 162 | — |
| Religious | 6 | 16 | 66 | 1000% |
| Educational | 10* | 24 | 112 | 1430% |
| Cultural | | 5 | 41 | |
| Health and Medical | 16 | 31 | 168 | 950% |
| Fraternal, Foreign Interest, Nationality, and Ethnic | 10 | 4 | 29 | 190% |
| Veterans, Hereditary, & Patriotic | 7 | 8 | 16 | 129% |
| Legal, Governmental, Public Administration and Military | NA | 3 | 18 | — |
| Labor | NA | NA | 3 | — |
| Hobby and Avocational | NA | 1 | 4 | — |
| Athletic and Sports | 1 | 1 | 9 | 800% |
| Unclassified | 6 | 0 | 0 | — |
| ALL CATEGORIES | 112 | 309 | 1474 | 1216% |

Source: *Encyclopedia of Associations*, Vol. 1: CD-ROM, 1998; Paper Editions 15, 1980; and 2, 1959 (Detroit, MI: Gale Reserch).
Note: NA indicates data not available.
* Educational and cultural associations were combined into one category in the 1959 data but were later separated.

more likely to seek other kinds of constituents. Indeed, many of the groups in the *Encyclopedia* that have small numbers of members actually serve other organizations, rather than individuals.

Staff-led associations engaged in child and family advocacy have proliferated along with many other kinds of advocacy groups since the 1960s. These groups usually enlist modest numbers of citizen adherents, or none at all. Social and technological changes have made it possible to organize advocacy centrally without a large volunteer corps. Many experts are happy to work for important causes under the tutelage of well-known leaders, such as CDF's Marian Edelman, who can amass foundation grants. Meanwhile, new political conditions and media

Table 5.3  *Membership in National Children and Family Associations by Founding Year Periods, 1998*

| Size of Membership | Number of Associations Founded in Each Period | | | Total Associations (All Years) |
|---|---|---|---|---|
| | *1960–98* | *1930–59* | *<1930* | |
| 1,000,000 or more | 3 | 3 | 6 | 12 |
| 100,000 – 999,999 | 25 | 5 | 12 | 42 |
| 50,000 – 99,999 | 18 | 4 | 13 | 35 |
| 10,000 – 49,999 | 64 | 14 | 20 | 98 |
| 5,000 – 9,999 | 61 | 10 | 11 | 82 |
| 1,000 – 4,999 | 189 | 32 | 21 | 242 |
| 0 – 999 | 770 | 110 | 48 | 928 |
| TOTAL | 1130 | 178 | 131 | 1439 |

Source: *Associations Unlimited CD-ROM* (Detroit, Mich.: Gale Research, 1998).

opportunities make it possible for advocates to influence public policy by addressing congressional leaders and reporters rather than by persuading millions of citizens and hundreds of legislators in local communities.

Family and child advocates face some special dilemmas, as well as new opportunities, in America's transformed civic environment. Traditionally, advocates for children and families have worked in partnership with locally based membership federations, allowing advocates to reach out to families with children and to the recreational, educational, and health institutions on which families rely (even in the age of the Internet). But by the late 20th century, the organized civic world became more loosely connected (Wuthnow 1998). Both local groups and nationally organized professional groups exist today, but few bridges connect the two sets of groups. This lack of integration can hurt the prospects of new national measures that support families and children.

Causes such as universal health care, improved schools, or paid family and medical leave may be popular; they may even be essential for thousands of families. But how can advocates get the message out to people, and how can they arouse large numbers of Americans to press for such innovations? Business and professional groups can often deploy large amounts of money to buy media time or activate nationwide networks of professionals or corporate employees to promote their causes. But for advocates seeking new social supports for parents and children, nothing can substitute for sustained grassroots pressure. Advocacy in general will suffer if the chasm between professional advocates and locally oriented associations widens.

## Responding to New Social and Civic Challenges: Four Case Studies

The dilemmas described have not been lost on the civic groups that currently advocate for children and families. Groups are developing innovative tactics to bridge divides and recreate old connections in new ways. The following case studies cover some of these approaches, the lessons they suggest, and the challenges that remain.

- *National Parent Teacher Association.* An old-line membership federation responds to demographic changes and competition from local parent-teacher groups.
- *Children's Defense Fund.* A 1970s advocacy group launches its Stand For Children initiative, which devises a new way to mobilize broader support on behalf of children's and family issues.
- *National Partnership for Women and Families (formerly the Women's Legal Defense Fund).* Like the Children's Defense Fund, a 1970s advocacy group transforms itself in response to political opportunity and develops a revamped mission.
- *Texas Industrial Areas Foundation.* A grassroots group of organizers and religious congregations develop fresh strategies for popular mobilization on children's issues.

### *The National Parent Teacher Association*

The National PTA is still the largest volunteer child advocacy organization in the United States. On its Web site, the PTA says that it prides itself for being "a leader in reminding our nation of its obligations to children," having actively done so for more than a century. The PTA pursued a pattern of organizational growth typical of early civic associations, amassing large numbers of members—12 million in its heyday—in a nationwide federation complete with branch congresses in most states and thousands of local groups. Its causes have included enacting pensions for mothers, opposing child labor, running popular service programs, supporting day care, and taking an activist stance in public education, the activity for which the organization is now most widely known.

PTA membership soared from less than 3.5 million in 1945 to more than 12 million in 1960, according to Crawford and Levitt (1999). The organization reaped the rewards of a societal emphasis on traditional families, the post-war baby boom, and concerted membership drives that included door-to-door canvassing, newspaper and radio ads, publicity drives, and letters and phone calls to parents. Middle-class stay-at-home wives and mothers, in particular, made up most of the PTA's membership (Crawford and Levitt 1999, 263). But after 1963, PTA membership began a steady decline that lasted two decades. Membership had dropped nearly 50 percent by 1975, and only 5.5 million members remained by 1985. Meanwhile, the number of local PTA chapters decreased from a peak of 47,000 in the 1960s to a low of 24,400 in 1984 (*ibid.*).

In seeking to explain the PTA's massive loss of membership and local units, Crawford and Levitt point to several converging factors. First, they note that the decline corresponds to a period when large numbers of middle-class mothers entered the paid labor force and when rising divorce rates led to an increase in female-headed households. Both of these trends created additional time constraints for women and made it more difficult for them to participate in the PTA. Declines in school enrollment after the baby boom era and the corresponding school consolidations in the late 1970s reduced the need for PTA chapters and shrank the organization's traditional recruiting pool.

A consolidation also occurred as a result of the Supreme Court's *Brown v. Board of Education* decision, which led to the racial integration of the PTA itself. In 1970, the PTA absorbed the National Congress of Colored Parents and Teachers and desegregated all state PTA groups. This organizational shift likely contributed to a membership drop, particularly in the South. Crawford and Levitt found that "28 percent of the total national membership loss in 1970–71 came from just seven southern states; close to 18 percent came from Mississippi, Florida and North Carolina alone" (1999, 277). Moreover, they argue, mandatory busing programs—which physically removed children from local schools—may have unintentionally made it harder for parents to participate in PTA activities, since the events were held at distant schools.

Ladd (1999) attributes part of the membership drop to the rise of competitor organizations, namely parent-teacher organizations (PTOs) that perform functions similar to those of local PTA chapters but do so as independent groups. Ladd found that by the mid-1990s, less than a quarter of all public and private K-12 schools had PTA affiliates. At the same time, his survey of school officials found that most schools still had active parent-teacher associations, although only a minority were affiliated with the PTA.

Ladd argues that many parents' desire to maintain local control and keep "all the dues money for local use" likely explains the large-scale defection to other groups (1999, 33). Some observers, however, contend that the PTA's specific political positions and its affiliation with teachers' unions explain the decline in membership. For example, Crawford and Levitt argue that along with the overall societal trends, dissatisfaction with the PTA—particularly concerns about its effectiveness—played a role. They cite a growing perception among the general public that the PTA has become "an increasingly irrelevant 'punch and cookies group'" and comprised of "supporters of the status quo" (Crawford and Levitt 1999, 275).

The PTA did not simply lie dormant during these developments. The organization pursued several strategies for adapting to new family, racial, and civic realities, including modifying its operations and assuming new functions. Since the 1980s, as Crawford and Levitt (1999) show, the PTA has devoted significant additional resources to accommodate dual-career and single-parent families. In the 1990s, the PTA distributed more than 750,000 copies of *The Busy Parents' Guide to Involvement in Education*, a pamphlet that encourages the creation of PTAs in workplaces, the provision of babysitting services during parent-teacher conferences, and the development of meeting schedules that accommodate the needs of working parents. The PTA even began running after-school child-care programs.

The PTA continued to make parental involvement in education an organizational priority throughout the 1990s, convening a major national summit on the issue in 1992 and working to pass the Goals 2000: Educate America Act of 1994, which named parental involvement in education as one of the eight National Education Goals. The organization also supported expansion of the Family and Medical Leave Act to enable parents to attend school activities held during workdays.

The PTA advanced new efforts to reach out to urban families in order to build a more racially and economically diverse membership. In 1998, Lois Jean White became the first African-American president of the PTA in the organization's 100-year history. Under her leadership, the PTA sought to enter previously ignored communities and developed new public education materials for those constituents, especially for minority and non-English-speaking parents, to encourage their involvement in their children's schooling.

These kinds of efforts by the PTA have thus far met with some success. In the 1980s, PTA membership rebounded somewhat, reaching more than 7 million by 1990 (1.5 million more members than in 1985), but between 1990 and 1997, membership declined again by about a half million members, and almost 2,000 local chapters folded (Crawford and Levitt 1999). Today, membership is about 6.5 million. Like other large civic federations founded in the early 20th century, the PTA has only partially recovered its influence and may never recapture its role as the preeminent parent-teacher organization. Indeed, Ladd (1999) concludes that the PTA should now be considered a minority player in an increasingly fragmented group of autonomous PTOs.

One concern raised by the reliance on PTOs is that most of these groups are not integrated into an organizational network at the national or even the state level (Crawford and Levitt 1999). Instead, they tend to focus on serving individual schools and on encouraging parents to concentrate on their own children's welfare, rather than on bringing together representatives from diverse schools to address broader system issues. In the context of the changed civic universe, this fragmentation and localism may exacerbate the class and racial divisions that the PTA has worked hard to bridge.

### The Children's Defense Fund and Its Stand For Children Initiative

From its founding in 1973 through the mid-1990s, the Children's Defense Fund (CDF) functioned as a professional research and lobbying association focused primarily on influencing national officials and the national media. By the late 1980s, CDF's communication network and annual meetings involved a few thousand direct supporters, including many social-service professionals, and the organization had contact with church groups in various parts of the country. But CDF did not try to function as a membership organization. Rather, it directed its expertise, foundation financing, and Marian Wright Edelman's compelling personal reputation and political savvy toward gaining influence in Washington, D.C. The organization sought to defend and expand Great Society–era social programs including Medicaid, Food Stamps, and Head Start.

After Ronald Reagan became president, however, CDF had to play defense as much as offense in advancing its cause. The legislative situation became dire in 1994, when the Democrats lost control of Congress. During 1995 and 1996, CDF joined with other liberal advocates in a last-ditch defense of Aid to Families with Dependent Children, but it failed to prevent the abolition of federal guarantees to poor mothers and children.

As inside strategies met with increasing resistance, CDF looked to protests and to organizing beyond the nation's capital. CDF's most ambitious effort to date has been the launch of Stand For Children. Orchestrated by CDF and cosponsored by more than 3,500 organizations, Stand For Children began as a mass demonstration in Washington, D.C., on June 1, 1996, not long after the Million Man March succeeded in generating wide participation and media interest. Close to 300,000 supporters gathered at the Lincoln Memorial to pledge their commitment to children, while more than 100 local Stand For Children events took place across the nation, making it the largest public demonstration for children in U.S. history.

At the outset, Stand For Children was given an identity and tax status separate from CDF. But it was not until 1997 that Executive Director Jonah Edelman, Marian Wright Edelman's son, and Eliza Leighton began to develop Stand For Children into more than an annual march. Their vision was to transform Stand For Children into a national membership organization "where local people choose local issues to work on," with chapters linked statewide and nationwide (Edelman 1999). Stand For Children now recruits and trains a growing number of parents, teachers, child care professionals, church congregations, and others to offer services to parents, to organize communities and empower them to raise awareness about children's issues, and to advocate for policy changes.

Initially, Stand For Children supporters were loosely organized into Children's Action Teams that essentially planned annual local events associated with the national Stand For Children rally (e.g., cleanups of after-school centers, rallies, book drives) or recruited additional supporters for the annual demonstration. In 1999, 130 Children's Action Teams covered 35 states, and 1,700 local events were planned for Stand For Children Day. To develop these supporters into an effective force for change, the national Stand For Children officers began to structure the teams into formal chapter affiliates of the organization's 501(c)(4) arm. This arm enables lobbying activity beyond that allowed under the organization's 501(c)(3) component, which focuses on education and training.

The national Stand For Children organization now collects dues from local chapter members and sets minimum standards, values, and principles on various issues pertaining to children. Stand For Children's membership was formalized in 1999; it grew to 4,000 members by 2000, with 16 chapters in seven states. The organization's goal is to enlist 40,000 members by 2002, and Edelman envisions a membership of at least 150,000 in the longer term (Edelman 1999; Edelman 2000).

Given Stand For Children's relatively limited budget (about $1 million), the scale of chapter organizing has been small. In early 1999, only six organizers were doing field work in four states (Oregon, Maryland, Tennessee, and Texas), but the group's organizing activity is always intensive. Stand For Children organizers identify local leaders through small meetings, and then work with these leaders to explore issues and develop action strategies, offering technical assistance and training as needed, on topics including team-building strategies, generating media coverage and turnout, fundraising, and using the Internet effectively. Over several months, these professional organizers participate actively in local meetings to nurture the development of chapter leaders and to help build community among chapter members. Over the longer term, Stand For Children organizers work on linking local chapters to state federations that can advocate for statewide issues. Stand For Children targets its organizing efforts at locations deemed "swing" districts when it comes to child-related state legislative activity.

Stand For Children chapters have led several successful local organizing campaigns. For example, the Centre County, Pennsylvania, chapter recruited 100 community members to convince the town council to fund a youth center and a skateboard park. Other chapters have organized to provide services to children, such as helping to enroll children in a new state health insurance program (Boston, Massachusetts) and recruiting dentists to provide free dental screenings for low-income children (Wilmington, Delaware). Generally, organizers hope that small victories like these will help generate interest and attract new members.

Stand For Children's largest effort to date has been the formation of the Salem-Keizer, Oregon, chapter. The effort began when Stand For Children organized a public meeting of 380 community members to convince county commissioners to restore funding for mental health specialists serving vulnerable children. Stand For Children targeted the area because it had recently swung from Democratic to moderate Republican control, putting funding for some child programs at risk. In addition, because the state capital is in the area, Stand For Children organizers had a good chance of expanding activity that might have been seen as merely local to other parts of the state.

After targeting the area, the Stand For Children organizer—in this case, Jonah Edelman himself—held personal meetings with pastors and other active citizens to seek out potential leaders for a new Stand For Children chapter. Edelman then helped these leaders to target cuts in the county's budget for children's therapists—an emotional issue that was seen as concrete, immediate, and winnable. After the victory, Edelman stayed to help local leaders build the chapter's membership and organization. By early 2001, Stand For Children had 300 members in Salem, as well as 400 members in three other Oregon chapters (Albany, Corvallis, and Hillsboro). It was in the process of forming four more chapters.

During the 2001 legislative session, Stand For Children sought to link its Oregon chapters on a statewide issue: improving the quality of child care in Oregon by attracting and retaining more qualified child care providers. The proposed legislation, dubbed the Oregon Cares Program, was modeled on a proposal put forward by the Corvallis chapter to supplement the wages of qualified child care teachers based on their level of training.

Stand For Children's parent organization, CDF, has a $13 million budget, the capacity to frame issues on the national level, the skill to undertake sophisticated policy research, and influence inside Washington's Beltway. These features complement Stand For Children's strategy of focusing on local organizing efforts. But Stand For Children's labor-intensive approach is both time-consuming and costly, and, given the organization's limited budget, can only be conducted on a small scale. Moreover, Stand For Children receives half its funding from foundations, which tend to look for results within short time frames. Indeed, Stand For Children has debated whether it should select issues from CDF's list of initiatives and campaign for them at the local level—something Jonah Edelman has opposed. For now, the plan is for Stand For Children's organizers to help the localized efforts to cross-fertilize and connect to form statewide and, eventually, national initiatives. Jonah Edelman, however, acknowledges that Stand For Children needs to build many more chapters and that it is headed down a very long road, and not a well-trodden path (Edelman 1999).

## National Partnership for Women and Families

The expense and difficulty of building a national membership network led the Women's Legal Defense Fund (WLDF), now known as the National Partnership for Women and Families, to broaden its outreach by building inter-association ties at the national and state levels. Founded by a group of feminist lawyers in Washington, D.C., in 1971, WLDF originally was an all-volunteer service organization providing pro bono legal representation and counseling for D.C.-area women (e.g., for divorce and domestic-violence cases). The political, legal, and networking skills of its executive director, Judith Lichtman, and the expertise of WLDF's staff quickly propelled the organization from being a local service provider to its current status as a leading national advocate for women's rights that was known for its involvement in precedent-setting sex-discrimination litigation.

WLDF's goal was to acquire 10,000 members nationwide to ensure the organization's financial independence and to encourage organizational accountability to a national feminist community (WLDF 1979). Membership, however, remained relatively flat, between 1,000 and 2,000 people. According to Donna Lenhoff, general counsel for the National Partnership, WLDF's early legal focus may have been too narrow to appeal to a large number of Americans, especially given the recruiting efforts of other women's groups, such as the National Organization for Women (Lenhoff 1999). In addition, WLDF faced the dichotomy of a predominantly elite membership and a less-advantaged constituency; WLDF's leadership feared that an active membership would steer the organization toward a focus on "glass ceiling" issues rather than on issues such as a lack of child-support policies.

After some early attempts to increase its membership, WLDF found that mass membership recruitment was "very labor intensive and hard to do," not cost effective (especially for direct mail), and out of step with the expertise of key staff (Lenhoff 1999). So the organization never committed a significant portion of its resources to membership development. Instead, it raised funds primarily through foundation grants and large individual donations. Rather than recruit large numbers of individual citizens, WLDF sought to build and lead coalitions of organizations, including membership groups, to develop the grassroots support needed for its national advocacy campaigns.

Throughout the 1970s and 1980s, the organization retained its early model of direct legal service provision at the local level, a model grounded in the concept that advocacy is best informed by field experience. Direct services continued to be an integral component of WLDF's advocacy strategy until 1990, when, in a major restructuring, the organization decided to dedicate its energies to national legislative advocacy. By then, WLDF had begun to shift its emphasis from women's legal rights to a broader policy agenda encompassing family and work issues, including family and medical leave benefits (paid and unpaid), universal health care, pay equity and fairness, and child care and support. According to Lenhoff (1999), this new emphasis partly reflected the organization's recognition of "the limits of litigation as a social change strategy" as Reagan-appointed judges became more influential. The organizational change also reflected an awareness of an increasingly diverse and time-burdened audience.

The new direction was influenced perhaps most of all by WLDF's long, successful campaign to enact the Family and Medical Leave Act (FMLA). This precedent-setting piece of legislation ended the United States' status as the only advanced industrialized nation without a federal maternity leave policy. The passage of FMLA during a period that seemed adverse to major social legislation was considered remarkable. WLDF wrote the first draft of FMLA in 1985, deliberately giving it a comprehensive and universal design (e.g., extending benefit coverage not just to mothers, but also to caretakers; addressing child care needs as well as spouse and parent care needs) to inspire a broad constituency to advocate for and defend its provisions.

In leading the coalition of more than 150 organizations that fought for the FMLA's enactment for more than eight years, WLDF recognized that it could be an effective national policy advocate. However, it also realized that such efforts required additional organizational resources. The direct services WLDF was providing seemed to drain existing resources without generating comparable impact, and thus were spun off (Lenhoff 1999). The election of a Democratic president in 1992 and the FMLA's enactment in 1993 convinced WLDF that conditions were favorable to its legislative program. But the 1994 Republican takeover of Congress changed that view, prompting WLDF to once again reassess its mission.

As a result, in 1998 WLDF repositioned itself and became the National Partnership for Women and Families. As part of this strategy, the National Partnership streamlined its programmatic activity into two major areas—work/family and health care—and increased the percentage of its budget allocated for public education efforts. The organization also formed a small Action Council, a base of new members/donors that the organization could call on to help target congressional swing districts.

Thus far, the National Partnership's new focus has enabled it to reach out more easily to other organizations, including businesses and religious associations that may have perceived WLDF as too "radical feminist"

(Lenhoff 1999). This kind of outreach will be especially important for the organization's first major initiative as the National Partnership: the campaign for family leave benefits, an effort focused initially on having individual states expand the FMLA's family and medical leave to include partial wage replacement during the leave period. By 2001, 24 states had introduced paid family leave bills. The National Partnership is drafting model legislation and offering other forms of assistance to spur more states to act and, ideally, to create a positive feedback loop between state and federal advocacy efforts, as it did during the FMLA campaign.

But in the current political atmosphere, the creation of a paid leave benefit program will involve organizing challenges larger than those faced by WLDF during the campaign for FMLA. During deliberations for unpaid leave, conservative and business opponents were able to secure major concessions from the bill originally written by WLDF, including the exemption of small businesses from the new regulations. Such forces have already mobilized to oppose the expansion of state unemployment insurance programs to offer partial wage replacement for employees unable to work during periods of FMLA leave.

As the debate over paid family leave moves from individual states to the national level, the National Partnership will need a base of grassroots supporters to persuade legislators from the country's more conservative corners to support the effort. Because such mobilization often depends on ties to other organizations, many of which have declining memberships, the task seems daunting.

## Texas Industrial Areas Foundation

The PTA, CDF, and the National Partnership are all committed to national strategies for influencing the well-being of children and families, and each has developed innovative ways to combine legislative lobbying with broader mobilization efforts. The Texas Industrial Areas Foundation (IAF) provides an alternative approach, working directly to unify diverse urban communities throughout Texas and the adjacent Southwest to fight to improve children's lives using the communities' own collective power (see Shirley 1997; Warren 2001).

IAF's organizers are professionals inspired by the ideas of the late Saul Alinsky. Over the past generation, IAF staff in the Southwest and in other regions of the United States have focused on using resources and people from religious congregations to create power blocs able to win local, state, and regional battles to improve the quality of life for families and communities. IAF's efforts are not considered purely grassroots, because professional organizers are on staff. Church leaders, especially Catholic bishops, and some foundations are also crucial supporters. Moreover, much of the financial support for IAF organizing comes from dues paid as a proportion of the budgets of member religious congregations. IAF's organizers are not professional advocates, however, because they never speak out on behalf of constituencies. Instead, they ask men and women from member congregations to become "leader-organizers" in their own communities. Leader-organizers work together to foster personal relationships across racial, denominational, local, and class boundaries and to identify shared concerns that can be addressed jointly.

Unlike most of the politics surrounding advocacy efforts in America today, this type of mobilization avoids media coverage and takes a long time to mature. IAF organizers do not court media attention, believing that the media is likely to focus on individual leaders and on personal issues in ways that undercut group mobilization. Only after months or years of "relational" organizing—i.e., thousands of person-to-person meetings in people's homes—do leaders publicly voice shared grievances and launch policy campaigns. Public officials and business leaders are then pressed by mass movements to address community needs in new ways.

Past IAF campaigns have succeeded in establishing job training programs that lead to paid positions with full benefits, creating new after-school programs, and enhancing school curricula. Family needs, as defined by people in one-to-one or small-group settings, are always at the center of IAF campaigns. The organization has found that this approach arouses moral energy and fosters cooperation among different racial, ethnic, and religious groups.

Both local and state politics have been influenced by IAF organizers. IAF has built a statewide Alliance Schools campaign to involve low- and moderate-income parents in reforming schools and improving community conditions in dozens of troubled Texas school districts (Shirley 1997). In contrast to the usual practice of local PTAs, IAF is willing to challenge existing school administrations and practices. The organization also affects safety and economic conditions in school environments by leveraging resources that teachers and administrators alone probably could not mobilize.

IAF is, in fact, political in a completely different way than either the PTA or national advocacy groups like CDF and the National Partnership for Women and Families. Although it does not form direct electoral or interest group alliances and has little influence on national media campaigns or national legislation, IAF concentrates on changing power configurations at the local and state level and on empowering citizens who might not participate otherwise. The advantage of this approach is that it brings fresh moral and popular energy into democratic life. To reverse the ebbing of citizen participation in advocacy, IAF is taking new, deliberate approaches to involving a cross-section of grassroots participants. Families are directly in touch with IAF campaigns through church and neighborhood networks, and it is common to see secretaries or laborers playing leading roles in IAF campaigns.

The limitation of the IAF approach, however, is that its groups, even its regional alliances, have little visibility in national politics and thus little capacity to influence federal legislation. Many of the workplace and economic conditions that affect IAF families need to be addressed at the national level. Step by step, IAF regional movements do aim to link their efforts, but this kind of relational grassroots organizing is a long-term proposition.

## Conclusion

The four organizations described here illustrate some of the ways that groups advocating for children and families are responding to today's new civic practices and challenges. The PTA exemplifies the rise and decline of many large, locally rooted civic associations founded in the early 20th century. It remains the largest child advocacy organization in the United States, but has lost some of its earlier influence. With school enrollments now surpassing record levels, the PTA has an important opportunity to expand its membership and influence. But amid the new social and political realities, the organization must do more to adapt and reach out to new constituencies. The PTA, as Crawford and Levitt (1999) point out, will also need to work cooperatively with new groups—including parent-teachers organizations—and broaden some of its legislative positions to adapt to the needs of modern families.

In this respect, the PTA and other child advocacy organizations could learn from the National Partnership for Women and Families, which broadened its focus from women's rights litigation to building national coalitions to advocate for universal social supports for all families. The passage of the Family and Medical Leave Act demonstrates such coalitions' potential power to enact progressive social legislation even in unfriendly times. In the case of FMLA, the coalition of more than 150 organizations led by the WLDF included the PTA and CDF, unions, women's and civil rights associations, senior citizens and disability groups, and religious organizations.

At the same time, the coalition's diminished ability to activate grassroots support, given the overall declines in membership among associations like the PTA, made the fight to pass FMLA much more lengthy and onerous, and resulted in a bill weakened by important concessions to small businesses. The National Partnership's need to motivate grassroots supporters is even more essential for its new campaign for paid family leave, which is sure to present even greater advocacy challenges. The same can be said for child care and universal health insurance campaigns.

The partnership between the Children's Defense Fund (CDF) and Stand For Children, though still fairly new, presents an innovative advocacy approach that has some potential for breathing new life into the movement for children and families. As CDF continues its important Washington, D.C.–based lobbying and public education efforts, Stand For Children aims to ground the national advocacy in local roots. Stand For Children's organizing style is similar to that of IAF; in fact, Stand For Children organizers attend IAF training courses. Down the road, if Stand For Children is able to expand its membership and chapter units, it might become a force on a par with the conservative, powerful Christian Coalition. Achieving the capacity to act both on national and local issues at the same time would allow each effort to enliven and energize the other. Of course, pressure to get instant results could threaten the organization's ability to expand its grassroots organizing. While Stand For Children is well positioned, its partnership with CDF gives it the national visibility that other chapter-based advocacy groups must struggle to gain.

A revitalized movement for children and families in America will depend on the ability of advocates to find new ways to link their efforts nationally and across state and local lines, and to reach out more effectively to parents and communities. The experiences of the organizations described here demonstrate that such efforts, while challenging in the current climate, can proceed, and may prove pivotal in the struggle to put children and their families first in American society.

# NOTE

1. Children and family associations include all public affairs; social welfare; cultural; educational; health/medical; hobby; labor; legal/governmental/public administration/military; religious; fraternal/foreign interest/nationality/ethnic; veterans/hereditary/patriotic associations; and athletic/sports organizations in the 1998 *Encyclopedia of Associations* with the following keywords in their title or description: child, family, parent, mother, father, daughter, son, homemaker, maternal, paternal, marriage, divorce, pregnancy, birth, adoption, abortion, and their variants (e.g., childhood, grandparent, married, or maternity).

# REFERENCES

Bennett, Michael J. 1996. *When Dreams Came True: The GI Bill and the Making of Modern America.* Washington, D.C.: Brassey's Inc.

Berry, Jeffrey M. 1999. *The New Liberalism: The Rising Power of Citizen Groups.* Washington, D.C.: Brookings Institution Press.

———. 1997. *The Interest Group Society,* 3rd ed. New York: Longman.

———. 1977. *Lobbying for the People: The Political Behavior of Public Interest Groups.* Princeton, N.J.: Princeton University Press.

Bordin, Ruth. 1981. *Woman and Temperance: The Quest for Power and Liberty, 1873–1900.* Philadelphia, Penn.: Temple University Press.

Brown, Richard D. 1974. "The Emergence of Urban Society in Rural Massachusetts, 1760–1830." *Journal of American History* 61 (1): 29–51.

Crawford, Susan, and Peggy Levitt. 1999. "Social Change and Civic Engagement: The Case of the PTA." In *Civic Engagement and American Democracy,* edited by Theda Skocpol and Morris P. Fiorina (249–96). Washington, D.C.: Brookings Institution Press; and New York: Russell Sage Foundation.

Dunlap, Riley E., and Angela G. Mertig. 1992. *American Environmentalism: The U.S. Environmental Movement, 1970–1990.* New York: Taylor and Francis.

Edelman, Jonah. 2000. Personal Communication to Jillian Dickert, September.

———. 1999. Interview conducted by Jillian Dickert, July.

Gamm, Gerald, and Robert D. Putnam. 1999. "The Growth of Voluntary Associations in America, 1840–1940." *Journal of Interdisciplinary History* 29 (3): 511–57.

Gelb, Joyce, and Marian Lief Palley. 1982. *Women and Public Policies.* Princeton, N.J.: Princeton University Press.

Godwin, R. Kenneth, and Rondo Cameron Mitchell. 1984. "The Implications of Direct Mail for Political Organizations." *Social Science Quarterly* 65 (3): 829–39.

Jenkins, J. Craig. 1998. "Channeling Social Protest: Foundation Patronage of Contemporary Social Movements." In *Private Action and the Public Good,* edited by Walter W. Powell and Elisabeth S. Clemens. New Haven, Conn.: Yale University Press.

Joyce, Michael S., and William A. Schambra. 1996. "A New Civic Life." In *To Empower People: From State to Civil Society,* 2nd edition, edited by Michael Novak. Washington, D.C.: AEI Press.

Ladd, Everett C. 1999. *The Ladd Report.* New York: The Free Press.

Lenhoff, Donna. 1999. Interview conducted by Jillian Dickert, July.

Morris, Aldon D. 1984. *The Origins of the Civil Rights Movement: Black Communities Organizing for Change.* New York: Free Press.

Putnam, Robert D. 2000. *Bowling Alone: The Collapse and Revival of American Community.* New York: Simon and Schuster.

Schlesinger, Arthur M., Sr. 1944. "Biography of a Nation of Joiners." *American Historical Review* 50 (1): 1–25.

Schlozman, Kay Lehman. 2000. "Did Working Women Kill the PTA?" *The American Prospect* 11 (20): 14–15.

Shirley, Dennis. 1997. *Community Organizing for Urban School Reform.* Austin: University of Texas Press.

Skocpol, Theda. 1999. "Advocates without Members: The Recent Transformation of American Civic Life." In *Civic Engagement in American Democracy,* edited by Theda Skocpol and Morris P. Fiorina. Washington, D.C.: Brookings Institution Press; and New York: Russell Sage Foundation.

———. 1997. "The GI Bill and U.S. Social Policy, Past and Future." *Social Philosophy and Policy* 14 (2): 95–115.

———. 1992. *Protecting Soldiers and Mothers: The Political Origins of Social Policy in the United States.* Cambridge, Mass.: Harvard University Press.

Skocpol, Theda, with Marshall Ganz, Ziad Munson, Bayliss Camp, Michele Swers, and Jennifer Oser. 1999. "How Americans Became Civic." In *Civic Engagement in American Democracy,* edited by Theda Skocpol and Morris P. Fiorina (27–80). Washington, D.C.: Brookings Institution Press; and New York: Russell Sage Foundation.

Skocpol, Theda, Marshall Ganz, and Ziad Munson. 2000. "A Nation of Organizers: The Institutional Origins of Civic Voluntarism in the United States." *American Political Science Review* 94 (3): 527–46.

Skocpol, Theda, Ziad Munson, Andrew Karch, and Bayliss Camp. Forthcoming. "Patriotic Partnerships: Why Great Wars Encouraged American Civic Voluntarism." In *Shaped by War and Trade: International Influences on American Domestic Politics,* edited by Ira Katznelson and Martin Shefter. Princeton, N.J.: Princeton University Press.

Walker, Jack L., Jr. 1991. *Mobilizing Interest Group Politics in America: Patrons, Professions, and Social Movements.* Ann Arbor: University of Michigan Press.

Warren, Mark R. 2001. *Dry Bones Rattling: Community Building to Revitalize American Democracy.* Princeton, N.J.: Princeton University Press.

Wells, Mildred White. 1953. *Unity in Diversity: The History of the General Federation of Women's Clubs.* Washington, D.C.: General Federation of Women's Clubs.

Women's Legal Defense Fund (WLDF). 1979. *Report on Long-Range Planning of the WLDF Board of Directors.* Washington, D.C.: Women's Legal Defense Fund.

Wuthnow, Robert. 1998. *Loose Connections: Joining Together in America's Fragmented Communities.* Cambridge, Mass.: Harvard University Press.

# 6

# The Politics of Preschool Advocacy: Lessons from Three Pioneering Organizations

*Barbara Beatty*

"Politics are quite perplexing," Bessie Locke wrote in her "Executive Secretary's Report" to the National Kindergarten Association in 1939, when a national kindergarten bill was being debated in Congress. Although politics have certainly perplexed preschool advocates, who have been striving to establish programs for young children in this country for more than two centuries, they have achieved some remarkable political victories. The most notable success is the nearly universal adoption of kindergarten for five-year-olds by American public schools.

When the National Kindergarten Association was founded in 1909, day nurseries had existed for at least 100 years, and nursery schools were just starting to appear. But like all early childhood care and education programs, kindergartens had to overcome a lack of public support and familiarity with caring for children outside the home. What other kinds of obstacles did day-nursery, kindergarten, and nursery-school organizations encounter? What advocacy strategies can be learned from examining how kindergarten, in particular, became a standard part of early education throughout the nation? An analysis of preschool organizations' differing approaches to advocacy for early childhood care and education can provide useful answers to these questions.[1]

This chapter compares the history and experiences of three influential early childhood care and education organizations: the National Federation of Day Nurseries (NFDN), the National Kindergarten Association

(NKA), and the National Association for Nursery Education (NANE). These three groups were "maternalist" voluntary organizations that modeled the provision of social services to young children on women's traditional role in the family.

In the beginning, none of these groups exactly resembled the large, three-tiered, voluntary organizations, such as the National Congress of Mothers, that spread rapidly throughout the United States in the late 19th century and had national, state, and local branches. NFDN maintained local affiliates and individual members in the Northeast and Midwest. Although it had members scattered in other parts of the country, it did not have state chapters. The NKA worked through a network of partnerships with other voluntary associations but did not establish state or local chapters. The NANE had no affiliates in its early years of operation, but it gradually evolved into a comprehensive, three-tiered organization.

The overlap, cooperation, and competition among these organizations was characteristic of the divided history of early childhood care and education. Some of the same individuals served on the boards of all three and worked together on various advisory committees. NFDN, NKA, and NANE all collaborated with the federal government at different times (often subsidizing government activities), and they also all faced resistance from federal agencies. But despite their similar missions, NFDN, NKA, and NANE often had different ideas about what young children and families needed to thrive, and members sometimes criticized the quality and effects of the other groups' services. This disunity among the three organizations added to the fragmentation and lack of coordination evident in the children's services movement.

The strategies NFDN, NKA, and NANE used to promote their respective programs and to overcome resistance greatly shaped the progress of the reforms they advocated. All three organizations needed to convince politicians, policymakers, and the public that early childhood care and education were necessary to support families. All three organizations needed to secure financial support. All three sought to maintain some control over the types of early childhood care and education available to young children and families. But each organization met these challenges differently, and each helped shape the provision of early childhood care and education in the United States in its own way. The past cannot provide simple answers to the problems facing child advocates today, but a comparison of these pioneering organizations' histories can help us set priorities in advocating for early childhood care and education.

## Organizational History

### The National Federation of Day Nurseries

The National Federation of Day Nurseries was founded in 1898 by Josephine Jewell Dodge, the daughter of a Connecticut governor and the wife of Arthur Dodge, a Charity Organization Society founder and one of the wealthiest men in New York. Members of NFDN and its local affiliates included John D. Rockefeller's wife Laura Spelman Rockefeller, Mrs. Andrew Carnegie, Mrs. J. Pierpont Morgan, and other women in the social elite.

Many members of NFDN were mothers who believed that women with children should not work outside the home. Dodge, an organizer of the National Association Opposed to Woman Suffrage, thought that women should also stay out of politics. Dodge and most other members of NFDN considered contributing to private day nurseries an act of charity and saw serving on day nursery boards as an appropriate way to help less-fortunate women as well as society in general. According to Dodge, a woman should remain "exempt from political responsibility" so as to be "free to render her best service to the state" in ways "for which her nature and training fit her" (Durst 1989, 135–36).[2]

NFDN grew out of a committee organized by Dodge to plan an exhibit of day nurseries at the World's Columbian Exposition in Chicago in 1893. The exhibit gave day nurseries, which had existed since at least the end of the 18th century, national prominence. The exhibit committee that Dodge convened in 1892 eventually became the Association of Day Nurseries of New York City, and in 1898, Dodge founded the national organization. Affiliates soon sprung up in Chicago, Philadelphia, Cleveland, and other cities (Michel 1999). NFDN held national conferences and published a regular newsletter, and also conducted fundraising activities, provided training sessions for day nursery matrons, and organized mothers' meetings.

NFDN members saw day nurseries as temporary expedients to prevent needy families from sending their children to orphanages or other institutions. Day nurseries, conceived as home-like environments that might also improve the homelife of the poor, were not intended to replace children's real homes. Because NFDN members worried that some mothers might "shirk the burden of child-rearing to earn money for the gratification of selfish ends," NFDN conducted home inspections to confirm genuine need (Dodge 1897, 61). "Only children who cannot be cared for otherwise" were to be admitted; "hard times, scarcity of work for men, illness, insanity, desertion" were the kinds of conditions and exceptions used to determine eligibility (Dodge 1897, 61–62).

In the early 1900s, a movement to provide pensions to indigent mothers to help them care for their children affected the evolution of NFDN. Progressive reformers such as Jane Addams and Florence Kelley argued that giving poor mothers financial support to enable them to care for their children at home was preferable to providing child care. Although Addams had initially supported a day nursery at Hull House, she later changed her mind because she thought that raising children while supporting a family was a terrible burden. The day nursery was at best "a necessary evil," according to Addams, and in the influential journal of the Charity Organization Society, she stated that nurseries might tempt a single mother to attempt the impossible, "to both care for her children and support them financially" (Addams 1905, 411).

Like critics of day nurseries, members of NFDN worried about the effects on children of care outside the home. Dr. Lee K. Frankel advised NFDN members at a 1905 conference that "the home was the proper place for development" (Frankel 1905, 777). Although NFDN attempted to make its nurseries as homelike as possible, day nursery matrons were underpaid and often untrained, and the quality of care varied enormously. Concerned about these conditions, Addams reported that her investigation into the careers of children after leaving day nurseries in Chicago "had disclosed results which are neither encouraging nor reassuring" (Addams 1905, 411). Social workers and other reformers, including Julia Lathrop, director of the Children's Bureau and leader of the campaign for mothers' pensions, agreed.

NFDN's own ambivalence toward the effectiveness of day nurseries probably explains why the organization did not mount an active defense against its critics, even though World War I increased the need for child care. In 1922, Dodge went so far as to tell a convention of the Philadelphia Association of Day Nurseries (PADN) that NFDN was working for the "prevention of its own work" (Durst 1989, 174). Despite NFDN's inaction, governmental resistance to day nurseries, and the rapid enactment of mothers' pension legislation in many states, the number of NFDN-affiliated day nurseries increased between 1910 and 1920: In 1912, there were almost 500 day nurseries, double the number in 1902 (Durst 1989, 134), and by 1916, charitable organizations operated some 695 day nurseries (Tank 1980, 150–51).

Some groups and local NFDN affiliates strongly supported day nurseries despite the lukewarm support of the national organization. African-American philanthropists and women's clubs wholeheartedly favored day nurseries, in part because the African-American community largely accepted the idea of mothers working outside the home. Although faced with limited fundraising possibilities, the National Association of Colored Women and local African-American women's groups worked hard to raise money for day nurseries.

The PADN was also more proactive than NFDN. In 1905, the PADN sent a letter to school principals and attendance officers explaining that school-age children were being kept home to care for younger siblings and that day nurseries were greatly needed. Like other day-nursery associations, the PADN did not directly request public funding, but the letter, which was sent out on Board of Education stationery, generated eight proposals to start day nurseries. In the 1920s, Los Angeles' public schools sponsored 28 day nurseries, and a few other day nurseries existed in public schools around the country (Rose 1999, 19, 80).

Support from public school officials, however, was sporadic at best. In Philadelphia, the school superintendent and the teachers' union pushed for funding under the Lanham Act, which authorized federal funding for child care centers during World War II. But following the war, the PADN did not actively fight to maintain public child care in Philadelphia. Worried about the risks of becoming involved in politics, some PADN members said that they needed to "be careful of maintaining their nontax status and not become too active in propaganda and politics," a concern that is still voiced by child advocates today (Rose 1999, 190–91).

Eventually, however, mounting criticism and increasing support for mothers' pensions caused the number of day nurseries to decline. Although estimates vary, one source reports that the number of day nurseries peaked at 800 in 1931 and fell to 600 by 1940, probably in part because widespread unemployment during the Depression reduced the need for child care (Michel 1999). The decrease forced NFDN to merge with its New York chapter in 1938 to form the National Association of Day Nurseries. The National Association of Day Nurseries was in turn absorbed by the Child Welfare League of America in 1942.

Although NFDN's influence declined, stronger advocacy for day nurseries emerged from other organizations. For example, mothers in Philadelphia whose children had attended the wartime children's centers mounted a successful campaign to maintain public support. After militant demonstrations at City Hall and much bureaucratic wrangling, these women pressured the mayor's office to fund the child care centers. The Philadelphia public schools operated about 10 child care centers during the 1950s and 1960s (Rose 1999, 265). In addition, public child care centers in California continued to operate after the war, and there were a few centers in operation elsewhere. Although the day-nursery movement ended, child care advocacy regained momentum in the 1970s, when the rise in the number of working mothers from all backgrounds created great demand and a politically powerful constituency for child care.

## The National Kindergarten Association

Like the NFDN, the NKA was formed before women in most parts of the country could vote. But unlike the NFDN, the NKA eagerly entered the political arena to promote the cause of universal kindergartens. Begun in 1909 by Bessie Locke, the NKA, whose motto was "Kindergartens for all the nation's children," grew out of the New York Free Kindergarten Association. Locke, born in 1865 in West Cambridge, Massachusetts, came from a very different background than Josephine Dodge. The daughter of a printer, Locke attended a public kindergarten in Brooklyn. As an adult, she worked as a bookkeeper and store manager and took business courses at Columbia University. Having seen the effects of a charity kindergarten firsthand, she was converted to the kindergarten cause and became the financial secretary of the Brooklyn Free Kindergarten Association and the New York Kindergarten Society (Beatty 1999).

Locke was particularly interested in having kindergartens be made available to children in small cities and towns throughout the country. According to an 1898 Bureau of Education survey, almost 3,000 public and private kindergartens were attended by about 200,000 children in the United States (Beatty 1995). Most of these kindergartens, however, were in metropolitan areas and were often seen as a way to prevent crime and teach manual training. Early on, public kindergartens, like day nurseries, were stigmatized as urban programs for socializing poor and immigrant children.[3]

The NKA was a political action group, rather than a charity or professional organization. Structured as a national umbrella organization, it had broad representation from academia, elite society, and educational organizations. Honorary vice presidents, all male, included college and university presidents G. Stanley Hall of Clark, David Starr Jordan of

Stanford, A. Lawrence Lowell of Harvard, and Benjamin Ide Wheeler of the University of California. As in the NFDN, many wealthy New Yorkers served on the organization's board of directors. The NKA's Education Committee was made up of influential female kindergarten experts from around the country. The NKA was formally affiliated with the Chicago Kindergarten College, the National Education Association, the International Kindergarten Union, the General Federation of Women's Clubs, the National Congress of Women, and the National Congress of Mothers. John Dewey joined the Executive Committee in 1912 and served as president for three years.

The NKA's success was due in large part to Locke's fundraising ability, administrative acumen, and promotional skills. As executive secretary of NKA, a position she held for 41 years, Locke raised $700,000 for kindergartens in New York City; secured a $250,000 donation from John D. Archbold, president of Standard Oil of New Jersey; and appealed to tycoons Andrew Carnegie, John D. Rockefeller, and Cornelius Vanderbilt for help. As the NKA's leader, Locke knew that networking was the key to political lobbying. She obtained the dates of state teachers' conventions, found out when state legislatures convened, and corresponded extensively with state and local superintendents and kindergarten directors. Rather than try to establish a large national organization, she worked through other organizations to build the NKA's influence.

One of the NKA's most effective relationships was with the U.S. Bureau of Education. In an effort to organize kindergartens in the South, the region of the country with the fewest kindergarten programs, Locke began corresponding with University of Tennessee education professor Philander P. Claxton. When Claxton became U.S. Commissioner of Education in 1912, he suggested that the NKA establish and fund a kindergarten office within the Bureau of Education. Locke served as the director of the Kindergarten Bureau throughout its existence, from 1913 to 1919.

With the imprimatur of the federal government now affixed to the campaign for public kindergartens, the Kindergarten Bureau was able to collect detailed statistics, publish a series of kindergarten circulars, and provide information to other government agencies. Claxton and Locke even discussed plans for a Kindergarten or Children's Building, which Claxton hoped John D. Rockefeller might fund. It is not clear why the NKA's relationship with the Bureau of Education ended in 1919, but Claxton continued to support the extension of public kindergartens and to send out pamphlets at great savings to the NKA.

The NKA was far ahead of its time in using public-relations techniques to lobby political support. Locke sent out thousands of mailings and press releases and commissioned kindergarten experts to prepare articles for local newspapers. The NKA also used the new medium of film effectively. The organization's first film, *At the Threshold of Life*, was a clever marketing device that focused on an upper-class young businessman whose fiancée taught in a charity kindergarten and refused to marry him unless he contributed financially to the kindergarten cause. The NKA sent information about the film to school superintendents, women's clubs, and professional education groups, with advice on how to use the film.

Above all, Locke understood that extending the reach of public kindergartens would require intense political lobbying at all levels of government. The NKA began by focusing on state-level lobbying to enact permissive legislation that would allow public monies to be spent on children under six years old. The organization then sent a model kindergarten statute to the governors and the superintendents of public instruction in three states, with no results. Locke realized that considerable preliminary work would be necessary to get kindergartens on the legislative agenda.

This preliminary work was done locally; by 1912, the NKA had field secretaries in 37 states. The NKA relied heavily on its relationships with women's voluntary associations, especially the National Congress of Mothers (which later became the Parent Teacher Association [PTA]). A local PTA would be persuaded to start a demonstration kindergarten, and then it would request that the school board assume responsibility for the program's funding. If no PTA existed in a particular locality, the NKA asked church groups and other organizations (see Skocpol and Dickert, this volume) for support. The grassroots organizing required much effort, time, and ingenuity.

Once permissive state legislation was passed, the next step was to require local school systems to provide kindergarten programs. Locke knew that this would be more difficult because "securing legislation which makes it *compulsory* to establish kindergartens when parents petition for them" meant dealing "with the fear of a strain on the purse strings" (National Kindergarten Association 1925, 7). As the NKA soon found out, innumerable roadblocks hampered state legislation. Although enabling legislation was passed relatively easily in 1913 in California, the law put forth by the NKA in North Carolina was declared inoperative because of a minor technicality. It took seven attempts before a kinder-garten bill was passed in South Carolina. In Utah, Locke wrote in 1929, through "a cleverly arranged plan on the part of some male members of the Legislature, our bill was killed by changing *shall* to *may*." And in Massachusetts, where the first public-school kindergarten class in the country had opened in Boston in 1870, the NKA was advised by the Civic League to hold off on a legislative campaign because "the state was not ready for this step."[4]

The NKA was even more frustrated in its efforts to pass federal kinder-garten legislation. The Depression's impact on preschool education led the NKA to seek national support. Although some new kindergartens were established during the early 1930s, many more were closed. At the same time, the federal government began sponsoring emergency nursery schools as part of its efforts to revive the economy.

To forestall further kindergarten closings and to obtain federal fund-ing for kindergartens, the NKA hired a professional Washington lobbyist. As a result, a bill was drafted requesting annual funding for kindergartens and nursery schools in increasing increments, starting with $6 million and increasing $2 million dollars every year up until $16 million. The object of the bill was to obtain federal money, but not federal control. The bill stipulated that insofar as possible, kindergartens and nursery schools were to be "conducted by graduates of kindergarten or nursery-school courses for teachers at accredited institutions of learning," and that the act was intended "to leave all supervision, management, control, and choice of kindergarten and nursery-school education means, processes, and programs to State, Territorial, and local governments" (Locke 1947, 2).

The federal kindergarten bill was introduced in 1934 by Congress-man Sol Bloom (D-NY), but it encountered endless obstacles; although it was introduced repeatedly over the next 15 years, it never passed. Locke also tried unsuccessfully to get wording about kindergartens added to the federal school-aid bill lobbied for by the National Education Association. Locke and her coworker and lifetime companion Florence Jane Ovens got to know the secretaries of senators and congressmen, and stationed themselves outside of politicians' offices. Democratic Sen-ator Claude Pepper of Florida, who introduced the bill in 1939 and 1940, called them "two of the most indefatigable workers" he had ever seen.[5] The main roadblock to federal legislation was the longstanding tradition of local control and funding of education. When Locke wrote to Works

Progress Administration administrator Harry Hopkins in 1935, emergency nursery school coordinator Grace Langdon wrote back saying that kindergartens had been explicitly left out of the new federal program. "We carefully protected the kindergarten . . . by taking only children from two to four years," Langdon wrote, leaving the kindergarten "as it always has been, a function of the community" (Locke 1935, 2–3). After petitioning Eleanor Roosevelt and others, NKA was finally told that kindergartens would receive no emergency funding because of the fundamental policy of not treating regular accepted public school functions on a relief basis.

Ultimately, kindergartens' acceptance as a state and local rather than federal responsibility would prove beneficial, but kindergartens suffered through a difficult transitional period. In 1937, Acting Secretary of the Interior Charles West wrote that it was not the federal government's role "to establish financial assistance to education in general in the states." Since the kindergarten "merely represents another grade level of general education," he saw "no more reason for subsidizing that level than any other complete grade level in the regular school course" (Locke 1935, 2). In 1947, when the kindergarten bill was voted down for the last time, Senator Claude Pepper said that it was no longer necessary because the war was over and the "release of mothers for employment in war industries is no longer a problem" (National Kindergarten Association 1947, 6). Although not yet a universal offering in the American education system, the kindergarten was considered too universal to receive targeted federal aid or to be perceived as an emergency program.

Although the federal kindergarten bill was defeated, NKA persisted in its state and local efforts, and the number of public kindergartens grew steadily. In 1954, two years after Locke died, an NKA survey found that 1,265,189 children were enrolled in public kindergartens—an increase of more than 300 percent since 1910, when the U.S. Census counted 396,341 children under the age of six attending public and private kindergartens (National Kindergarten Association 1954; U.S. Bureau of the Census 1913). Still, progress was uneven. Many states in the South had few if any public kindergartens. In progressive California, only 147,123 five-year-olds attended public kindergartens in 1963, out of a kindergarten-age population of 240,999, although some of these children were attending private kindergartens (National Kindergarten Association 1963).

NKA continued to lobby for universal public kindergartens until the 1970s. The education of five-year-olds had by that time become an established public responsibility in most parts of the country. In 1975, the NKA board of directors decided it had fulfilled its mission and dissolved the organization.

## The National Association for Nursery Education

In 1929, the National Association for Nursery Education (NANE) was formally organized as a modern professional association, neither a charity nor a political action group. Unlike NFDN and NKA, NANE was run by elected officers who served set terms, rather than by a director or executive secretary who ran the organization for life, as Josephine Dodge and Bessie Locke did.

The idea behind NANE, however, did begin with one woman, Patty Smith Hill, who in 1925 called together a group of nursery school educators to discuss forming an organization. Hill, however, never served as president of NANE. A nationally known leader of the kindergarten movement's progressive wing, Hill had taught in charity kindergartens in Louisville, Kentucky, where she was born in 1868. Although she had no formal college or graduate degree, she began lecturing at Teachers College at Columbia University in 1905, where she spent a long career, and helped introduce the nursery school movement to the United States (Hewes 1976).[6]

The NANE's organizers were part of a rapidly expanding, fragmenting field of children's professionals. The subcommittee appointed to consider the organization's structure included Arnold Gessell of the Yale University Psycho-Guidance Clinic, Lois Hayden Meek Stolz of the American Association of University Women, and Abigail Eliot of the Ruggles Street Nursery Training Center in Boston. Attendees at early conferences included members of at least 35 other child-related organizations (Davis 1964, 108).

Why the organizing committee chose not to merge with the International Kindergarten Union, a relationship that might have fostered closer ties with public schools, is unclear. Hill was opposed to public school adoption of kindergartens and may have wanted to maintain autonomy and independence among nursery schools. Indeed, the competition between kindergarten and nursery school interests created a perennial tug-of-war among preschool advocates. The presence of male psychologists, who played an active role in NANE but were wary of older, predominantly female kindergarten organizations, also might have kept the two organizations separate (Senn 1975, 20).

Because nursery school children are younger than kindergarteners, the question of whether young children should be away from their mothers, and for how long, was more problematic for the NANE than for the NKA. Although nursery educators believed that attending nursery school was beneficial to children, they turned to scientific research for proof. Much of the money for this research came from philanthropy, particularly the Laura Spelman Rockefeller Memorial, which by 1925 was spending more than $1 million a year on child development, child guidance, and other parent- and child-related education and nursery school projects (Schlossman 1981, 297). Lawrence K. Frank, who directed these foundation initiatives, hoped that child-development research conducted in special university-affiliated institutes and campus nursery schools would generate useful information about child-rearing. College-educated, middle-class mothers increasingly relied on science and nursery educators for ideas about how to raise "normal," healthy children, but nursery schools were less accepted by other segments of the population.

While some NANE members urged caution, others thought the mounting scientific evidence justified moving forward and seeking public support. At the 1931 NANE conference, Iowa Child Welfare Research Station Director George Stoddard said that "hypothesis, theory, observation, and experiment all seem to point . . . to a strong need for organized, professional public- and private-school education for children, three or four years below the conventional primary age" (Stoddard 1931, 7).

Unlike NFDN members and their critics a decade earlier, Stoddard thought that a mother's desire for "personal freedom . . . to work for pay or to develop more intensively various cultural and recreational activities" was the best answer to the question of need, and dismissed concerns about mother-child separation (ibid., 9). Sounding like Bessie Locke from NKA, Stoddard said that nursery educators needed "clever sales people, from copywriters to public relations counsels" to help with promotion (ibid., 9). He also believed that nursery educators should not rely on public school administrators, who would always worry about costs, but should reach out to the general public and educate whole communities about the need for nursery schools. If NANE members were serious, according to Stoddard, they "must be prepared to recommend an expenditure of possibly half a billion dollars per year on the systematic education of 5 million preschool children" (ibid., 10).

The evolution of NANE was much affected by the Depression and World War II. At the height of the Depression, Stoddard told NANE members that nursery schools could serve as public works programs that would contribute to the national economy and "lead to new construction, new employment, new careers" (*ibid.*, 10). When it was announced at the fifth NANE conference in Toronto, in October of 1933, that the federal government had authorized funds for emergency nursery schools, NANE members were ready to provide support.

In line with the broader, multidisciplinary approach to child advocacy, all nine members of the National Advisory Committee on Nursery Schools appointed to oversee the federal emergency nursery schools belonged to NANE, and most belonged to other organizations as well (Michel 1999). The Committee raised private funds to allow Mary Dabney Davis, on loan from the U.S. Office of Education, to direct the program. Members of NANE also served as regional supervisors, putting in long hours visiting emergency nursery schools throughout the country. By 1934, some 3,000 emergency nursery schools with enrollments of more than 64,000 children had been established. At their peak in 1935, the emergency nursery schools served some 75,000 children (Beatty 1995, 181).

NANE hoped that the emergency nursery schools would become part of the public schools, where many of the programs were located. Stoddard told NANE members, "We have before us the hard task of welding, once and for all, the needs of 5 million preschool children to the great body of public education" (Stoddard 1935, 261). But little welding took place. In fact, Stoddard announced further fragmentation that year, when formation of the Society for Research in Child Development drew many psychologists out of NANE.

Although NANE members believed that emergency nursery schools had proved their worth and deserved permanent and universal application, the Roosevelt administration continued to view the schools as temporary relief measures, and public schools showed little interest in picking up the tab. Mary Dabney Davis and other U.S. Office of Education specialists later concluded that public schools saw emergency nursery schools as separate, expensive, targeted programs that could only be adopted with federal help. The emergency nursery schools "left the double impression that nursery schools were good things for the economically underprivileged but that they were a service which local schools could not undertake without federal aid" (Goodykoontz, Davis, and Gabbard 1947, 61).

Members of NANE were also involved in the design and supervision of federally supported wartime children's centers. Rose Alschuler, who was appointed head of the National Commission for Young Children that advised the centers, traveled across the country giving lectures and advice. The children's centers provided full-day care—and sometimes around-the-clock care—as well as comprehensive services such as medical care and take-out meals. Despite this broader scope, nursery educators made these centers seem like nursery schools. Again, many NANE members hoped that the wartime children's centers would become public preschools, and a few did. But as before, most public schools were unwilling, or perhaps financially unable, to take on the responsibility for educating and caring for young children. NANE membership had fallen below 100, so the association was in no position to mount a national campaign.

Although much reduced in size, NANE continued to seek public support, and it became more involved in politics and public relations efforts. The first *NANE Bulletin,* which appeared in 1945, argued for federal "aid to education which will bring about equal and improved educational opportunity to all children of all ages with maximum state and local control by educational agencies." At the state level, NANE promoted "the extension of public education to include the education of young children" (NANE 1945, 5–7). In California, Docia Zavitkovsky, who directed the Child Care Centers in the Santa Monica Public Schools, provided political leadership for the national organization through her legislation column in the *NANE Bulletin.* Some state chapters of NANE became very involved in political lobbying. The New York State Association for Nursery Education (1939) pushed for a permissive bill for nursery schools in 1939, and NANE members in other states worked on national lobbying efforts.

NANE created a new public relations committee as well as several subcommittees on magazines and newspapers, motion pictures, and radio, which began working hard to gain the attention of the general public. Articles on nursery schools were placed in popular women's journals, such as *Good Housekeeping* and *Glamour,* and in some city newspapers. A popular radio program, "The Baby Institute," developed with the help of an advisory committee of NANE members, disseminated information about nursery schools.

As a result of these efforts, membership began to increase, and in 1964 NANE voted to change its name to the National Association for the Education of Young Children (NAEYC), just as the federal government was gearing up for Project Head Start. Today, the NAEYC is an enormous, national professional association with state and local affiliates all around the country. Many of NAEYC's efforts focus on the accreditation of preschool programs and on professional development and licensing for teachers, including those in public and private nursery schools and child-care centers. The NAEYC is still strongly associated with developmental psychology, as demonstrated by its journal *Young Children* and by its influential manual on developmentally appropriate practice.

The organization has also retained its link to private nursery schools. Although members talk of blurring boundaries between public and private care, and sessions at NAEYC's national conferences address different types of programs, the historical divisions of public versus private child care and nursery schools have continued to shape the organization's dialogue.

## Lessons Learned

What helpful lessons for today's preschool advocates can be learned from the histories of the National Federation of Day Nurseries, the National Kindergarten Association, and the National Association for Nursery Education? Examination of the evolution of these three organizations reveals four common external challenges and a number of different strategies for overcoming these challenges. In addition, the three organizations' histories show how organizational dynamics affected how they carried out their respective missions. These pioneers' experiences in fighting for early childhood care and education in the first part of the 20th century hold important lessons for child advocates today.

### Societal Opposition to Working Mothers

All three organizations faced societal opposition to the idea of mothers of young children working outside the home, a pervasive, controversial debate that continues in American culture. Members of NFDN themselves believed that mothers should not work outside the home except in dire circumstances, and then only temporarily. NFDN's critics also did not see institutionalized child care as a pressing need, in part because a very small percentage of mothers of young children, probably less than 5 percent, worked outside the home during the first decades of the 20th century, and because mothers' pensions were proposed as an alternative (Durst 1989, 11).

Since the mid-1980s, however, more than 50 percent of mothers of children under the age of six have worked outside the home (Gormley 1995, 17). Moreover, today there is a shortage of affordable child care. Lower-income families that pay for child care spend about 33 percent of their income on child care, while middle-income families spend about 6 percent. This differential leaves lower-income families particularly disadvantaged in the private child care market (Bergmann 1999; Hofferth 1999). The growing number of mothers in the labor force and the increasing need for child care bode well for future advocacy efforts.

The organizations each found a way to counter societal opposition to child care outside the home. NKA and NANE avoided some criticism because kindergartens and nursery schools were perceived as education programs for young children rather than as child care for working mothers. NKA and NANE also argued that preschool education enriched young children and that mothers and their children both benefited from being away from each other for discrete periods.

Opinion research shows that the public still views early childhood education more positively than child care (Bales 1999; Blood and Strategies for Children 2000). The extended-day options offered by some nursery schools were very popular, as all-day kindergartens and after-school programs are today, suggesting that advocacy for flexible hours and "wraparound" programs may be a successful approach to combining child care and preschool education. Some researchers argue that blurring the distinction between child care and early childhood education may hinder the public's acceptance of a mother's right to work (Michel 1999). It seems more likely, however, that acceptance of early childhood care and education will promote greater acceptance of working mothers.

## Perceived Effects of Out-of-Home Care on Young Children

Historically, much of society's opposition to mothers working has been based on concerns that out-of-home care may harm young children. This perception, which was a problem particularly for NFDN, continues to affect child care policy, despite studies showing that high-quality child care can help many children (National Center for Early Development and Learning 1999; Zaslow 1991). NKA was able to mitigate criticism by presenting kindergartens as a positive benefit, a "right" for all children. Although kindergarten advocates did not view kindergartens as academic preparation for school, the public increasingly saw them that way, making school readiness another strong rationale for these programs. Kindergarten supporters had a broader vision, seeing kindergartens as preparation for life, and prevention of social problems continues to be a strong rationale for public preschools.

Concern about the effects of outside care on children appears to be less of a barrier today than in the past. There is growing awareness of public preschool programs in others countries, such as France's *ecoles maternelles* (Michel 1999; Richardson 1994; Richardson and Mary 1989). More U.S. school officials and politicians are promoting universal preschool education as a way of boosting early literacy and later academic achievement. The American Federation of Teachers ranked providing high-quality preschool education as its first priority for 2001 (Feldman 2000); the National Education Association ranked strengthening early childhood education as its third goal (Chase 2001). Some eligible school districts are choosing to use federal Title I funds for educationally disadvantaged children to support school readiness efforts in public preschools.

This heightened interest suggests that concerns about child care's possible ill effects on young children have abated, although quality control will always be a major issue. While school readiness is a persuasive rationale for early childhood care and education, there is increasing pressure on kindergarten and preschool teachers to meet requirements for academic standards and accountability testing. Preschool advocates should be cautious about employing excessively didactic teaching methods, which could spark adverse public reaction to early education efforts (Elkind 1987), but they should also be aware that promoting early childhood care and education as part of comprehensive education reform efforts is a promising approach.

NANE tried to use scientific research as a defense against concerns about the effects of preschool on children and to prove that early education is beneficial. Although research results can persuade some politicians and well-educated voters, public opinion analysis shows that scientific arguments for early childhood care and education are not well understood by the public (Bales 1999). Findings may also be exaggerated, as was the case with the much touted "new brain research" and the impact of Head Start on IQ, leading to unrealistic expectations and then disillusionment (Bruer 1999; Vinovskis 1999; Zigler and Muenchow 1992). Because the literature on the long-term effects of preschool education is mixed (Barnett 1995), overreliance on scientific evidence seems ill-advised.

## Perceived Stigma and Effects on Family Rights

A third roadblock to these organizations' success was the stigma associated with public preschools, and their perceived infringement on private family rights. Members of NFDN would not have placed their own children in one of their day nurseries; they considered these programs appropriate only for "other people's children" (Rothman 1973). By contrast, one of NKA's main goals was to destigmatize urban kindergartens, originally seen as poverty-track programs. Most of the private nursery schools run by NANE members served children from upper- and middle-class backgrounds, although some of its nursery schools served poor children. Most preschool programs will probably continue to be segregated along racial and social class lines, as are most K–12 schools, but promoting universal, rather than targeted, preschools will help ease this problem. However, the pressing need to provide preschool education for more children from low-income families suggests that advocacy efforts should use targeted programs as an interim strategy and promote universalization as soon as possible.

Concern about intrusion into the private domain of the family is largely ideological. Preschool education involves the implicit and explicit teaching of values that may not always concur with individual family views (Joffee 1977). While media analysis indicates that privacy-related objections to preschool education are waning (EDK Associates 1999), some conservative groups continue to criticize the push for universal preschools. But conservatives are not the only ones concerned about private child-rearing becoming a state function; some liberals and progressives express similar reservations (Bloch and Popkewitz 2000; Joffee 1977). Preschool advocates should be respectful of these differing views and wary of efforts that imply compulsory attendance or that are seen as promoting family dependency. Advocacy that both emphasizes public access to programs (rather than direct provision of services) and encourages the participation of public and private preschools has a greater chance of being effective. The existence of a large lobby group for private preschools leaves little space for a unilateral approach.

## Cost of Early Childhood Care and Education Programs

The fourth issue challenging all three organizations was cost. The cost of universal preschools is in fact high, a barrier that preschool advocates have not been able to circumvent. One source estimates that it would cost $30 billion per year to provide two years of high-quality preschool education to children from low-income families (Sawhill 1999, 7). Most estimates for providing high-quality early childhood care and education for all three- and four-year-olds fall in the $40–50 billion range; some are considerably higher.

The history of NKA and NANE suggests that this money is unlikely to come from the federal government, except during times of perceived national emergency (Takanishi 1977). Congressional focus on children living at or near the poverty level remains high, and concern about school readiness and early literacy has moved up on the national agenda. Moreover, the amount of discussion about increased preschool funding in both political parties suggests that funding attitudes may be changing. The impressive increase in Head Start funding, from $2.5 billion in 1992 to $5.3 billion in 2000, made the program a close third in federal education programs, behind Title I grants for the disadvantaged and special education (OECD 2000, 18, 24). The budget surplus and the current decline in birth rates may make preschool advocacy easier at the national level.

As in the past, preschool advocacy continues to be most successful at the state level. Many preschool advocates seeking new sources of funding and attempting to diversify costs are watching Georgia's Universal Prekindergarten program as a model. The program was launched in 1993 by Governor Zell Miller and is underwritten by lottery revenues. By 1998, the program had succeeded in covering the costs for prekindergarten programs for 60,000 children, or about 80 percent of Georgia's four-year-old population (Raden 1999, 21). Although Alabama voters rejected a similar plan, South Carolina recently passed an education lottery.

In some states, preschool funding is embedded within education budgets, a strategy that is probably more desirable over the long run than reliance on outside sources (Gallagher, Clayton, and Heinemeier 2001). New York passed legislation for universal programs in 1997 (Hicks, Lekies, and Cochran 1999). But so far, the public preschool initiatives funded by state taxes in the New York tristate area (New York, New Jersey, and Connecticut) are primarily targeted to low-income children and underperforming school districts.

Some public school systems have begun charging tuition for preschool programs in order to attract middle-class parents. In January 2001, Chicago Public Schools began offering full-day preschool programs for three- and four-year-olds in select schools. Tuition for these programs is $5,700 per year, with a sliding-fee scale for parents who cannot afford to pay the full amount. Initiatives in Illinois, Massachusetts, and other states and cities suggest that focusing advocacy in areas that can promote inter- and intrastate awareness, which NKA often did, may be a promising approach to building local capacity and infrastructure.

## Organization-Specific Challenges: Structure, Leadership, and Collaboration

Other lessons can be learned by comparing the organizational strategies of NFDN, NKA, and NANE. Differences in centralization, leadership style, governmental relationships, and collaboration all influenced how each organization achieved success.

The relatively decentralized structure of NFDN, which had a national office and independent boards scattered around the country, made it difficult for the organization to mount a national campaign. This structure, however, allowed for a good deal of local variation and autonomy. NKA, by contrast, functioned effectively by networking with other organizations, but it was sometimes too dependent on Bessie Locke's one-woman national bandwagon. NANE (now the NAEYC) began as a national professional group and gradually brought affiliates into its fold. Although regional, state, and local NAEYC chapters and the national office engage in some political advocacy, the organization still functions primarily as a professional organization for teachers. Of the three organizations, NKA was probably the closest to the current model of national advocacy groups. Like today's groups, it had no formal membership but relied instead on paid organizers. Its success, however, largely reflected its ability to work with other organizations at the grassroots level, something that modern professional advocacy groups sometimes find difficult.

The three organizations' leadership styles reflected their goals. NFDN was an old-style charity of elite society women trying to serve the public good. The aura of noblesse oblige surrounding the organization meant that some of its members were likely as interested in the social cachet of serving on a board as they were in the services offered. Of course, NFDN members' accomplishments should not be dismissed; wealthy women volunteers continue to be a central group promoting children's causes.

NKA, a forerunner of a today's political interest groups, was directly involved in political lobbying around a single issue, and was directed by an executive secretary who understood the importance of face-to-face advocacy and who knew how to use the media effectively, something

THE POLITICS OF PRESCHOOL ADVOCACY 185

early childhood care and education advocates are trying to do today. The NKA model and the success of public preschool programs in Georgia and elsewhere suggests that strong leadership, usually on the part of the governor, is critical (Gallagher et al. 2001). NKA also benefited from remaining independent from teachers' groups, which were continuously embroiled in pedagogical controversies, and by maintaining good relations with these groups.

NANE adopted a professional leadership style and relied on a hierarchy of academic experts, using a structure similar to that of today's research foundations. This strategy is attractive to middle- and upper-class parents as well as to corporate leaders and business groups, all of whom tend to be very influential in the policymaking arena. This strategy is less successful, however, for building a broad constituency among parents, grandparents, and other taxpayers in less-educated segments of society, where child care needs are often most pressing. As Doug Imig (this volume) describes, grassroots advocacy is an important and appealing strategy. But it is also a difficult and time-consuming one, and less-advantaged groups may be unable to find ways to be politically active. This gap in accessibility suggests that preschool advocates should try to attract as wide a constituency as possible.

All three organizations experienced difficulties in dealing with governmental agencies. For example, NFDN faced significant opposition from the Children's Bureau. Both NKA and NANE were able to overcome some governmental resistance by sponsoring public-private partnerships; in these arrangements, the organization paid the salaries of staff who essentially functioned as federal employees. The current atmosphere of devolution and deregulation suggests that supporting local partnering efforts and public-private initiatives are effective strategies.

Finally, child advocates continue to operate in a competitive environment. Historically, NFDN, NKA, and NANE competed with each other to provide early childhood care and education services. Many other children's organizations, child-related advocacy groups, and foundations also competed to find and capture a "needs niche" that would allow them to control a particular type of service. While understandable, given the decentralized nature of education and public welfare in America, such competition tended to fragment child advocacy efforts (Steiner 1976; Kagan 1991).

The recent increase in collaborative models and state and local partnerships suggests that greater integration is beginning to take place. But the lure of competition is difficult to overcome, and the presence of many providers does have some positive effects, including the stimulation of new ideas. Moreover, coalitions can be hard to establish and maintain, given the patchwork of existing organizations and agencies. Making comprehensive, integrated services available to young children and families should be a strategic priority for all preschool advocates.

Among these three organizations, the focused, flexible strategies of NKA appear to have been the most successful. NKA formed coalitions with other organizations and was able to work with different groups at the national, state, and local levels. Not all of these partnerships held up in the face of intense competition for funding, but NKA remained inclusive and persistent throughout its history. Today, no single-issue interest group is promoting universal early childhood care and education as effectively as NKA promoted universal kindergartens. If one lesson can be learned here, it is that intensive, explicit political advocacy that links national, state, and grassroots efforts can achieve wide reform.

The recent increases in federal and state funding for early childhood education and care will require more coordinated political advocacy to maintain and monitor the progress of different programs. As the chapters in this volume demonstrate, competing priorities will continue to vie for public funds. Advocates will need to convince the public that continuing to increase investment in preschool education is a wise choice. Supplying universal access to high-quality early childhood care and education will be an important goal. The histories of the National Federation of Day Nurseries, National Kindergarten Association, and National Association for Nursery Education demonstrate that advocates for early childhood care and education have made great progress through ingenuity, persistence, and their commitment to children and mothers. Different approaches to organizational structure, leadership, and collaboration greatly influenced the outcomes of these organizations' advocacy work. Their successes and challenges can serve as helpful models to today's proponents of early childhood care and education.

## NOTES

1. I am grateful for the comments of Emily Cahan, Ruby Takanishi, and Sheldon H. White. I want to especially thank Ruby Takanishi for involving me in this project and for sending me many helpful papers and articles. I also appreciate the comments of the other

authors in this volume, participants at the Conference on the Roles of Child Advocacy Organizations held at the Urban Institute in December 1999, and the outside reviewer.

2.  I am indebted to Sonya Michel and Elizabeth Rose, upon whose research much of my information about the NFDN is based. Most NFDN records are at the New York Public Library; many are on microfilm. Some NFDN records are held at the Social Welfare History Archives at the University of Minnesota. Further information on NFDN records and documentation is available from the author on request.

3.  The NKA records are held in Special Collections at Milbank Memorial Library, Teachers College, Columbia University, Manuscript Group 16. I am especially indebted to David Ment and to the gracious staff of the archives, who made my stay informative and pleasurable. The NKA began as the National Association for the Promotion of Kindergarten Education. Its name was changed to the National Kindergarten Association in 1911. Further information on NKA records and documentation is available from the author on request.

4.  Information on South Carolina is from the "Executive Secretary's Report for March 19," 1919; on Utah and Massachusetts, from the "Annual Report for 1926–29," on North Carolina from the NKA's "1915 Annual Report." See endnote 3 for more information on the NKA's archives.

The first public kindergarten class in Boston was short-lived, although Boston did establish public kindergartens in 1888. St. Louis started public kindergartens in 1872.

5.  *Report of the Executive Secretary,* May 7, 1990.

6.  I am indebted to Dorothy Hewes, who chaired the NAEYC Organizational History and Archives Committee that wrote "NAEYC's First Half Century, 1926–1976," upon which I based much of my understanding of the early days of the NANE. Dorothy holds a wealth of knowledge on the history of early childhood education and generously shared information with me, including NANE files. The NAEYC archives are housed in the Special Collections at the Cunningham Memorial Library at Indiana State University. Further information on NANE records and documentation is available on request from the author.

# REFERENCES

Addams, Jane. 1905. "Day Nurseries—Do They Foster Parental Irresponsibility?" In "The Day Nursery Discussed by Miss Addams." *Charities* 15 (December 30): 410–11.

Bales, Susan. 1999. "Communicating Early Childhood Education: Using Strategic Frame Analysis to Understand Child Care as a Public Issue." Washington, D.C.: Benton Foundation.

Barnett, W. Steven. 1995. "Long-Term Effects of Early Childhood Programs on Cognitive and School Outcomes." *The Future of Children* 5 (3): 25–50.

Beatty, Barbara. 1999. "Bessie Locke." In *American National Biography,* edited by John N. Garraty (798–99). New York: Oxford University Press.

———. 1995. *Preschool Education in America: The Culture of Young Children from the Colonial Era to the Present.* New Haven: Yale University Press.

Bergmann, Barbara R. 1999. "Making Child Care Affordable." *The Silent Crisis in U.S. Child Care: The Annals of the American Academy of Political and Social Science* 563 (May): 208–19.

Bloch, Marianne N., and Thomas Popkewitz. 2000. "Constructing the Parent, Teacher, and Child: Discourses of Development." In *The Politics of Early Childhood Education,* edited by Lourdes Diaz Soto (7–32). New York: Peter Lang.

Blood, Margaret, and Strategies for Children. 2000. *Our Youngest Children: Massachusetts Voters and Opinion Leaders Speak Out on Their Care and Education.* Boston: The Stride Rite Foundation.

Bruer, John T. 1999. *The Myth of the First Three Years: A New Understanding of Early Brain Development and Lifelong Learning.* New York: The Free Press.

Chase, Bob. 2001. "A New Deal for Children." *Education Week* (January 17): 9.

Davis, Mary Dabney. 1964. "How NANE Began." *Young Children* 2 (2): 106–09.

Dodge, Mrs. Arthur M. 1897. "The Development of the Day Nursery Idea." *The Outlook* 56 (May): 60–64.

Durst, Anne. 1989. "Day Nurseries and Wage-Earning Mothers in the United States, 1890–1930." Ph.D. dissertation, University of Wisconsin-Madison.

EDK Associates. 1999. "Evaluation of the Media Strategies Group: A Five-Year Effort to Unify the Voices of Child Care Advocates." New York: EDK Associates.

Elkind, David. 1987. *Miseducation: Preschoolers at Risk.* New York: Knopf.

Feldman, Sandra. 2000. "A Holiday Wish List." *New York Times,* "Week in Review" (December 17): 9.

Frankel, Dr. Lee K. 1905. "Why Is It Necessary for the Mothers to Work?" *Charities* 14 (9): 777.

Gallagher, James J., Jenna R. Clayton, and Sarah E. Heinemeier. 2001. *Education for Four-Year-Olds: State Initiatives.* Chapel Hill: University of North Carolina, FPG Child Development Center, National Center for Early Development and Learning.

Goodykoontz, Bess, Mary Dabney Davis, and Hazel F. Gabbard. 1947. "Recent History and Present Status of Education for Young Children," *Forty-Sixth Yearbook of the National Society for the Study of Education,* vol. 2, *Early Childhood Education.* Chicago: University of Chicago Press.

Gormley, William T., Jr. 1995. *Everybody's Children: Child Care as a Public Problem.* Washington, D.C.: Brookings Institution.

Hewes, Dorothy W. 1976. "Patty Smith Hill-Pioneer for Young Children." *Young Children* 31 (4): 297–306.

Hicks, Susan A., Kristi S. Lekies, and Mon Cochran. 1999. *Promising Practices: New York State Universal Prekindergarten.* Ithaca: The Cornell Early Childhood Program, College of Human Ecology, Cornell University.

Hofferth, Sandra L. 1999. "Child Care, Maternal Employment, and Public Policy." *The Silent Crisis in U.S. Child Care: The Annals of the American Academy of Political and Social Science* 563 (May): 20–38.

Joffee, Carol. 1977. *Friendly Intruders: Childcare Professionals and Family Life.* Berkeley: University of California Press.

Kagan, Sharon L. 1991. *United We Stand: Collaboration for Child Care and Early Education Services.* New York: Teachers College Press.

Locke, Bessie. 1947. "Highlights of the Bill." In "Report of the Executive Secretary," May 28. National Kindergarten Association Collection, Box 7, Folder 8.
———. 1935. "Report of the Executive Secretary," November 14. National Kindergarten Association Collection, Box 7, Folder 6.
Michel, Sonya. 1999. *Children's Interests/Mothers' Rights: The Shaping of America's Child Care Policy.* New Haven: Yale University Press.
Muenchow, Susan. 1996. "The Role of Media in Child and Family Policy." In *Children, Families, and Government: Preparing for the 21st Century,* edited by Edward F. Zigler, Sharon Lynn Kagan, and Nancy Hall. Cambridge: Cambridge University Press.
National Association for Nursery Education (NANE). 1945. *Bulletin of the National Association for Nursery Education* 1 (1).
National Center for Early Development and Learning. 1999. "Children of the Cost, Quality, and Outcomes Study Go to School," *Executive Summary.* Chapel Hill: National Center for Early Development and Learning.
National Kindergarten Association. 1911–63. *Annual Reports for 1914, 1909–1911, 1925, 1947, 1954, 1963.* New York: National Kindergarten Association.
New York State Association for Nursery Education. 1939. "Report of the First Annual Conference." New York State Association for Nursery Education.
OECD Country Note. 2000. *Early Childhood Education and Care Policy in the United States of America.* Washington, D.C.: Organization for Economic and Cooperative Development, Office of Education Research and Improvement.
Raden, Anthony. 1999. "Universal Prekindergarten in Georgia: A Case Study of Georgia's Lottery-Funded Pre-K Program." Working paper series. New York: Foundation for Child Development.
Richardson, Gail. 1994. "A Welcome for Every Child: How France Protects Maternal and Child Health—A New Frame of Reference for the United States." Arlington, Va.: National Center for Education in Maternal and Child Health.
Richardson, Gail, and Elisabeth Marx. 1989. *A Welcome for Every Child: How France Achieves Quality in Child Care: Practical Ideas for the United States.* New York: The French-American Foundation.
Rose, Elizabeth. 1999. *A Mother's Job: The History of Child Care, 1890–1960.* New York: Oxford University Press.
Rothman, Sheila. 1973. "Other People's Children: The Day Care Experience in America," *Public Interest* 30 (winter): 11–27.
Sawhill, Isabel V. 1999. "Investing in Children." *Brookings Children's Roundtable Report* 1 (April): 1–8. Washington, D.C.: Brookings Institution.
Schlossman, Steven L. 1981. "Philanthropy and the Gospel of Child Development." *History of Education Quarterly* 21 (fall).
Senn, Milton. J. E. 1975. "Insights on the Child Development Movement in the United States." *Monographs of the Society for Research in Child Development* 40 (3–4).
Steiner, Gilbert Y. 1976. *The Children's Cause.* Washington, D.C.: Brookings Institution.
Stoddard, George. 1935. "Emergency Nursery Schools on Trial." *Childhood Education* 11 (March): 260–63.
———. 1931. "Conferences Issues." *Proceedings of the Fourth Conference of the National Association for Nursery Education.* New York: National Association for Nursery Education.

Takanishi, Ruby. 1977. "Federal Involvement in Early Childhood Education (1933–1973): The Need for Historical Perspectives." *Current Issues in Early Childhood Education* 1: 139–63.

Tank, Robert. 1980. "Young Children, Society, and Family in America since the 1820s: The Evolution of Health, Education, and Child Care Programs for Preschool Children." Ph.D. diss., University of Michigan.

U.S. Bureau of the Census. 1913. "Abstract of the Census with Supplement for Massachusetts." *Thirteenth Census of the United States, Taken in the Year 1910.* Washington, D.C.: Government Printing Office.

Vinovskis, Maris A. 1999. *History and Educational Policymaking.* New Haven, Conn.: Yale University Press.

Zaslow, M. 1991. "Variation in Child Care Quality and Its Implications for Children." *Journal of Social Issues* 47: 125–38.

Zigler, Edward, and Susan Muenchow. 1992. *Head Start: The Inside Story of America's Most Successful Educational Experiment.* New York: Basic Books.

# 7

# Mobilizing Parents and Communities for Children

*Doug Imig*

On the eve of the June 1996 Stand for Children Rally in Washington, D.C., *Time* magazine ran a cover story documenting the plight of American children and asking why there was so little public outrage over children's welfare (Gleick 1996). Responding to this question, Marian Wright Edelman, president of the Children's Defense Fund, predicted that the Stand for Children rally would be the first step in a nationwide mobilization on behalf of children. Edelman explained,

> I knew it would take . . . 25 years to seed a movement. You just have to keep planting and watering and fertilizing. And then, when it is time, you do what you have to do. But you have to stand up—win, lose, or draw. And it's time (Gleick 1996, 31).

Not long after the Stand for Children rally, Theda Skocpol offered a view on how such a national mobilization might gain momentum. Reviewing the success of earlier waves of children's advocacy, she argued that mobilizing parents "is the best route toward effective advocacy for children in the United States today" (Skocpol 1997, 14).

Similarly, Hewlett and West believe that parents stand ready to demand major changes in child and family policy. They argue that the concerns of parents cut across racial and economic lines, and that this shared concern will soon galvanize a "parent's movement that crosses the divides of race, class, and gender" in this country (Hewlett and West 1998, 257).

These calls for a widespread political mobilization of parents and communities on behalf of America's children are tantalizing. But the national mobilization these researchers describe has yet to materialize, even as the number of children endangered by poverty, unstable home lives, and unraveling communities remains high.

Since 1974, when children became the poorest group of Americans, child poverty has deepened (U.S. Congress 1985; Kagan and Rubin 1998). In 1997, 14.7 million children (21 percent of all children) lived in poverty, nearly double the poverty rate of the elderly. And the percentages are significantly higher for minority children and children born to single mothers (KIDS COUNT 2000). These figures have shocked individuals across the political spectrum. As one advocate observes, "they offend our sense of what is good, decent and just, and . . . they threaten our future as a prosperous society" (Schorr 1993, 78–79).

Why, five years after the first Stand for Children rally, have Americans remained silent despite repeated calls to action on behalf of children? This question has no simple answer. However, a review of the factors required to stimulate social movement mobilization, along with examples of past advocacy successes, can help us begin to assess the current state of child advocacy.

## Waves of Child Activity: The Influence of Mobilization Factors

Americans have not always been so complacent about the plight of children. Over the past century, concerted nationwide reform movements have emerged several times in order to fight to strengthen the families and communities in which children live. These waves of social reform led to the development of the Settlement House, the national movements for kindergartens and day schools, compulsory public schooling, passage of child labor laws, consideration of mother's pensions and governmental support for prenatal care, the development of federal programs such as Aid for Dependent Children, and the War on Poverty. In each of these waves of reform, children's issues, however briefly, captured the public's imagination and, in turn, leveraged political concessions.

Children's concerns were defined and given political voice in the context of a broader wave of social movement mobilization. The resulting public policies bore the mark of social protest. As one observer notes, government policies for children were "created not only in the context of suffering but also in the turbulence of vociferous protest" (Gordon 1994, 209).

In theory, widespread concern with a policy problem in and of itself should lead the media, concerned experts, and the public to rally around an issue. Mobilized by their shared concerns, interest groups and social movement organizations should cohere and attract members, funding, prestige, access to policymaking, celebrity and elite support, and policy legitimacy (Dahl 1956; Truman 1951; Wilson 1995).

In practice, however, the link between policy problems and political mobilization is much more tenuous, and it only imperfectly reflects enduring social and political inequities. The emergence of social movements—including the shape and activity of movement organizations, the venues for action available to activists, and the reception they receive—depends on many factors. For advocacy organizations, effective networking and dynamic leadership are essential to successful mobilization. More broadly, factors such as patterns of social change, dramatic and critical events, shifting political landscapes, the efforts of influential allies, policy shifts, and the focus of public attention all affect how strongly a society mobilizes in response to a cause.

## Networks

Social movements tend to develop along the lines of communication and organization established by existing organizational networks. These defined structures allow individuals to form a collective identity and to recognize their shared grievances. This commonality serves as the basis for further organization and collective action (McAdam 1982; Tarrow 1998). For example, the successful efforts of children's advocates in the first two decades of this century were built upon networks of organizations operating at national, state, and community levels (Skocpol 1997; Skocpol and Dickert, this volume). These networks provided an infrastructure for mobilizing community support for children's policy, and also offered a route through which to translate public sentiment into both state and federal policy agendas.

Communities also need networks of interaction and engagement at the local level. When members of a community come together, they invariably discover shared concerns and establish constructive patterns of interaction. The venue for this interaction is probably much less important than the fact that the interaction takes place. By establishing networks of association, the group naturally arrives at norms of "generalized reciprocity" (Putnam 2000). Local organizing networks are stronger in some contexts than in others. For example, strong local networks tend to form around existing community assets, particularly in faith-based communities and neighborhood schools (Cortes 1996). In other cases, networks emerge when a neighborhood bands together against an external threat, such as gentrification or urban renewal (Shaw 1996; Stoecker 1994).

### Entrepreneurial Leadership

Social movements are fueled by the strategic vision and political acumen of activist leaders. Amidei (1993) emphasizes the importance of strategic leadership in the campaign for federal child-care provisions in the late 1980s. The campaign was successful, she argues, precisely because advocates chose to concentrate their efforts on building a sophisticated, national, grassroots campaign. Charismatic, tireless leadership and managerial acumen can help organizations thrive and gain access to policymakers (Pope 1989; Salisbury 1984). In short, strategic action and effective leadership are essential to translating general discontent into a specific political agenda.

### Social Trends

The fight for children's rights has often occurred during tumultuous periods in U.S. history. For example, the Great Depression brought record rates of adult unemployment and heightened public and political support for child labor restrictions (Hawes 1991). The women's suffrage movement also raised the public's awareness of children's rights. As women fought for the right to vote, national political attention helped define an agenda of "women's issues," which included mother's pensions, child care, and public education (Amenta 1998; Skocpol 1992).

In recent decades, the percentage of American women in the labor force has increased—from 25 percent in 1950 to more than 65 percent in 1998. In addition, the growing number of one-parent families, the recession of the late 1980s, and declines in real wages among men have led to an increase in the number of middle-class dual-earner families. The presence of more women in the workforce has given specific issues, such as the quality and cost of child care, greater political priority than in the past (Michel 1999; Wildavsky 1998). But the greater number of relatively affluent women in the workforce may also have helped diffuse political support for income assistance to low-income mothers (Imig 1996a, 1996b). Indeed, a marked difference in policy toward low-income mothers has occurred over the past three decades. In 1969, President Nixon vetoed the Family Support Act, in part because of fears that it would encourage poor mothers to leave their children and enter the workforce. Today, however, welfare-to-work programs mandate that low-income mothers with young children return to work.

## Critical Events

Certain "triggers" can lead to surges in social movement mobilization and policy attention. In 1911, a fire at the Triangle Shirtwaist Company in New York City led to the death of more than 140 young women and children. According to historians, that critical disaster focused media and public attention on child labor and unsafe factory conditions, and contributed to passage of the 1916 Keating-Owen Act, an attempt to regulate child labor (Hawes 1991; Sarbaugh-Thompson and Zald 1989). Similarly, the outbreak of World War I proved critical in sparking concerns over the "Americanization" of immigrant children, and helped promote the adoption of kindergarten programs across the country (Beatty 1995; Beatty, this volume; Skocpol and Dickert, this volume). In the 1950s, pediatricians' increasing use of X-ray machines, along with legislation mandating that pediatricians and social workers report instances of suspected mistreatment, led to widespread public awareness of child abuse and to child-protection campaigns (Besharov and Laumann 1996).

## Political Alignments

The emergence and power of social movements also depends on the level of uncertainty within dominant political coalitions. When elections are highly contested or existing political alliances are unstable, parties and candidates must reach out to less institutionalized or less well-known voices in an attempt to establish a winning, stable power base (Hansen 1991; Piven and Cloward 1979). Children's advocates can use these periods of electoral instability to gain leverage and amplify their voices in politics.

The political uncertainty inherent in granting women the right to vote, for example, challenged the power base of many political figures and caused them to devote more attention to child and family policies. As they competed for these new votes, political parties began to give serious consideration to such issues as child labor, infant health, and maternal health policies (Hawes 1991; Sutton 1996). Similarly, the massive dislocations caused by the Great Depression increased support for child labor regulation, prompted the creation of the New Deal, and expanded the federal government's role in social services. The civil rights and antiwar movements of the 1960s forced political elites to respond to domestic unrest; their reconfigured agendas led to the Great Society and War on Poverty initiatives.

## Influential Allies

Social movements draw power and legitimacy from their mass base, but they also gain shape, find direction, and acquire needed resources by attracting the support of allies, including faith-based communities, philanthropic foundations, and members of the media. The historical relationship between children's advocates and their powerful allies is a critical and complicated one. Children themselves are represented in politics only by proxy. Moreover, the marginalization and political silence of low-income communities mean that those families with children most at risk are doubly removed from direct participation in politics.

Medical and family-care professionals have been powerful allies to the children's movement. In particular, the professionalization and institutionalization of pediatrics, social work, and public education have influenced child advocacy (Michel 1999). For example, Barbara Beatty (this volume) demonstrates ways that professional groups and factions within particular professions fought for different approaches to early childhood care and education policy in the early 1900s. Similarly, tensions between medical doctors and social workers fueled debates over maternal and infant health policy in the early 20th century (Skocpol 1992; Stone 1996).

Some of child advocates' most powerful allies have come from within government agencies. Edwin Amenta (1998) outlines the importance of government supporters in the initial development of the Aid for Dependent Children program (ADC), which later became Aid to Families with Dependent Children (AFDC). ADC, he argues, was largely a product of a reform-oriented regime and the efforts of state policy administrators working under the aegis of the Children's Bureau. More recently, Georgia

Governor Zell Miller and his staff built a universal prekindergarten program funded by lottery revenues (Radin 1999). These examples suggest that political elites can successfully organize a program that, once understood and implemented, will generate both public commitment and political support.

Efforts driven by powerful political figures alone, however, are more difficult to sustain than those built through widespread community investment. Amenta found that the lack of a mass support base ultimately led to lower levels of funding and administrative support for ADC than for other programs with strong bureaucratic *and* social movement support (Amenta 1998, 257). Furthermore, causes that are championed by government agencies may actually suffer a loss of public support. When the government appears responsive to a cause—even if that responsiveness constitutes symbolic concessions—the public may see political action as irrelevant (Piven and Cloward 1979).

## The Policy Environment

Public policy agendas and the political rhetoric of the times also shape the opportunities available to advocates. Highly charged debate and the presence of visible antagonists, for example, can serve as lightning rods for mobilization (Imig 1998). Marian Wright Edelman pointed to this dynamic in building support for the 1996 Stand For Children rally: "Without Newt Gingrich . . . we would never have been able to bring folks together in this way" (Gleick 1996, 31).

Mobilization is much more likely to occur when well-established programs and the groups they serve are threatened, or when new policy initiatives raise expectations that advocacy efforts can succeed. In Michigan in 1999, the governor's office planned to simplify and streamline the state's licensing requirements for child care centers. Children's advocates believed that these efforts would weaken Michigan's standards, which ranked among the toughest in the industry. Within a month, advocates had delivered 3,200 petitions calling for protection of the child care standards to Governor Engler, and almost every newspaper in the state had endorsed the advocates' cause. Governor Engler agreed to pull the proposal for reconsideration and revision (Imig 1999).

New initiatives can also fuel mobilization and inspire activism. The formation of the Children's Bureau in 1912 gave child advocates an avenue for expanding the federal government's role in child policy. Similarly,

President Johnson's declaration of the War on Poverty both legitimized vigorous federal intervention into welfare politics in the United States and expanded the range of federal grants available to advocates for social justice (Katz 1989). During its existence, the Select Committee on Children, Youth, and Families provided both an opportunity and a target to advocates eager to gain congressional attention.

## Raising Public Consciousness

Ultimately, social movements' power lies in their ability to mobilize mass public support. Doing so requires that advocates present a cause that resonates with the public and create an agenda capable of moving people from complacency to action. William Gamson and Adria Goodson (2000) note that the causes that have been most successful in mobilizing people for collective action are characterized by *injustice, agency,* and *identity.* Injustice, they explain, raises the moral indignation the public feels over a social and political wrong. Agency refers to the awareness that conditions can be altered through collective action. Identity occurs when a group defines itself collectively against a common target.

The media are critical agents to the process of raising public support. Extended media coverage of a policy issue can help generate resources for advocates and relax barriers to government access. Media coverage can also link social problems to particular causes as well as to potential solutions (Stone 1997). Media attention can rally supporters around certain positions and behind policy demands. But advocates seldom control the way the media frames events, and they certainly cannot control how the public will interpret coverage of these events.

Public awareness is also shaped by the efforts of foundations, research groups, and government agencies. For example, the Annie E. Casey Foundation's annual KIDS COUNT *Data Book* and the Federal Interagency Forum on Child and Family Statistics' publication *America's Children: Key National Indicators of Well-Being* establish a comprehensive picture of the conditions in which American children live. The Benton Foundation's Connect for Kids E-Zine provides a weekly newsletter on advocacy efforts for communities and families. Goal One of the National Education Goals effort provided a political dimension to the growing academic consensus surrounding the importance of early childhood care and education. As Kagan and Rubin (1998) argue,

"Goal One served as a beacon of hope that the national posture towards young children would change not only for those who had long been committed to the well-being of young children, but also for those who may have been somewhat skeptical of the importance of the early years."

## Opportunity Structures and Public Policy for Children

Returning, then, to the central question of this chapter, do we stand on the brink of a social movement for children in this country? Under current social and political conditions, it will be difficult to build and sustain a social movement for children.

This assessment is shared by many individuals in the child advocacy field. As a Michigan advocate observes, community mobilization "is not happening in any systematic way . . . and it has to happen to move us off the dime." A member of the executive staff of the National Parent Teacher Association offers a similar opinion: "Today, there really is no grassroots mobilization for kids in this country." And a leader in the Children's Aid Society agrees: "Communities that have mobilized around children's issues are few and far between . . . and without bottom-up organizing, not much is possible" (Imig 1999; 2000a; 2000b).

Today, children's advocates face ambiguous, at times antagonistic, political conditions. State and national policy objectives often conflict, the public is divided over policy priorities, and the role that government should play in social policy is debated on all sides. Despite the growing number of children living in poverty, both state and federal support structures are slipping. The 1996 phase-out of AFDC marked the end of a guaranteed minimum income for poor families. This end came after the program had already been cut by more than 42 percent from 1972 to 1992 (see Rosenbaum and Sonosky, this volume). And political initiatives of the 1990s, including the Contract with America and the Personal Responsibility and Work Opportunity Reconciliation Act, revealed a desire to reduce the federal government's role in social policymaking. According to one commentator, both politicians and the public increasingly view the social safety net as an unwanted form of paternalism (Starobin 1999).

Child advocacy efforts also face an uphill battle because the public itself appears conflicted about the needs of children and families. Survey after survey has shown that Americans are concerned about the problems facing children. Parents, across income and racial groups, worry about a wide range of questions, including the amount of time they are forced to spend away from their children, the negative influences in their children's lives, the high cost of quality day care, and the uncertain future their children face (Hewlett and West 1998). The public is also frightened by youth crime, and parents worry that other adults are not taking responsibility for raising their own children. At the same time, the public is unsure whether government should play a larger role in child policy (Public Agenda 1999a; 1999b; Yankelovich 1998).

This difficult social landscape is further complicated by religious differences. Roughly one-third of all Americans identify themselves as fundamentalist Christians. Although this group identifies strongly with a pro-family political orientation, it is generally opposed to social policies that accommodate or seem to promote nontraditional family structures, mothers in the labor force, or expanded reliance on child care. As a result, this cohort is alienated from a significant share of child advocacy efforts (Hardisty 1999; Media Strategies Group 1999; Talbot 2000).

As the economic and social threats to children have increased, the political power base of families—particularly among families in need—has declined. This decrease in influence reflects two developments. First, the percent of families with children under the age of 18 is shrinking and is expected to drop from approximately 46 percent of American households in 1998 to less than 42 percent of households by the year 2010 (U.S. Census Bureau 1998).

Second, the emergence of a growing geographic divide between poor and middle-class families has diffused support for children. This is significant because the mobilization of social movements requires that individuals begin to identify, and take action, collectively. According to the current pattern of American urban development, most middle-class parents live in the suburbs, far removed from the concerns that urban families face (Waste 1998). This geographic distribution undercuts the potential to mobilize parents around a shared identity. Moreover, poverty and joblessness are increasingly concentrated in America's central cities, while political power is increasingly concentrated in the suburbs, which have higher population growth rates and higher tax bases (Moe and Wilkie 1997). The effect of this geographic separation is an urban housing pattern that divides Americans along racial and economic class lines. These residential patterns undermine efforts to unite parents as a broad-based coalition or political force for children.

## Efforts to Mobilize Communities for Children

The difficulty of mobilizing concerned citizens in a fragmented, contentious policy environment does not mean that advocacy efforts are unproductive. These efforts may be, in fact, the best way to push beyond the current policy impasse. Political opportunity structures, by their nature, are constantly in flux. As demonstrated by the success of the civil rights, women's rights, and antiwar movements, the process of mobilizing social support around a cause is itself a significant factor in shifting opportunity structures (Tarrow 1998). Efforts to organize advocacy efforts are critical to building collective identification, a necessary first step in sparking collective action and mobilizing success.

A number of smaller, promising initiatives demonstrate how mobilization efforts have the power to effect change even without the support of an overarching child advocacy movement. Although dozens of organizations list efforts to mobilize parents and communities for children among their principal concerns,[1] few of these organizations' activities are explicitly focused on the political work necessary to build a nationwide movement for children. A review of these organizations, however, reveals several important exceptions.

The first exception is the set of organizations concentrating on community capacity-building. These groups are helping link social service providers and families, and are creating community-based organizational networks that may serve as critical resources for a national children's movement. By arguing that children cannot succeed without the active support of their families and communities, family resource center advocates have focused on improving and coordinating the delivery of existing social services to the youngest children and their families (Hook 1996). One such promising program is the Healthy Family Partnership in Hampton, Virginia. The Partnership offers home visiting support; parent education classes; parenting newsletters; parent resource centers in the public libraries; programs to prevent teen pregnancy; and infant, maternal, and family health programs.

The second exception is the set of organizations focusing on building collective identification within selected communities and identifying internal and external assets that may prove to be potent sources of community power. The Academy for Educational Development, the Asset-Based Community Development Institute, and the Search Institute at Northwestern University are prominent examples of such organizations.

The third exception is the set of initiatives that link three kinds of processes: building collective identity, developing networks and infrastructure, and mobilizing collective action in a targeted way. Some of these efforts build on the community-school model developed by the Mott Foundation in the 1930s and focus on strengthening the partnerships between schools and communities. The Mott Foundation envisioned community schools as "nerve centers" that would provide 24-hour, year-round activities for residents of all ages. Today, community-school partnerships are working to create programs that include on-site medical and dental care, mental health counseling, family support services, extended day tutoring, and recreation and education programs for students, families, and community residents (Blank and Steinbach 1998; Coltoff 1998; Melaville 1998).

The community-school initiative is particularly promising because it acknowledges the central role that schools play in people's lives, and works to expand that role. According to recent figures, 89 percent of all school-age children (approximately 53 million children) attend public school in the United States (KIDS COUNT 2000). This high percentage, and the importance of education in general, ensures that the quality of our public schools will continue to be a major social concern. Community-school partnerships attempt to link parents with educators, religious leaders, governmental officials, and other groups that, together, can help improve public schools. The Children's Aid Society has been instrumental in encouraging the development of community-school efforts. Currently, it is working with eight schools in New York City and an additional 70 sites throughout the nation to develop community schools. Another recent initiative built on the community-school concept is the Alliance Schools Project, coordinated by the Industrial Areas Foundation (IAF) and the Texas Education Agency.

The Alliance Schools Project is based on the premise that families and communities are in the best position to mobilize resources on behalf of their children's future (Blank and Steinbach 1998; Cortes 1996). The project has linked children's successes—in school as well as in other contexts—to parental involvement (Mapp 1997). IAF, in conjunction with the Texas Education Agency, has created a network of some 118 schools that work to draw parents and community groups into the process of child-related decisionmaking (Hatch 1998; Interfaith Education Fund 1998; Shirley 1997).

These kinds of initiatives could prove instrumental in developing networks within and between communities that are defined by shared concerns about children. Ultimately, these efforts may prove to be important precursors to the development of a larger social movement for children in this country.

## Promoting Advocacy for Children

Predictions that we will soon see a national social movement for children are premature. Social movements require more than the presence of shared grievances to develop and sustain momentum. Advocates can succeed only when grievances are channeled into political action through organizational networks and when favorable conditions advance their cause. This chapter identifies several factors that promote wide-scale mobilization, including social change, wide public awareness of the issues, shifting political alignments, the presence of influential allies, and targeted political rhetoric.

But current efforts to mobilize on behalf of children are occurring in a complex, fractured political and social context. Conservative political gains at the federal level, the public's struggle to define the best standards for children's education and well-being, the growing geographic divide between urban centers and the suburbs, and weakening community-level organizational networks have all hampered communities' efforts to confront the enormous difficulties facing children. In this kind of fragmented environment, efforts tend to focus on forming local, immediate solutions to critical problems rather than building a collective vision of the nation's child policy.

Nonetheless, current initiatives that focus on mobilizing communities to address children's issues have tremendous potential to build political will for future mobilization efforts. Advocates need to consciously work on building out individual school or neighborhood mobilization efforts toward the goal of forming broad community identities and community consensus around children. In other words, mobilization efforts need to work through the existing infrastructure of communities. Ignoring this existing social capital is an expensive proposition for advocates. As Ernesto Cortes (1996) argues, the two neighborhood institutions that do seem to work for most residents of most communities are schools and churches.

Ultimately, to build a true community-based agenda for children, advocates must assign roles and responsibilities not only to government, but also to individuals, community groups, and businesses. Although policy discussions are increasingly framed in terms of either state-level or market-based solutions, the reality of social life is more complex. In practice, people's responses to policy problems reflect the interplay between communities, states, and markets.

As history demonstrates, however, even small action can beget change, and small steps may begin to bridge the political divides within communities. The examples discussed in this chapter suggest that this type of work has already begun. They suggest ways of bringing together parents and families around shared concerns and, in turn, may be the first steps in building a nationwide mobilization on behalf of a shared political agenda for children.

## NOTE

1. This section is based on material collected from groups that reported working to mobilize parents and communities around children's issues and on interviews with representatives from several of these organizations. For each organization, I tried to identify programmatic successes and efforts to mobilize communities around children's policy and examined the roles community groups played in each organization's efforts. Advocacy organizations reviewed were the Academy for Educational Development; the Alliance Schools; the Asset-Based Community Development Institute; Beacon Schools; the Children's Partnership; the Children's Aid Society; the Institutional Grassroots Advocacy Campaign at Children's Memorial Hospital in Chicago; the Children's Defense Fund; Connect for Kids; the Essential Schools; Families and Work Institute; Family Care; Family School Community Partnerships; the Greater Kansas City Community Foundation; the Healthy Families Partnership; Healthy Steps; I Am Your Child; the Institute for Education Leadership; the Institute for Responsive Education; JumpStart Michigan; the Manitoba School Improvement Project; the National Parent Information Network; the National Parent Teacher Association; Off the Street; the Parent Institute; Parents for Public Schools; the Search Institute; and Stand For Children.

## REFERENCES

Amenta, Edwin. 1998. *Bold Relief.* Princeton: Princeton University.
Amidei, Nancy. 1993. "Child Advocacy: Let's Get the Job Done." *Dissent* 40 (spring): 213–20.
Beatty, Barbara. 1995. *Preschool Education in America.* New Haven: Yale University.
Besharov, Douglas J., and Lisa A. Laumann. 1996. "Child Abuse Reporting: The Need to Shift Priorities from More Reports to Better Reports." In *Social Policies for*

*Children,* edited by Irwin Garfinkel, Jennifer L. Hochschild, and Sara S. McLanahan (257–73). Washington, D.C.: Brookings Institution.

Blank, Martin, and Carol Steinbach. 1998. "Communities: Powerful Resources for America's Youth." In *The Forgotten Half Revisited,* edited by Samuel Halperin (59–82). Washington, D.C.: American Youth Policy Forum.

Coltoff, Philip. 1998. "Community Schools: Education Reform and Partnership with Our Nation's Social Service Agencies." Washington, D.C.: Child Welfare League of America Press.

Cortes, Ernesto, Jr. 1996. *A Community of Stories: Involving Citizens in Education Reform.* Washington, D.C.: American Association of Colleges for Teacher Education.

Dahl, Robert. 1956. *A Preface to Democratic Theory.* Chicago: University of Chicago Press.

Gamson, William A., and Adria Goodson. 2000. "Social Movements and CYF Policy," Forum on Building Constituencies: Achieving Supportive Social Policies for Children, Youth and Families, June 8. Sponsored by the Grantmakers for Children, Youth and Families, Washington, D.C.

Gleick, Elizabeth. 1996. "The Children's Crusade." *Time* (June 3): 30–35.

Gordon, Linda. 1994. *Pitied but Not Entitled: Single Mothers and the History of Welfare.* Cambridge and New York: Harvard University Press.

Hansen, John Mark. 1991. *Gaining Access: Congress and the Farm Lobby.* Chicago: University of Chicago Press.

Hardisty, Jean. 1999. *Mobilizing Resentment: Conservative Resurgence from the John Birch Society to the Promise Keepers.* Boston: Beacon Press.

Hatch, Thomas. 1998. "How Community Action Contributes to Achievement." *Education Leadership* (May): 15–16.

Hawes, Joseph M. 1991. *The Children's Rights Movement.* Boston: Twayne.

Hewlett, Sylvia Ann, and Cornel West. 1998. *The War against Parents.* New York: Houghton Mifflin.

Hook, Lynn B. 1996. *Working Together for Our Youngest Children: Four Collaboratives in Early Childhood Education.* BellSouth Foundation (www.bellsouthfoundation.org).

Imig, Doug. 2000a. Interview with executive of National Community School Partnerships. The Children's Aid Society.

———. 2000b. Interview with senior staff member of JumpStart Michigan.

———. 1999. Interview with executive of National Parent Teacher Association.

———. 1998. "American Social Movement and Presidential Administrations." In *Social Movements and American Political Institutions,* edited by Anne Costain and Andy McFarland (159–70). Boulder Colo.: Rowman and Littlefield.

———. 1996a. "Advocacy by Proxy: The Children's Lobby in American Politics." *Journal of Children and Poverty* 2 (1): 31–53.

———. 1996b. *Poverty and Power: The Political Representation of Poor Americans.* Lincoln, Nebr.: University of Nebraska.

Interfaith Education Fund. 1998. "Alliance Schools Concept Paper." Austin, Texas: Interfaith Education Fund.

Kagan, Sharon L., and Ronnie Rubin. 1998. "Examining Children's Readiness for School." Yale University working paper, December.

Katz, Michael. 1989. *The Undeserving Poor: From the War on Poverty to the War on Welfare.* New York: Pantheon.

KIDS COUNT. 2000. *KIDS COUNT Data Book.* Baltimore, Md.: The Annie E. Casey Foundation.

Mapp, Karen. 1997. "Making the Connection Between Families and Schools." *Harvard Education Letter: Research Online* (September/October). Http://www.edletter. org/past/issues/1997-so/connection.shtml. (Accessed May 10, 2001.)

McAdam, Doug. 1982. *Political Process and the Development of Black Insurgency.* Chicago: University of Chicago Press.

Media Strategies Group. 1999. "Evaluation of the Media Strategies Group: A Five-Year Effort to Unify the Voices of Child Care Advocates." New York: Communications Consortium Media Center.

Melaville, Atelia. 1998. *Learning Together: The Developing Field of School-Community Initiatives.* Washington, D.C.: Institute for Educational Leadership and National Center for Community Education.

Michel, Sonya Alice. 1999. *Children's Interests/Mothers' Rights.* New Haven, Conn.: Yale University Press.

Moe, Richard, and Carter Wilkie. 1997. *Changing Places: Rebuilding Community In the Age of Sprawl.* New York: Owl Books.

Piven, Frances Fox, and Richard A. Cloward. 1979. *Poor People's Movements.* New York: Vintage.

Pope, Jacqueline. 1989. *Biting the Hand That Feeds Them.* New York: Praeger.

Public Agenda. 1999a. *Kids These Days '99: What Americans Really Think about the Next Generation.* Washington, D.C.: Public Agenda.

———. 1999b. *Playing Their Parts: Parents and Teachers Talk about Parental Involvement in Public Schools.* Washington, D.C.: Public Agenda.

Putnam, Robert D. 2000. *Bowling Alone: The Collapse and Revival of American Community.* New York: Simon and Schuster.

Raden, Anthony. 1999. "Universal Pre-Kindergarten in Georgia; A Case Study of Georgia's Lottery-Funded Pre-K Program." Working Paper Series. New York: Foundation for Child Development.

Salisbury, Robert H. 1984. "Interest Representation: The Dominance of Institutions." *American Political Science Review* 78: 64–76.

Sarbaugh-Thompson, Marjorie, and Mayer N. Zald, 1989. "Child Labor Laws: A Historical Case of Public Policy Implementation," Mimeo.

Schorr, Lisbeth B. 1993. "Daring to Learn from Our Success." *AQ: The Aspen Institute Quarterly* 5 (1): 78–107.

Shaw, Robert. 1996. *The Activist's Handbook: A Primer for the 1990s and Beyond.* Berkeley: University of California Press.

Shirley, Dennis. 1997. *Community Organizing for Urban School Reform.* Austin: University of Texas Press.

Skocpol, Theda. 1997. *Lessons From History: Building a Movement for America's Children.* Washington, D.C.: The Children's Partnership.

———. 1992. *Protecting Soldiers and Mothers: The Political Origins of Social Policy in the United States.* Cambridge, Mass.: Harvard University.

Starobin, Paul. 1999. "The Risky Society." *National Journal* (July 10): 2006–12.

Stoecker, Randy. 1994. *Defending Community.* Philadelphia: Temple University Press.

Stone, Deborah A. 1997. *Policy Paradox: The Art of Political Decision Making*. New York: W. W. Norton and Company.

————. 1996. "The Cultural Context of Health Insurance for Children." Paper prepared for the conference on First Steps for Children: Strategies for Universal Health Insurance for Our Nation's Youth, October 3–4.

Sutton, John R. 1996. "Social Knowledge and the Generation of Child Welfare Policy in the United States and Canada." In *States, Social Knowledge, and the Origins of Modern Social Policies*, edited by Dietrich Rueschemeyer and Theda Skocpol (201–30). Princeton, N.J.: Princeton University Press.

Talbot, Margaret. 2000. "A Mighty Fortress." *New York Times Magazine* (February 27): 34–85.

Tarrow, Sidney. 1998. *Power in Movement: Social Movements, Collective Action and Politics*, 2nd ed. New York: Cambridge University Press.

Truman, David. 1951. *The Governmental Process*. New York: Knopf.

U.S. Census Bureau. 1998. "Families by Presence of Own Children under 18: 1950 to Present." Http://www.census.gov:80/population/socdemo/hh-fam/htabFM-1.txt.

U.S. Congress, House Committee on Ways and Means. 1985. *Children in Poverty*. Washington D.C.: U.S. Government Printing Office.

Waste, Frank. 1998. *Independent Cities*. New York: Oxford University Press.

Wildavsky, Ben. 1998. "The Divide over Day Care" *National Journal* (January 24): 167–68.

Wilson, James Q. 1995. *Political Organizations*. Princeton, N.J.: Princeton University.

Yankelovich, Daniel. 1998. "Public Opinion and the Youth of America." In *The Forgotten Half Revisited*. Washington, D.C.: American Youth Policy Forum.

# About the Editors

**Carol J. De Vita** is a senior research associate in the Center on Nonprofits and Philanthropy at the Urban Institute. She served as principal investigator for The Roles of Child Advocacy Organizations in Addressing Policy Issues, the Urban Institute conference on which this book is based, and directs research on nonprofit organizations in low-income neighborhoods of the District of Columbia. Previously, Dr. De Vita was a senior demographer at the Population Reference Bureau, where she directed the data collection for the annual *KIDS COUNT Data Book,* produced by the Annie E. Casey Foundation.

**Rachel Mosher-Williams** is a research associate in the Center on Nonprofits and Philanthropy at the Urban Institute. She was the project manager for The Roles of Child Advocacy Organizations in Addressing Policy Issues. She is currently conducting a three-year evaluation of the Foundation Media Relations Project. Prior to joining the Center, Ms. Mosher-Williams was the editor in chief of The George Washington University's journal of public administration and a program associate at the National Council of Nonprofit Associations.

# About the Contributors

**Barbara Beatty** is an associate professor at Wellesley College, where she has taught since 1981, and is chair of the Education Department. Dr. Beatty is an associate editor of *History of Education Quarterly,* a board member of the Wellesley College Centers for Research on Women, and college coordinator of the Boston Higher Education Partnership. She is author of *Preschool Education in America: The Culture of Young Children from the Colonial Era to the Present* (Yale University Press 1995). She is currently writing a book on controversies over teacher education.

**Emmett D. Carson** is the president and CEO of the Minneapolis Foundation. Dr. Carson came to The Minneapolis Foundation from the Ford Foundation in New York, where he spent five years as a program officer, first in the area of social justice and then in governance and public policy. Prior to that he served as project director of the Study on Black Philanthropy at the Joint Center for Political and Economic Studies in Washington, D.C.

**Sally Covington** is the founding director of the California Works Foundation, a nonprofit organization dedicated to equitable economic development in California. Previously, Ms. Covington directed the Democracy and Philanthropy Project for the National Committee for Responsive Philanthropy.

**Jillian Dickert** is a Ph.D. candidate at Brandeis University in the Department of Sociology. She has written and conducted research on politics, public policy, work/family, and social movements for Harvard University and for the Center for Women in Politics & Public Policy at the University of Massachusetts-Boston. Her dissertation focuses on the sociopolitical development of family and medical leave policy in the United States.

**Doug Imig** is associate professor of Political Science at the University of Memphis. Previously, Dr. Imig was affiliated with the Public Administration and Political Science Departments at the University of Nevada-Las Vegas and with the Program on Nonviolent Sanctions and Cultural Survival at Harvard University. His research addresses issues of social movement mobilization and public interest advocacy.

**Elizabeth Reid** is a research associate in the Center on Nonprofits and Philanthropy at the Urban Institute. Ms. Reid has 20 years of experience in labor and community organizations, grassroots political education, and leadership training. Formerly, she served as the national political director for the American Federation of Government Employees, and more recently, as adjunct faculty to the Corcoran School of Art. She is author of "Nonprofit Advocacy and Political Participation," a chapter in *Nonprofits and Government: Collaboration and Conflict* (Urban Institute 1999).

**Sara Rosenbaum** is the Harold and Jane Hirsh Professor of Health Law and Policy at The George Washington University (GWU) School of Public Health and Health Services. Dr. Rosenbaum is also the director of the Center for Health Services Research and Policy and the Hirsh Health Law and Policy Program. In addition, Dr. Rosenbaum is a professor of Health Care Sciences at The GWU Medical School and a lecturer at The GWU National Law Center.

**Theda Skocpol** is Victor S. Thomas Professor of Government and Sociology at Harvard University, where she also serves as director of the Center for American Political Studies. Her books include *Protecting Soldiers and Mothers: The Political Origins of Social Policy in the United States* (Harvard University Press 1992); *Boomerang: Health Reform and the Turn Against Government* (W. W. Norton 1997); and *The Missing Middle: Working Families and the Future of American Social Policy* (W. W. Norton and the Century Foundation 2000). Dr. Skocpol's current research focuses on civic engagement in American democracy.

**Colleen A. Sonosky** is a senior research scientist and assistant director of the Center for Health Services Research and Policy at the School of Public Health and Health Services at The George Washington University Medical Center.

**Nicholas A. J. Stengel** is a former research associate at the Center on Nonprofits and Philanthropy at the Urban Institute who worked on data quality issues and arts projects.

# Index

215